Post-Weird

Post-Weird

Fragmentation, Community, and the Decline of the Mainstream

CALUM LISTER MATHESON

Rutgers University Press
New Brunswick, Camden, and Newark, New Jersey
London and Oxford

Rutgers University Press is a department of Rutgers, The State University of New Jersey, one of the leading public research universities in the nation. By publishing worldwide, it furthers the University's mission of dedication to excellence in teaching, scholarship, research, and clinical care.

978-1-9788-4017-1 (cloth)
978-1-9788-4016-4 (paper)
978-1-9788-4018-8 (epub)

Cataloging-in-publication data is available from the Library of Congress.
LCCN 2025008071

A British Cataloging-in-Publication record for this book is available from the British Library.

∞ The paper used in this publication meets the requirements of the American National Standard for Information Sciences—Permanence of Paper for Printed Library Materials, ANSI Z39.48-1992.

rutgersuniversitypress.org

For Jerrell Maurice Braden (1980–2012),
an anchor of stability in countless lives.
May his memory be eternal.

Contents

Post-Weird

Introduction

The Spolia of Babel

This book is about how anti-rhetorical readings shape communities in the wake of the decline of symbolic efficiency. Its key argument is that the communities that arise to fill a perceived void in shared culture bear unexpected structural similarities that are evident in their styles of interpretation, or reading, and that, while not all of these communities are insidious, cultivating rhetorical attitudes as a means of both accepting and navigating ambiguity and uncertainty is an important condition for us to find ways to live together.

But allow me to say more.

Four thousand years ago, the Sumerians had a story about a ruler who sought to build a tower and unite all the languages of the universe. It didn't work out, but along the way writing on clay tablets was invented as a new media technology.[1] The later versions of this story seek to explain how our languages were confounded in the first place. Again, there is a tower. The legend of Babel might have been inspired by an actual structure in Babylon called Etemenanki built from seventeen million bricks, many of them inscribed. It is now a ruin south of Baghdad—built, destroyed, rebuilt, redestroyed, and abandoned. In the Babel legend, the nations must "make us a name," lest they "be scattered abroad upon the face of the whole earth." But God sees the tower as a sign that with their "one language . . . nothing will be restrained from them, which they have imagined to do." "Go to," God says, "let us go down, and there confound their language, that they may not understand one another's speech." And "the LORD did there confound the language of all the earth: and from thence did the LORD scatter them abroad upon the face of all the earth."[2] This is the most famous version of the old story, just one of many that existed around the world.[3]

The notion that we might have a common language, including both common signifiers and shared protocols for interpreting them, is called symbolic efficiency. This is the capacity for signifiers to effectively stand in for absent referents, most notably abstract principles like power, authority, and sanctity. Symbolic efficiency is about learning to make a world out of the signifiers around us, out of the stories we tell together more than simply the conditions we perceive with our senses. The most important signifiers represent the authority to tell us how to read the other signifiers around us.[4] We all know, for example, that political leaders are not incorruptible demigods but people who eat, sleep, defecate, get bored, and harbor petty jealousies. Our social orders require that we forget these things and act *as if* they were not true, that the Emperor has a right to rule or that King Charles III is really something more than just an old man whose family history of incest is unusually public. Every institution—good, evil, and in between—relies on this suspension of disbelief. Slavoj Žižek, quoting a line from Groucho Marx, claimed that the central question of our social order is "Whom do you believe, your eyes or my words?"[5] Cultural critics have long theorized the demise of symbolic efficiency, telling the old story of Babel in new, increasingly urgent ways.[6] This demise occurs when we refuse to indulge the fantasy and start to trust our eyes, not more abstract codes of authority mediated by symbols. As Joy Williams put it in *Harrow*: "To see is to forget the name of the thing you see."[7]

A key point here is that the rules of a society don't have to reflect total agreement or fealty to a cause, only collective fantasy. Symbolic efficiency is not consensus. It is consensus to pretend that there is consensus, because authority is always symbolic in any case. Ultimately, what unites us is this willingness to pretend as if we are not pretending. In her book on comedy, Alenka Zupančič illustrates this point with the character of a pompous baron who, slipping on a banana peel, gets back up still assured of his superiority, stumbling from one comical accident to the next. The basic appeal of this bit is about shared illusion. It doesn't hinge on the fact that we, like the baron, have material bodies that are subject to frustration by concrete obstacles like the banana peel. Rather, the humanity that we share with the baron is his conviction that he is something more than just a naked ape. We are not laughing so much at the fall as the fact he gets up and continues prancing around like an aristocrat. After all, Zupančič reminds us, the idea of inherited superiority is much more prevalent in our daily lives than is the coincidence of a well-placed banana peel.[8]

Jacques Lacan, upon whose ideas Žižek and Zupančič draw, argued that the "non-dupes err"[9] in refusing to be tricked because authority's sleight of hand is what makes society function. Ultimately what is at stake is the rhetorical concept of propriety (*to prepon*), also called decorum. On the one hand, propriety means what is proper: social mores and norms, which we could understand as the regime signified by symbols of authority. On the other hand, propriety also refers to the individual's sensibility about how to position themselves within this regime.[10] We have to know not only what the rules are, but also when we are supposed to ignore them in service of other, unspoken ones. Many offers are supposed to be refused, for example, no matter how seriously they may be expressed (think of the graceful Persian *taarof*, or the indelicate American "let me pay for that" coupled with a glacially slow reach for the wallet). These are signals of goodwill even when they mean the opposite of what is said and as such serve a function in maintaining social bonds, and they exist as elements of culture whether we "believe" in them or not. The distance this implies—that we can know the rules but also navigate them in the concrete moments of contingency that compose our lives—necessitates both literal and rhetorical strategies of reading authority. Symbolic authority relies on the ability of a symbol to stand in for something else, to condense and proliferate meanings, a dynamic we experience at the level of individual words in trope and figure. We know that symbols aren't "just" what they appear to be but can mean a variety of things and connect to other symbols in a variety of ways. The rhetorical sensibility of propriety informs our judgments about how to interpret our symbolic worlds and when to take its laws with a grain of salt. Without this, we lose our capacity to live in community with one another.

If we do finally pull ourselves apart, future scholars sifting through our wreckage might discover the story of Kellyanne Conway buried just beneath a layer of discarded N95 masks, QAnon placards, and unused vaccines. In 2017, Conway defended a statement made by White House Press Secretary Sean Spicer about attendance numbers at Donald Trump's inauguration. Spicer had claimed that Trump inspired "the largest audience ever to witness an inauguration" and slammed "attempts to lessen the enthusiasm for the inauguration" as "shameful and wrong," although his conclusions seemed to be contradicted by visual evidence.[11] Conway defended Spicer by claiming access to "alternative facts," a phrase that topped the list of notable lines in *The Yale Book of Quotations* and launched a thousand hot takes across the wine-dark sea of the Internet. Trump's enemies latched on to the phrase, seeing it as a revelation about Trumpism's disregard for truth.[12] Meanwhile, some of his defenders claimed that their leftist opponents had inaugurated the decline of truth themselves through poststructuralism and allied movements: If they trash grand narratives and historical truth, who are they to point the finger when conservatives do the same?[13] A Facebook post by Dan Rather about the incident was shared more than two hundred thousand times: "These are not normal times," he wrote. "These are extraordinary times."[14] But in many ways they weren't. We were just repeating the old story of the confusion of tongues.

Perhaps what is remarkable about Kellyanne Conway's "alternative facts" comment is not that it represents a new era, but that it signals the end of an old one. Conway was relying on a basic deception that has served to hold us together rather than divide us. Explaining the meaning of her statement in an interview, she gave a number of examples. "Alternative facts are partly cloudy partly sunny," "glass half full," or like two media outlets claiming higher ratings based on different criteria.[15] Conway actually winked at the camera at one point in this conversation. "Everybody knew what I meant," she said. And they did. Kellyanne Conway was saying *believe what I say, not what you see*. This is the basic call of authority that has glued societies together since time immemorial under different guises: "Trust me, I'm an expert," "doctor's orders," "Daddy knows best," "because I said so," *Führerprinzip*. This is not new—Kellyanne Conway wanted us to trust in authority, not to ignore it and come to our own conclusions. She is a propagandist who knows that orthopraxy matters more than orthodoxy, just as Jacques Ellul could have told her.[16] No one needs "is" if they have "as if."

When symbolic efficiency begins to erode, we lose the rhetorical flexibility that allows us to navigate the world "as-if." We are surrounded by information, but without the old protocols of understanding and the common ground we need to connect meaningfully with one another. In retrospect, Conway's "alternative facts" line and the panic around it seem quaint. After a decade of fiercely contested elections, media bubbles, political violence, moral panics, and ideologies of open hatred, we seem past mere quibbles about the honesty of politicians. Society seems to have fragmented, and the division between Democrats and Republicans is only the beginning. It's not just about new terminologies, although they exist in abundance, with "red pills," "chuds," "snowflakes," "zoomers," "boomers," "doomers," and "consoomers." Beliefs that were once taboo are now openly shared, from neo-Nazism to occultism to skepticism about the moon landing. We cannot even agree on what constitutes a fact, much less whose are more persuasive. In rhetorical terms, we are missing a point of *stasis*—an acknowledgement amidst our strife that we can at least agree about what we are disagreeing about, and what would constitute evidence for one side or another. Even when there are points of commonality, our differences seem so stark as to be insurmountable. This is why the U.S. Democratic Party's strategy of labeling Republicans as "weird" failed in 2024: "Weird" matters only in context, and without shared norms, it may simply validate an oppositional community's sense of coherence and struggle, something that Democrats should have learned from the "basket of deplorables" epithet almost a decade before. It requires a shared sense of propriety, and that's in short supply.

Of course, one ought to be skeptical about how unified American culture ever really was. Michael Lee and Jarrod Atchison have argued that the desire to carve out new enclaves—geographically, culturally, or spiritually—is endemic to the history of the United States, a country itself founded by secession from the United Kingdom.[17] The "notion of national oneness" expressed in *E pluribus Unum* "has been haunted by its twin, *E pluribus pluria*" since its very birth, they write, and there "can be many functionally different nations in the same country at the same time without any formal secession declaration."[18] Narratives of dissolution are often exaggerated for different reasons, and one group's golden age may be another's time of misery. Nostalgia for unity tends to ignore racial, sexual, and gender differences, often mistaking oppression for consensus. In its worst form, this may manifest as a kind of psychosis for the establishment of an unquestionable order of singularity, something like Svetlana Boym's "restorative nostalgia."[19] Lamentations about the loss of a bygone era have a long history as props for cultural conservatism,[20] and much nostalgia imagines a past that never was, especially when it comes to "family values."[21] We have not lost some White, hetero, *Leave-it-to-Beaver* patriarchal time of yore, but rather the willingness to *act as if* we were all united. That's all the American cultural, political, and ideological mainstream ever was—a pact to pretend there was a pact, constantly enforced by agents of oppression that would not be necessary if that homogeneity was real. While enforced homogeneity was oppressive, it is becoming clear that its alternatives are far from pleasant. Freed from conformity and connected at the speed of light, we suddenly realized that it was more than we could handle, and we didn't like what the neighbors were saying anyway. So we didn't wait for anyone to finish knocking down the Tower—we pulled it apart brick by brick, stone by stone, death by a billion tweets. If you listen to the critics, we are unmaking the world—not by flood, not by fire, but by shitpost.

Building in the Ruins

So far, not much of this is news. There are more books about polarization and the death of shared values than Stephen Miller could burn in a lifetime. Many of them portray our situation in apocalyptic terms, like I just have. All of that is comprehensible from within the frame of the decline of symbolic efficiency. What is harder to explain is how new languages, new communities, and new beliefs rise to fill the gaps.

I wrote this book not to ruminate on the collapse of shared languages but because I want to know how splinter communities form in our current media environment, what they build from the ruins. When the actual tower of Etemenanki was finally pulled apart, locals hauled the bricks away to make their own buildings.[22] The practice of reusing old materials (*spolia*) in new construction has been common since antiquity. So this book is about what follows the tower's collapse: how practices of communication give rise to new communities amidst the decline of symbolic efficiency. *Spolia* is a means of thinking through how new structures emerge from the wreckage of the old, both literally and metaphorically. Paul O'Kane made this comparison when he wrote that our thinking, philosophy, and writing "have always redeployed the *spolia* of previous attempts to seek truth, cultivate knowledge and question preconceptions. The recycling of *spolia* is not an exception or curiosity but a rule in our philosophical and historical tradition. Not marginal but central."[23] As our present symbolic network seems to decline, new communities are coming together around shared texts and other media, often facilitated by the same Internet that helped to smash the most recent tower. Because all communities are to some degree "interpretive communities," discovering how they produce, interpret, and attach to shared texts and other media is an important part of understanding them more generally.[24]

What emerges, however, is not always a cause for celebration. While not all of the groups sprouting up in the vacuum of authority are vile, many are. The Internet once promised freedom, especially for marginalized identities who could find community no matter how isolated they might be. Instead, the World Wide Web and social media became vehicles for all manner of violence, from racial hatred to old-fashioned government tyranny, and among the groups who found each other were sexual predators, racists, and violent misogynists. As Ian Bogost put it, "social media creates communities at the fringe. In the best cases, these improve the lives of people who might otherwise struggle for connection; but they can also serve as bubbles." These places "where weirdos could connect" often end up flooded with conspiracy theories, disinformation, and bigotry, where every post becomes "an opportunity for some miscreant, mansplainer, or literalist to pick your words apart."[25] At the risk of coining a new Internet law, for every subjugated group that finds space for self-expression online, another finds space to advocate the extermination of that group. The groups studied in this book fall between those poles, although most are closer to one side than the other.

Each of the following chapters engages with representative communities who have created their own structures of authority and meaning. Following the mass shooting at Sandy Hook Elementary School in 2012, a group of doubters quickly converged who alleged that the massacre never happened, the "official version" being merely a ploy to seize weapons from the USA's armed citizenry. Holiness Pentecostal serpent-handlers are a somewhat older community that has responded to an increasingly secular world by pledging such a strict fidelity to the Bible's text that they often die in the service of their faith. Online pro-anorexia (commonly shortened to pro-ana) communities personify their condition as the basis for new forms of sociality organized, directly or indirectly, around control, death, and desire, themes that may animate all communities but are scarcely acknowledged by most of them. The fourth chapter analyzes a cluster of communities (incels, biological racists, and "trans investigators") that invoke the same signifier, "Science," in novel ways while paying only formal obeisance to it and evading responsibility for their choices.

In the process of researching, interacting with, and observing these groups, I concentrated on their relatively public practices of communication: what they say, write, record, and perform in specific contexts, but also their protocols for how to read, interpret, and orient themselves toward these shared media. I have chosen to focus on a particular set of communities for a variety of reasons. All of them believe significantly different things, which I thought was important to highlight that any structural similarities were not due simply to overlapping convictions. Pro-ana groups and Sandy Hook deniers still exist, but they reached their heyday on the Internet about a decade ago, providing a good balance between accessibility and distance for often ephemeral online cultures. Serpent-handling Holiness churches are older institutions than the others, providing a longer term perspective for a study that otherwise focuses on the Internet age. Anti-trans conspiracy theorists, incels, and biological racists are all influential as I write and are likely to remain so. All of these groups have produced enough to make them objects of study, and all think of themselves as outsiders to some extent, whether or not that judgment holds up in every instance.

The commonalities I found studying these groups are evident in many, many others, some of which I considered including and ultimately chose to omit. All of these communities are bound together by signifiers that define them and come to influence the subjectivities of their members. All of them sometimes destroy these subjects, whether it be physically through starvation and venom or socially through professional ostracism and isolation. These observations give rise to the central questions of this book: How do these communities constitute themselves through their interpretive practices around shared media objects, what function do they fulfill for their members such that they persist despite their costs, and how might we adapt our theoretical approaches to account for them?

To engage these questions, my research draws on tools from a variety of traditions including cultural studies, rhetoric, and media studies, but psychoanalytic thinking intersects them all. Psychoanalysis is a big, diverse, and messy field with a complex and often troubling history. This book employs psychoanalytic concepts but also criticizes them, sometimes in ways that would surely result in my excommunication if the Psychoanalytic Congregation of the Doctrine of the Faith ever got its act together. Psychoanalysis has often been too rigid, too narrow, too closely bound to slanted notions of sex, race, and gender masquerading as universals. Others share these critiques, and the response to them has transformed psychoanalytic thought over the last few decades, especially in Lacanian circles. And yet, psychoanalysis is full of insight. Psychoanalysis is an art of reversals and ambiguities. It's about turning things inside out only to discover that they had no inside or outside. It dissolves mysteries to find their impenetrable cores but stops before claiming to really *know*. The results of psychoanalytic inquiry are weird, upsetting, and counterintuitive, just like we humans are. As a means of hypothesizing the intersection of desire and language, it only flourishes in tandem with its equally misfit sibling art, rhetoric. To me, employing a psychoanalytic rhetoric is distinct from drawing on the authority of a static, exclusionary field, Psychoanalysis with a capital P. A psychoanalytic rhetoric is one that attends to the unconscious, that system of unspoken, unknown knowns that remains elusive even as it structures the contexts of our discourses. Although I will reference many specific concepts throughout this book, four have been particularly important for my inquiry.

First, presence and absence cannot be thought of without each other. In some ways, all of psychoanalysis begins with negation. Silences, lacks, cuts, holes, and refusals are *things* that *aren't there*, structural spaces marked by the absence of something that one would expect to find, like a gap in a bookshelf where a volume should fit. Psychoanalysts treat these as paradoxically active, present things, sometimes giving them a hypothetical presence as in Lacan's *objet petit a*, the impossible object that would hypothetically fill what he argued was a constitutive lack in the human subject. "The Lacanian subject is subjectivized lack,"[26] writes Patricia Gherovici, noting that the lack is active and productive of what and who we are. Alenka Zupančič explains this with a joke: A man orders coffee without cream at a café, but the server informs him that the café has no cream. Would he accept coffee without milk instead?[27] Desire depends on a lack because we could not *want*—note the various meanings of this word—if we were totally complete already. Repression (or the more definitive foreclosure) is also the presence of something through its absence, the disavowal and replacement of an often-traumatic thing that becomes literally unspeakable but still plays a dramatic role in organizing our minds. Understanding the unconscious, which is perhaps the defining object of psychoanalysis, requires attention to these subtle refusals of the presence/absence binary. Forgotten events, unrecognized assumptions, and deeply ingrained cultural values all influence us even when we do not bring them consciously to mind. So, too, do the many potential associations and meanings of words, the compositional qualities of images, and the hard-to-place affective resonances of sound.

All of this leads to a second idea: The unconscious is not a deeply buried and disavowed interior within each person's mind. It is best understood as the dynamic interaction of the symbolic order of human experience—our language, media, and everyday speech—and the subjective itinerary that someone takes through it.[28] The unconscious is simultaneously the most impersonal and most personal human encounter with language. On the one hand, it could refer to all of the hidden or overlooked meanings, associations, and connections woven together by a particular culture and operated in language, invoked and present even when they are not acknowledged. There is a certain objectivity to this in that it conditions and produces individual subjects but exceeds them all. On the other hand, each individual subject experiences this constellation of meanings from a particular location, so that symbols easily referenced by others might be pushed under due to the particularities of upbringing and experience, while other formations that are generally overlooked might form important parts of one's symbolic world. In other words, what is repressed by a culture might return for an individual while what is repressed by an individual might operate openly in a culture. The unconscious is like the night sky: We may share the same stars, but each viewer sees different constellations from where they stand, the names of which were chosen by people long dead but continue to shape what connections we make between the stars. The decline of symbolic efficiency relies on this notion: While a symbol like a judge's robe might signal authority in a culture, not every subject need accept that role, and those that do might attach quite different valences to it. Taking it seriously, though, shows that symbolic efficiency in general does not decline but is rather redistributed, for some subjects or subjectivities, differently across their plane of the Symbolic. The collapse of meaning for one signifier does not mean that all language dies at once, nor does the adoption of one mode of reading (e.g., literal) for one set of signifiers necessitate it for every signifier.

Third, we pay a price for language. Some variant of "speaking being" is common in English-language psychoanalysis, but the word Lacan used was actually the neologism *parlêtre*, which combines "to speak" (*parler*) with "being" (*être*),[29] perhaps to imply that the relationship isn't just a being that speaks but a being that exists for, and by virtue of, speaking. It resonates with "letter" (*lettre*), a signifier instantiated between language and speech, the material support of concrete discourse.[30] We can divide up the world by naming things and trade signifiers with other people, who we render into linguistic objects with their own names, but in doing so, we ourselves are turned into subjects that can be circulated in the same way. "Every subject is called to being, but it is not a summons from 'inside,'" writes Néstor Braunstein. "The injunction makes a subject, it subjectifies. A demand is made for the subject to speak" by the Other, our personification of the Symbolic order, which "confers life" by "mortifying" it. "The subject comes into being . . . but incurs a debt."[31] We are forever bounded, never complete, always lacking. We are subjects of language in every sense of this phrase. We might think we are wise when we recognize that language is a golem that could turn against us, but we fail to acknowledge that we are the golems ourselves and language is the master. The signifiers in our cultural systems are the agents, and we the *parlêtres* are their media.[32] Kenneth Burke famously wrote that we are "the symbol-using" and "symbol misusing" animal, "inventor of the negative . . . separated from [our] natural condition by instruments of [our] own making"; but the agency of language over us is one way to interpret our being "goaded by the spirit of hierarchy" or "moved by the sense of order."[33] I think of this definition of humanity in relation to Lacan's assertion that for Freud "man [*sic*] is the subject captured and tortured by language."[34] Made separate by the signifying order around us, we are doomed to seek wholeness through an endless series of things that stand in for one another, a function of the same system by which we were condemned. All of our specific traumas are prefigured by this more general one that we are always trying to convince ourselves can be overcome. This is essentially Carlo Michelstaedter's view of rhetoric as an "ornament of darkness," a "poultice for the pain."[35] It is also the origin of desire: We would not want if we did not *want*.

This leads to a fourth notion: Every symptom is a spontaneous effort at a cure. Besides the modern medical notion of "symptom" as a subjective feeling of some condition, the word is often used simply to designate some anomaly that points toward an underlying cause or condition, somewhat of a conflation with a medical "sign." Perhaps these are valuable uses of the term. Its most radical potential for psychoanalytic rhetoric, however, begins with the recognition that symptoms arise in *response* to underlying trauma and represent efforts to assuage or compensate for it. Even if they are maladaptive and cause suffering, symptoms are not the problem to be solved. As Zupančič puts it, the symptom is "a subjective *solution* to some contradiction or impasse.... The work of analysis consists in forcing out the contradiction 'solved' by the symptom."[36] This observation is important because efforts to resolve symptoms alone are almost doomed to fail, even though psychoanalysis "does not solve the contradiction; rather it solves its solution."[37] A subject's entire coherence may depend on the maintenance of their symptom such that disrupting it results only in more suffering. All psychoanalysis necessarily does is unwind that complex prior to any possible (re)construction. A key question about the seemingly inexplicable behaviors and fixations of the communities in this book is: What does it *do* for them?

These considerations have led me to engage serpent handlers, conspiracy theorists, pro-anorexia bloggers, and pseudoscientific reactionaries by attending closely to what they actually say (or write, or film, etc.), hoping to see in it how their discursive communities are woven together and what structures of desire might keep them that way. Lacan claimed that analysts should be "secretaries to the insane,"[38] by which he meant we should not simply ignore the details of what people experiencing psychosis believe, as the content of their speech reveals the structures of their worlds. As he asked his students, "Wasn't it because they didn't go far enough in listening to the insane that the great observers who drew up the first classifications impoverished the material they were given?"[39] A "scientific" approach that ignores the particularities of each subject's discourse can't tell us much about desire, which is vitally important but requires speculation. We catch glimpses of a subject's unconscious through their slips, word choices, habits, and repetitions. Drawing conclusions about the structures of desire and belief communities hold without deep engagement in their own communication is at best arrogant, repeating the unfortunate tendency to decide that we know what someone "really" means without regard to what they say. At worst, this may lead us to confirm our own biases or impose pet academic theories when better alternatives exist.[40]

By its nature, the present absences that condition communities are hard to study. This is precisely why the approach to media and culture in this book draws from the generative, sometimes wild, always uncertain intersections of psychoanalysis and rhetoric. Both look to the ways in which speech departs from the regular and expected by attending closely to its details. Both are theories of excess, the something-more that eludes easy categorization. We might think of psychoanalytic rhetoric as an effort to grasp for a particular audience what Jonathan Culler calls force: "the power of any text [which] . . . lies in those moments which exceed our ability to categorize, which collide with our interpretative codes but nevertheless seem right."[41] Following Shoshana Felman, psychoanalysis should not "grammatize rhetoric"—if everything unpredictable could be made predictable, rhetoric and psychoanalysis would both be unnecessary.[42] Aspiring toward a "scientific" psychoanalysis or rhetoric misses the point of both traditions and risks the kind of conceptual rigidity that underlies psychosis, an argument Lacan himself made in his essay "Science and Truth."[43] The basic problem is that we all know there are irrational, confounding, hidden knots of human experience that are too unique and complex for us to untie with the clumsy fingers of theory, but we have to try nonetheless. The constant reminder that categories are mutable and that we must live in ambiguity is how we prevent Dr. Lacan's couch from becoming a Procrustean bed.

A brief note on the method of my inquiry: As someone who attends to the outlandish, paranoid, reactionary, and obscure elements of culture, especially on the Internet, I am essentially an intellectual raccoon. Once I find the can and rip the lid off, I spend too many of my nights picking through trash, touching everything but only keeping the best bits. Surely, anyone who regularly visits these trash cans knows that they're being disturbed, but I try to be discreet. The more they know I'm there, the more likely they are to lock the bins, or throw things in the neighbor's dumpster, or even poison the bags to keep me away from the good stuff. Now and again, I'll sneak into the attic to see what the house is like on the inside, but if I bring anything back to show the others (that's you), it always comes from the unlocked cans. I eat the trash so you don't have to. That is to say, I spend a great deal of time immersing myself in the communications produced by the groups I study, navigating them as a consumer before I can be a critic. Although this sometimes means one-on-one conversations, observing offline interactions, or accessing closed forums, primary material I cite directly comes from publicly available sources where no password is necessary. Where I deem it appropriate, I will aggregate, describe, or cite forums rather than specific profiles, both to avoid overstating the importance of some Internet rando and because it's often impossible to really know who they are. My attitude is less "oppositional lurking" and more "evenly suspended attention,"[44] aimed at understanding the ways that communities understand themselves, although this endeavor is necessarily judgmental sometimes. Although I try to experience the haptics of these communities—the practice of scrolling, the bodily composure of reading, typing, serial video watching, and so on—I am first and foremost a scholar of communication focused on media and language. Therefore, I base my conclusions on images, texts, videos, and other media objects, although I also try to communicate the structures of feeling in which they are embedded because protocols of interpretation often rely on a kind of familiarity that cannot be easily reduced to tangible and discrete pieces of evidence. I have long been immersed in analog weirdness from cryptozoology to occult bookstores to underground zines and lived through a formative era of Internet culture, from Rotten.com to Reddit. This is not exactly new territory for me, but this is not an autoethnography, either.

Psychosis and Modes of Reading

In what follows, I use the concepts, tools, and methods already mentioned to speculate about the structures of desire that might cohere communities against the backdrop of declining symbolic efficiency. I do that by attempting to analyze closely their various communicative acts to understand how and why these communities form and stick together. The conclusions formulated by this inquiry are all interconnected. One early realization was that all of the communities I have studied here are characterized by similar protocols for interpreting the world despite very different ideologies, values, and social effects. As the next four chapters demonstrate, all of the communities studied in this book are founded on a three-part move, beginning with their disconnection from mainstream symbolic efficiency; followed by the formation of their own symbols either by repurposing old signifiers or inventing their own and stitching together a new structure; and finally the investing of these symbols with absolute certainty. These groups insist consciously or unconsciously that their key signifiers be read not just literally but univocally without the possibility of alternative interpretations. The sense of some deeply buried meaning adheres to this new language, even when that meaning is obscure. Ultimately these readings are *anti-rhetorical*: there is no room for flexibility, ambiguity, multiplicity, or uncertainty: There is no "as-if," only "is."

This three-part move closely mirrors the structure of individual psychosis as it has been theorized by many psychoanalysts, including Lacan. Although people who encounter the world through psychotic frames do so in different ways, Lacanian thought has traditionally focused on "more organized psychotic problems" rather than those in which "disintegration and chaos are pivotal,"[45] and due to my focus on coherent groups, I follow suit. This variety of experience has three characteristic traits. The first is foreclosure, an act of negation more extreme than that found in neurotic repression. This is the complete rejection (Freud: *Verwerfung*) of the "Name of the Father," an authoritative signifier that structures the world we share with others (I will critique this term and others in chapter Four, but I preserve it here for clarity). For Lacan, the Name of the Father is a quintessentially symbolic function that exists as part of the shared symbolic world of a culture (which we might personify as the Other). Lacan chooses this metaphor because, before the advent of DNA testing, the paternal provenance of a child was always at least potentially suspect because it couldn't be verified in the same way that the maternal connection could—that is, by the observation of pregnancy and birth. The family names given to children in patriarchal societies therefore asserted a kind of continuity through the signifier (the name) that could not be definitively proved through shared substance ("blood"). It is therefore somewhat arbitrary—the key point of the Name of the Father is "name," not "father," in that it refers to a signifier that orders, separates, structures, and divides the world. In other words, it is a symbol founding and representing authority in a particular cultural milieu, a key that shapes how subjects read other signifiers, and this is precisely what is rejected in psychosis. In every place and time, what is normative and what can be rejected is dependent on culture, history, and tradition. The alternative to this sanction is not liberation now that anything goes, but a universal exception where everything is abnormal and nothing is fine because no authority can sanction anything. Our symbolic world is always irrational, contingent, confusing, and full of surprising intensities and occupations.

Foreclosing an authoritative signifier is like losing the proverbial nail by which the horse's shoe is lost, then the horse, the rider, the army, and the kingdom. Psychosis does not need to be understood as a deficit to understand this phenomenon. People experiencing psychosis aren't necessarily divorced from reality at this stage—rather, their reality has overwhelmed the filters that make it manageable. It's not that these people are delusional while the rest of us are normal. We are all delusional, but their delusions don't bear the same symbolic efficiency for everyone else in their culture—that is, they violate some sense of propriety. Signifiers like the Name of the Father are essentially a means of staving off the formlessness and horror of an experience where everything means too much and too little. This wild excess of unfiltered reality is called the Real in Lacanian parlance, and as I have argued elsewhere, we are both attracted and terrified by it simultaneously, seeking to experience its authenticity through the safe remove of media, including but not limited to language.[46] Without their bearings, people experiencing psychosis may interpret common phenomena as having deep *significance*, in the sense that they seem to be inarguable symbols of something, having an aura of meaningfulness that is not arbitrary at all but perhaps signals some great truth of the universe. Signifiers no longer stand in for something else or open themselves to interpretation—they are what they are, absolutely if mysteriously. This ushers in two more key elements of psychotic experience: novelty and certainty.[47]

Upon the bedrock of meaningful portents, auguries, and signs, psychotic subjects begin to weave together new maps from which they can live in the world of the symbolic. Hallucinations and other intrusive experiences are examples of Lacan's maxim that "whatever is refused in the symbolic order . . . reappears in the real."[48] Annie Rogers—an analyst who has experienced psychosis herself—relates that "[w]ords become the floating signifiers of a mad Other who takes up a place in speech. Speech elements connect to nothing, have no meaning whatsoever, and disrupt the meaning that was unfolding. These elements . . . are foreign to the speaker and create a profound sense of disorder."[49] In the immediate aftermath of foreclosure, a subject's moorings snap and they are exposed to the press of an immense occulted meaning. "What is the psychotic phenomenon?" Lacan asks in one of his clearest expositions. "It is the emergence in reality [i.e., the Real] of an enormous meaning that has the appearance of being nothing at all—in so far as it cannot be tied to anything, since it has never entered into the system of symbolization—but under certain conditions can threaten the entire edifice."[50] "In the face of such a pervasive change in language," Rogers writes, "the psychotic subject, confounded by nonsense, begins to create a proto-order with connotations of a linguistic order."[51] Especially in paranoid psychotic subjects—the ones with whom Lacan was primarily interested—networks of new words grow together to plaster over the void of a missing signifier, like scar tissue closing a wound.

New names and terminology connect to one another and become the basis for deeply held systems of belief that seem to depart radically from whatever ordering signifier was foreclosed. In Freud's "talking cure," speech is the classic means by which structures like psychosis manifest, but all forms of communication—drawings, writings, gestures, YouTube videos—become the evidence through which the structural causes and consequences of psychosis are indirectly revealed. While neurotics hide one traumatic thing beneath another signifier, for psychotics, novel language operates as a set of signs, not signifiers.[52] Signifiers are essentially arbitrary things, although they tend to occupy us through affective bonds. A neurotic knows on some level that a signifier could be replaced and that, through metaphor, it might mean something else. The poetic function of language essentially relies on this capacity for substitution, which creates new meanings in excess of the signifiers involved.

This is why Lacan claims that the famous psychotic Daniel Paul Schreber was not a poet. While Dante Alighieri, for example, might have described intricate supernatural systems full of rich meaning, the *Divine Comedy* is largely allegorical and was almost certainly understood by Dante as such. Schreber's visions of God operate in a different way. At least to him, they were revelatory, not creative. While Dante's poetry is *signifying*, Schreber's delusions are full of *significance* with no alternative reference possible. As Lacan put it, "The meaning of these words . . . has the property of referring essentially to meaning *as such*. It's a meaning that essentially refers to nothing but itself, that remains irreducible. . . . Before being reducible to another meaning it signifies within itself something ineffable."[53] This is essentially the function of a signal, not a signifier: something that indicates in a direct and nonarbitrary way another presence, rather than something that simply stands in for it in a linguistic system. Subjects experiencing psychosis may adopt what Rogers calls "incandescent alphabets," the "elements of language that are creatively adopted when one must find a new way in language with respect to a strange world one has entered and cannot exit."[54]

The language of psychosis is part of its distinctiveness. Sometimes words used in this discourse are neologisms or novel combinations, but they are also frequently terms that already exist and simply emanate a different kind of significance for a psychotic subject. Listening to subjects caught up in psychotic discourse, one often hears scraps of language that come directly from the Other seemingly out of context and without mediation. Underground punk musician Wesley Willis, for example, frequently employed slogans from advertising campaigns in his music ("Wheaties: It's the breakfast of champions," "Folgers: It's good to the last drop") combined with atypical profanity (e.g., "Suck a polar bear's funky ass"). The subjective function of these phrases is explained in his own music: Willis sang about the intrusive, persecuting thoughts that plagued him in times of silence.[55] He gave these "demons" names like Heartbreaker, Nervewrecker, and Meansucker and used scatological lyrics to drown them out, changing a bad "war hell ride" to a better "joyride," restoring some semblance of order to his world.[56] The lyrics of Willis's music demonstrate the breakdown of language, the return of signifiers in the Real, and the development of a special argot full of significance that helps to find some semblance of bearings for a psychotic subject.[57] This is why, Freud says, "the secret" is that psychotics "*love their delusion as they love themselves*"—delusions are scraps of flotsam bobbing in a rough sea, something to which a drowning mariner can cling and hope to stay above water.[58]

Of course, words and phrases pop into our minds unbidden with great frequency, which most of us would not take as evidence of psychosis. Lacan tells of an interlocutor who was almost hit by a car who had the phrase "brain damage" occur suddenly to him as he escaped—evidence, Lacan says, that a "latent discourse" of the unconscious is always ready to surface.[59] In my first year as chair of the Department of Communication, I heard a sentence in my mind as

I walked down a busy street regarding a colleague about whom I do not frequently think: "[Colleague Name] is a smooth baby." What distinguishes this episode from a psychotic experience of language is that I brushed it off as an aberration, whereas a psychotic reading might have interpreted it as a revelation from God or a message from the CIA. My capacity to read language as meaning otherwise permitted me to hold this intrusive thought at arm's length and understand it as bizarre poetry, not occult truth. This capacity defines neurosis. As Lacan puts it, the neurotic "subject is essentially someone who is placed in the position of not taking the greater part of his internal discourse seriously. . . . The principal difference between you and the insane [i.e., psychotic] is perhaps nothing other than this."[60]

Here we see the third major element of psychosis: certainty. In psychosis, there is no room for ambiguity. Novel words tie together in delusional structures that can only mean one thing, even if it's not clear what it is. I don't know what "[Colleague Name] is a smooth baby" means, and I don't have a particular sense that it means *anything*, despite training as both a rhetorician and a psychoanalyst. Even were I sure that the words probably meant something, my path of inquiry would be metaphorical: The words aren't intrinsically meaningful but, quite the opposite, stand in for some other set of signifiers that they represent in my conscious mind. Certainty is the "rarest of things" for non-psychotic subjects, for even when faced with realities about which one is "in no doubt," one still does not "take them fully seriously."[61] There is no such ambiguity for the subject of psychosis. Psychotic reading is about certainty—more specifically, the certainty that the phenomenon is about the subject, whether it is "real" or not. The psychotic has "radical certainty" because even if they don't "believe in the reality of [their] hallucinations," they are "certain of something, which is that what is at issue—ranging from hallucination to interpretation—regards [them]."[62] The subject is not even sure of themselves but is absolutely convinced of an Other who is directly concerned with them. This is one meaning of a joke of which Slavoj Žižek is fond. A psychoanalyst sees a patient who will not leave his house because he believes that he is a grain of wheat and that a giant chicken outside will eat him. The analyst leads him to realize that he is not a grain of wheat, but weeks later, he is still locked inside. When the analyst hears of this, he confronts the man: "Come, now, you know that you are not a grain of wheat!" "Yes," the man replies, "*I* know that, but the *chicken* doesn't know that!" Reality is not the issue. The certainty of reference remains—the man is just a grain of wheat unless the Other agrees that he is a man.

Lacan used the concepts of metaphor and metonymy to explain how foreclosure, novelty, and certainty relate to one another. Subjects like Schreber foreclose metaphor, a replacement of one signifier with another that relies on juxtaposition and ambiguity to create new meaning. The Name of the Father, Lacan argues, is an example of metaphor as its work of connection and order operates through signifiers—words, labels, names—that stand in for one another, and that is precisely what is foreclosed in psychosis.[63] The distinction between language and speech is important: An absence of metaphor describes the lack of a symbolic anchor in someone's experience with the world, not necessarily a total absence of tropes and figures in their speech.[64] Novel elements of speech in psychosis, Lacan argues, are metonymic. These links can operate based on shared substance, whole-for-part substitutions, or even phonetic aspects of different signifiers, all of which make them appear not to be arbitrary. In compound terms, for example, elements that are dropped from new words remain relevant for their unconscious connections. Some objects in language "fracture" easily, Lacan says, and in their recombination "metonymic ruins" persist. Metonymy is distinguished from metaphor for Lacan partly because the former is a process of combination while the latter is substitution, but he is careful to note that every substitution or combination is not the same, meaning that careful attention to the subject's contextual ties to language is important.[65]

Foreclosure, novelty, and certainty are evident in each community studied in this book. For conspiracy theorists who claim that the Sandy Hook mass shooting was staged, first there is a meltdown in media trust and authority, followed by a complex set of detailed beliefs strung together by a web of idiosyncratic interpretive practices, all of which are held together as irrefutable signals of a hidden truth. For serpent-handling Christians, secularism and social change disrupted old lifeways, but an anti-rhetorical interpretation of biblical signs cemented a new set of practices and social order, a faith so deeply held that public spectacles of death cannot shake it. Pro-anorexia communities refuse to acknowledge their dependence on outside objects, filling the lack instead with the "object nothing," a hunger for meaning that is so literal it may result in bodily starvation. Biological racists, incels, and transvestigators all reject mainstream interpretations of science, but cling to its signifier almost like a magic word that might defend them against ambiguity, invoking it in the service of fiercely held and exclusive social hierarchies. From this observation I will argue that we should consider the ways that the collective structures arising to fill the void in this age of declining symbolic efficiency resemble the patterns seen in psychosis.

The concepts of "normal," "everyday," "ordinary," or "cold" psychosis already exist to describe ways that perhaps most or all of us are subjects of psychosis, and Josh Gunn has argued persuasively that this moment of American culture combines a baseline psychosis with eruptions of perversion, making for "speech that is both nutty and predictable *at the same time*."[66] Jodi Dean and others have already analyzed conspiracy theorists in terms of symbolic efficiency and psychosis.[67] My work builds on this foundation by arguing for a revision in our concept of psychosis as it applies to communal practices. Instead of metonymy,

I will argue that psychotic communities rely on anti-rhetorical figures to disavow any ambiguity in their central terms. Instead of foreclosing metaphor, they experience the loss of symbolic efficiency, which is closely related to rhetorical notions of propriety and psychoanalytic notions of the Other, a kind of personification of the overall system of signifiers that make up our cultural and linguistic worlds. Where my argument perhaps differs the most from the psychoanalytic mainstream is in the claim that neurosis, psychosis, and perversion should be understood most fundamentally as strategies of reading that give rise to particular subjectivities and structures of desire, not vice versa. Literal readings can coexist with figurative ones, but in the cases I examine here the insistence on absolute truth crowds out every alternative. The tools of textual interpretation are still useful, but they should account in much more nuanced ways for differences in media, form, and technological affordance. To capture this most clearly while retaining their insights, "text" should include any media object, and "speech" could be any contingent expression coming from a shared "grammar" of possibility.

Before we go any further, I should be clear that my argument is that the anti-rhetorical readings that structure emergent communities are *like* psychosis. I am not claiming that each member of each community *is* psychotic. One reason is that, as my research demonstrated, people have different modes of interpretation for different signifiers, so no one *is* psychotic, even though they have psychotic styles of connection in some places and times. Further, the strategies of reading characteristic of psychosis are not the sum total of what it is to *experience* psychosis. The work of Annie Rogers mentioned above is a good entry point into thinking about the excesses of this experience that theory cannot capture (and that it can). My use of psychosis as a conceptual frame for new strategies of reading is not meant to mark them as aberrant or "crazy." To the contrary, psychotic reading is not a pathology to be cured. We are all psychotic readers in relation to something, and whether we are labeled as such is mostly a result of a social judgement about whether our particular fixations are acceptable or not (i.e., whether they can be sanctioned by some kind of propriety). When someone calls a serpent handler "crazy" for risking their lives in worship but is willing to kill and die for an abstract concept of nationhood, we should ask how propriety crafts a difference between the two, not what's "wrong" with the Holiness pastor. As Darian Leader writes, "psychosis is still too often equated with the ways in which some people fail to fit the norms of society."[68] Calling the pastor crazy helps to legitimize our own rigid beliefs in contrast, but when it comes to some symbols that anchor you in the world, you are psychotic. So am I. Just not all the time. No one is.[69]

Psychotic readings are not inherently dangerous and, if this is not clear already, I am more sympathetic to some groups than others. The decline of symbolic efficiency made us all weird and exposed the fiction that we ever weren't. I chose to call this book *Post-Weird* for this exact reason: "Post" signifies present intensification at least as much as it signifies an absent break, just as in "poststructuralist" and "postmodern," both terms that describe diffusion to the point of ubiquity, not obsolescence. Still, recognizing that no one is normal is not a declaration that all things should be permitted, because great malice and violence can be authorized by anti-rhetorical certainty, even though the correlation is not total. Even when these readings don't produce bigotry and death, there is something diminishing about anti-rhetorical sensibilities. My concern is not that psychotic readings happen at all, but that they are becoming the default. Ambiguity and uncertainty are the conditions of possibility for novelty, beauty, curiosity, and possibility. Rigid readings of the world foreclose them, at least in relation to particular signifiers, and rob us of the already meager tools by which we try to find joy in the world without giving us truth in return.

Each chapter of this book also contributes to a psychoanalytic "B-story." This is largely a tale about media, identity, and desire. Most of the communities in this book would be impossible without the Internet, at least in their current form. Desire is the mortar of community: Ultimately, we will see these groups orbiting together around the same occupations and attachments as potential poultices for their constitutive wounds. Media and desire intersect to color our fantasies in new ways. As Francesco Casetti writes of cinema,

> direct exposure to the world triggers discomfort, to which spectators attest when they flee from their everyday milieu, when the movie is slow to start, when troubles in projection break the enchantment of the spectacle, and when screened images are mistaken for real people. Reality can be threatening. . . . The world must be kept at a distance. At the same time, the situation in which spectators are put . . . allows reality to reappear through images that look like epiphanies and that can even be taken as direct perceptions. Contact with the world is reestablished, a contact that appears safe and that remedies or remediates the distance and deferrals previously created.[70]

What is more protective than the Internet, which promises to bring the whole world to us while containing it safely behind a screen—compelling, addicting, but ultimately providing the illusion that we are in control? Discussing our ubiquitous mobile screens, Casetti writes that we "no longer reach the world, but . . . retreat from it. . . . At the same time, we remediate this regressive move duet to virtual connections that allow us to project ourselves beyond the ideal enclosure in which we have found refuge. The severance is thus broken thanks to a screen."[71] As I speculate about the patterns of desire that hold these communities together, I will endeavor to show how attention to media can help us understand what ends up being built in the Tower's ruins.

Chapter 1 covers conspiracy theorists who argue that the Sandy Hook massacre never took place, focusing on interpretation across multiple media, the resonance between their fixations and those found in classic delusions, and the role of guns as (symbolic) defenses. Chapter 2 engages Appalachian serpent-handling churches who demonstrate the clearest fidelity to the letter I have found and sometimes die for it, reflecting also on the propensity of their detractors to exhibit sadism about their fates. Chapter 3 analyzes pro-anorexia communities, focusing on their consumption of the "object nothing" and the inadequacy of sexual binarism to explain their desire, ultimately proposing hunger as an alternative metaphor for the drive that has often been reduced to sex. Chapter 4 traces several communities that deploy the signifier of "science" in ways that resemble psychotic obsession, arguing that the style of attachment developed by these groups—all of which deny the sanctity of others—should be an occasion to reflect on the limits of purely structural worldviews that come at the expense of agency. Another theme suffusing these chapters is the similarity—and difference—between these groups and mainstream academia, which is possessed of plenty of its own weirdness.

The conclusion uses the case studies of various communities to revise and reinterpret psychosis as a rejection of ambiguity. A truly rhetorical theory must militate against ossification and certainty. My aim is primarily to develop a theory of psychotic communication to better understand the communities studied in this book and others emerging in the wake of symbolic efficiency, but I also draw attention to the need to think of rhetoric as an attitude or "equipment for living" to embrace ambiguity and uncertainty. The question of how we, thrown together into collective life, will navigate the decline of symbolic efficiency will probably not be answered by academics, and for good reason. But because we fleeting-improvised subjects read the world through language and other media, our theories are still important, however provisional they are, and I take this opportunity to reflect on how we might read the world differently, including a new look at propriety as an undertheorized concept of rhetoric. In examining how communities form in the wake of symbolic efficiency, it is my hope that someone somewhere will find something in this book to help them be more comfortable in ambiguity and foster a more flexible understanding of the world, one that might point toward new perspectives on community and difference.

1

Sandy Hook

Guns and Anti-Rhetoric

On December 14, 2012, a teenager named Adam Lanza murdered his mother; he then drove to his old elementary school and in the space of about five minutes killed six school employees, twenty children, and himself. While the world ended quite literally for twenty-eight people, events were set in motion that transformed it figuratively for everyone else. Within hours of the shooting at Sandy Hook Elementary School a sizeable contingent of people declared that the event was staged, and within hours this view took root across the Internet, growing in the rich soil of conspiracism that lay fallow as if specially prepared for this day. Alex Jones, one of America's most prominent conspiracy theorists, often gets the blame for this phenomenon, but records of those calling in to his show make it clear that he acted as a human megaphone, amplifying sounds that he was not the first to make.[1] The conspiracy theories surrounding the Sandy Hook massacre grew rhizomatically from obscure origins.

Phenomena like Sandy Hook denialism cannot be reduced to a clear set of causes and effects. Nonetheless, there is a sense of this moment as a watershed, if not causal then symptomatic of larger transformations in the media ecosystem.[2] On the tenth anniversary of the massacre, Amanda Crawford called it "a pivot point that marked the start of a new era in misinformation and political polarization,"[3] while Elizabeth Williamson claimed that "Sandy Hook was the first mass tragedy to spawn an online circle of people impermeable and hostile to reality and its messengers, whether the mainstream media, law enforcement, or the families of the dead."[4] Sandy Hook increased the mainstream profile of

Alex Jones and inaugurated a yearslong legal struggle by the victim's families against him, resulting in verdicts totaling over one billion dollars that few believe will do much to end disinformation[5] and Jones himself has somewhat confusingly called a "victory for truth."[6] Conspiracy thinking is an ancient phenomenon and there are certainly precedents even for this specific incarnation of it, but whether or not one thinks the world "really" changed after Sandy Hook, the fact that it is often presented as a key inflection point makes it worthy of another look in the context of ongoing concerns about "fake news," disinformation, social media, and "alternative facts." At the very least, Sandy Hook was one of the most prominent conspiracy discourses between the bookends of 9/11 and QAnon.

Sandy Hook is still a frequent topic of discussion in conspiracy theory circles as a reference point for key ideas. "Crisis actors" and "false flag" narratives are advanced for virtually every high-profile mass murder event, especially school shootings. "False flags"—the notion that attacks are sometimes perpetrated by one group in the guise of another—have a long history in conspiracy circles, featuring particularly strongly for 9/11 "truthers." The claim that supposed victims were actually "crisis actors" who only pretended to die and often reappear in other public events was more novel in 2012. While Sandy Hook was not the first time this allegation was made, it is a particularly prominent one and apparently the template for future accusations made about school massacres at Parkland, Uvalde, Nashville, and likely many others that have occurred in the time between me writing these words and you reading them. The false flag and crisis actor narratives do not cover the whole field of conspiracy theories about Sandy Hook, but they are the most prominent and influential. As a result, I have chosen to make them the focus of my investigation of conspiracy discourses around this event. They are good illustrations of the relationship between delusion, media, and what I will argue is an anti-rhetorical mode of interpretation.

Conspiracy theorists are perhaps the clearest candidates for structurally psychotically organized communities outside a clinical setting, which Jodi Dean, Mark Andrejevic, and others have already noted.[7] Although "conspiracy theorist" is the conventional label, subjects in this discourse are critics as much as they are theorists: They criticize the dominant narrative through self-confirming research, building their alternative theories along the way. They are also prolific writers, producing texts and other media that serve to cohere communities of doubt and speculation that end up applying that doubt very selectively. While these conspiracy communities are suspicious of narratives they see as hegemonic, they demonstrate unwarranted certainty when it comes to their own narrative explanations of events. The assertion of crisis actors is one example of this certainty, operating like a rhetorical figure but closely resembling well-known individual delusions and rejecting the ambiguity that characterizes rhetoric as such. Due to their intolerance of ambiguity and uncertainty, I have labeled this kind of device anti-rhetorical. But language, either written or spoken, does not exhaust the media about Sandy Hook. Katharina Thalmann has argued that stigmatization of conspiracy thinking is new, not the practice, and if certain brands of "superconspiracy" are more common now it may be in reaction to the official scorn heaped on this mode of thinking.[8] New technologies have exponentially increased the possibilities for interconnection both between individual members of these communities and between different conspiracy ideas. The Internet distributed and enabled Sandy Hook denialism to such an extent that it would be difficult to imagine the movement existing, at least in the form it took, without this technology. Online platforms combine stasis and movement, reading and watching, image, video, speech, and text.

In the remainder of this chapter, I will make the case for analyzing Sandy Hook denialism as a kind of collective psychosis. While Andrejevic, Dean, and others make similar arguments at the level of overall structure, I will also consider the more granular devices from which this discourse is composed, focusing on the parallels between crisis actors and the classic Fregoli delusion. Lacan's explanation of psychosis is a helpful perspective but was built for an analytic environment of words, not YouTube videos and image macros. This requires a closer look at how the concept might apply to newer media. I will argue that considering the role of guns as defenses and fantasy objects might help us speculate about what is foreclosed in this discourse—that is, the intolerable encounter with uncertainty that conspiracy thinking serves to ward off. Finally, I conclude with a return to structure and form, suggesting that we academics might benefit by contemplating the ways in which conspiracy theories uncomfortably resemble our own practices.

What Happened

A succinct account of the Sandy Hook murders appears in the State's Attorney's final report. It reads:

> On the morning of December 14, 2012, the shooter, age 20, heavily armed, went to Sandy Hook Elementary School (SHES) in Newtown, where he shot his way into the locked school building with a Bushmaster Model XM15-E2S rifle. He then shot and killed the principal and school psychologist as they were in the north hallway of the school responding to the noise of the shooter coming into the school. The shooter also shot and injured two other staff members who were also in the hallway.
>
> The shooter then went into the main office, apparently did not see the staff who were hiding there, and returned to the hallway.

> After leaving the main office, the shooter then went down the same hallway in which he had just killed two people and entered first grade classrooms 8 and 10, the order in which is unknown. While in those rooms he killed the two adults in each room, fifteen children in classroom 8 and five in classroom 10. All of the killings were done with the Bushmaster rifle.
>
> He then took his own life with a single shot from a Glock 20, 10 mm pistol in classroom 10.
>
> Prior to going to the school, the shooter used a .22 caliber Savage Mark II rifle to shoot and kill his mother in her bed at the home where they lived at 36 Yogananda Street in Newtown.[9]

The shooter was Adam Lanza, aged twenty, a young man with a history of psychiatric diagnoses who seemed to enjoy guns, videogames, the Internet, and little else. Lanza was fascinated with previous school shootings and other acts of violence, but although he had himself once been a student at Sandy Hook, no motive for his carefully planned assault was officially determined.[10]

Events like the Sandy Hook massacre tend to be accompanied by chaos and confusion from the beginning. Reports of a man apprehended in the woods near the elementary school led to questions about a second shooter. The weapons used were sometimes misidentified. Adam Lanza was initially identified as Ryan Lanza, his brother. His mother, Nancy, was misidentified as a Sandy Hook Elementary School teacher. Adam Lanza was incorrectly said to have been buzzed in to the locked school. Social media went on a rampage, while some reporters from respected outlets relied on federal sources in New York and Washington rather than being on the scene themselves.[11] The demand for immediate news coverage mingled with the telephone game of social media to brew informational poison and distribute it around the world before basic facts could solidify. Some consumers interpreted these mistakes as deliberately false, rather than inevitable breakdowns in the face of such an unexpected and chaotic event.

Unanswered questions and seeming contradictions helped to spur the earliest conspiracy theories, which began with the simple affirmation that the event was faked. According to Williamson, one could listen to Alex Jones on December 14 grappling with this claim in real time on *Infowars*, as callers alleged that the shooting never happened before Jones himself had committed to the line.[12] But as time passed Sandy Hook denialism took on a more coherent shape. Rob Brotherton uses the term *anomaly hunting* to refer to this aspect of conspiracy thinking in which amateur epistemologists leap on inconsistencies to demolish the "official version" and establish evidence for a hidden alternate reality.[13] A new narrative emerges from the troubling gaps and lacunae and is always more comprehensive than the official version precisely because it is designed retroactively to provide a concrete explanation for every uncertainty. From initial chaos and confusion, then, order is imposed out of a variety of sources: news reports, social media posts, images, broadcasts, interviews, government documents, and so on, including ones about similar previous events or more general conspiracy literature. The goal of doing so is to reveal an ostensibly hidden truth, an invisible order that both arises from these scraps and explains their coherence—in the case of Sandy Hook denialists, this hidden truth is that some group of conspirators staged the attack as a pretense for seizing privately held firearms despite Second Amendment protections. The psychic function of this process is to avoid acknowledging that the world is ambiguous, traumatic, and out of our control. Even if an evil cabal might sound terrifying, it explains why bad things happen and reassures us that we do not live in a chaotic world that is complex beyond our comprehension where some obscure person can simply kill dozens of children for reasons that we can't understand. If acts like this are possible at all, they are always planned, even if we don't know the details of the larger order, and that belief may be less traumatic than the alternative.

Denialists advanced a broad range of evidence in favor of their theories. A common overall claim is that the building where the massacre is supposed to have happened was no longer operating as a school but was staged to look like one so that the attack could be staged there by some secretive entity, usually identified as one of the usual conspiracy theory suspects, like Mossad or FEMA. Discrepancies in which news stories about the massacre precede its occurrence are frequently cited, along with discrepancies in media coverage such as the alleged presence of multiple shooters.[14] That students, witnesses, and grieving parents are crisis actors is evidenced by unexpected affective responses, inappropriate performances, narrative inconsistencies, their professional backgrounds, and moments of preparation supposedly caught on camera. Images of children alleged to have died in the event are compared to photographs of children at public events like the Superbowl or other massacres.[15] The usual suspects behind the hoax are either Mossad, FEMA, or some other federal agency, sometimes in combination, motivated by the need to pacify the American public.[16] As in many American conspiracy theories, there is an antisemitic undertone to some versions of Sandy Hook denial in which "globalists" (i.e., Jews) want to disarm the American public to facilitate their own secret agenda. Sometimes, the history of Newtown, Connecticut, where the massacre occurred, is used to contextualize its choice as a setting due to its importance as an early location for weapons manufacture[17] or as a former host to "cruel experiments" at the Fairfield Hills psychiatric hospital.[18] The Connecticut community is alleged to go along with these schemes mostly for financial reasons as gifts and donations flooded into Newtown after Sandy Hook.

Among the most prominent texts produced by Sandy Hook denialists is the rather straightforwardly titled *Nobody Died at Sandy Hook: It Was a FEMA*

Drill to Promote Gun Control.[19] James Fetzer, coeditor of the book and author of several chapters, was once a Distinguished Professor of philosophy at the University of Minnesota Duluth. Fetzer cut his teeth on John F. Kennedy assassination theories, eventually moving on to Holocaust denial, skepticism about the moon landing, and work on Sandy Hook, for which he was sued by Lenny Pozner, father of one of the victims who also successfully challenged Alex Jones.[20] Fetzer's work exhibits a characteristic mix of suspicion and certainty. The official narrative—*any* official narrative—is necessarily suspect. "Knowledge of historical events," he writes, "can never be 'definitive and certain,'" as even today's date, parental DNA testing, and one's birthday could be "faked."[21] In the very next paragraph, however, Fetzer writes that "*there can be no doubt*" that the Warren Report on JFK's death was fabricated.[22] This pattern is repeated elsewhere, including in Fetzer's discussion of a press conference held by Connecticut's Governor Malloy on the day of the shooting, in which he mentioned that he had been "spoken to in an attempt that we might be prepared for something like this playing itself out in our state."[23] Asking himself what this could mean, Fetzer concludes that there are only two alternatives: that Malloy was warned in advance that there would be a shooting, or that he was told that a hoax would be implemented. No other possibility can be considered. "Mark my words," Fetzer concludes, "The evidence presented here demonstrates that the school was closed by 2008; that there were no students to evacuate; that Adam Lanza appears to have been a work of fiction; and that *the teachers, the parents, the Newtown School Board, the State Police, the Medical Examiner and the Governor were in on the hoax*."[24] James F. Tracy, former professor of communication at Florida Atlantic University, creates a similarly certain binary based on "multiple gaffes, discrepancies, and hedges" made by medical examiner H. Wayne Carver in an informal press conference, which "suggest that he is either under coercion or an imposter," again the only two options considered despite obvious alternatives.[25]

Fetzer's notion that Adam Lanza was fictional is also mentioned by the pseudonymous Vivian Lee, allegedly a professor, in a *Buzzfeed*-style "Top 10" list on the Sandy Hook hoax. Lee cites another Sandy Hook researcher to argue that Lanza was too weak to carry the gear he is supposed to have brought to the elementary school and therefore was perhaps not a real person.[26] Lee also alleges that photographs of Lanza are "ridiculously fraudulent" and "clearly do not depict a real person."[27] In support of the latter claim, Lee simply includes images, some of which appear to be inconsistent with each other. Even in book form, this visual approach to evidence is significant for many Sandy Hook denialists. Allan William Powell includes fifty "exhibits" in support of his claim that the school was closed at the time of the supposed shooting.[28] The video documentary format is often utilized, originally on YouTube before Sandy Hook denialism was deplatformed in the wake of Pozner's legal challenges. Influential videos such as *We Need to Talk about Sandy Hook* sometimes feature visual cues that add context to dialogue (such as a spinning Star of David to reference Jewish conspirators) or employ features unique to their media such as a deluge of overlapping videos and soundtracks to signal chaos and complexity. Twitter and Facebook were also key channels for multimedia conspiracism, a role now filled by reactionary social media (Gab, Rumble, BitChute, Truth Social, etc.).

The constellation of images, video, and text across multiple platforms provided the material from which the crisis actor theory could be assembled and evolve over time, but the process of building a community around a set of (relatively) coherent theories requires shared practices of interpretation and meaning-making. It is not enough to produce consistent tropes and to fit them together into persuasive texts—subjects who encounter them must know the protocols that make them legible within a particular discourse. While we might traditionally think of these practices as rhetorical, the insistence on univocal meaning in conspiracy thinking is ultimately contrary to rhetoric's acceptance of ambiguity, uncertainty, and polysemy as the foundations for speech. The interpretation of accidental connections as unshakable truths revealing a hidden order resembles delusional thought more than rhetorical interpretation. The next section will explore it in these terms with the aim of demonstrating how conspiracist communities mirror psychotic patterns of language at the level of the individual devices that combine to describe their larger discourses.

The Mask of Leopoldo Fregoli

Conspiracy theories have been analogized to genres of fiction in which the reader arrives at the solution of a mystery along with the characters by piecing together clues. Readers are trained by fiction to move in and out of a character's perspective and piece together a "big picture" that is not accessible to them. Fans are acutely aware of "bad readers," those who miss the deeper coherence of plot or the subtleties of its organization, much as conspiracy theorists accuse those who accept official narratives of being brainwashed, "useful idiots," "sheep" and so on.[29] Luc Boltanski has made this connection at some length by tying conspiracy theories to detective fiction,[30] an observation evidenced in the Sandy Hook case by Vivian Lee's reference to Sherlock Holmes.[31] From this perspective, the reader's enjoyment comes from unraveling the mystery along with the author and perhaps knowing the truth before the characters of the story do. A "good" reader is one who figures out the mystery, just as a "good" conspiracy theorist identifies a fundamental reality despite—even because of—the fragmentary information that serves to conceal it.

Sandy Hook denialists—like most communities discussed in this book—have a set of shared texts and media objects, but not every theorist has read every one, and different individuals may emphasize different elements of the theory while still falling within this tight-knit group. Rather than cohering around a single unitary text, conspiracy theorists assemble a narrative from a variety of fragmentary bits—news clips, social media posts, photographs, books, and radio shows like Infowars, among many others. This is not the same as reading a detective novel: The novel, written by a single author, usually has one correct solution to the mystery. Conspiracy theorists certainly feel like there is only one answer beneath the surface of these media fragments, but their participation is more active. In this sense they are like critics judging the quality of performative, literary, or rhetorical performances in relation to their genre. They perform criticism in at least two ways—as analysts of hegemonic narratives and active audiences for the conspiracy literature of others. Thinking of conspiracy theorists as critics helps us grasp how they render their judgments about plot and execution into new texts that form a basis for communal attachments, like critics writing reviews, though what is analyzed extends beyond what we traditionally characterize as texts and signifiers to include digital and other forms of mediation.

There are a series of movements in this work of conspiracy criticism. The would-be critic is first subjected to the deluge of information about Sandy Hook, a set of fragments so chaotic that they require some trust in authority to navigate and explain. With that trust lacking, these accounts are subject to close scrutiny and suspicion, which ultimately disproves (for the critic) the dominant story. The phrase "do the research," common in conspiracy circles, demonstrates that this process is largely self-confirming: that some hidden conspiracy is so obvious that the "facts" can only confirm what the conspiracy theorist believes, and anyone who examines them without bias can simply trust their own eyes. Next, the critic assembles a new theory of events, including a representation of the dominant narrative and the truth it conceals, authoring a new work analogous to a literary critic's interpretation of a text.

This criticism and writing are done in concert with others in conspiracy-friendly forums, creating the potential for community in two ways. First, the text is effectively written together, in the case of Sandy Hook a kind of exquisite corpse about how there are no corpses. Second, in addition to the bond of collective writing, conspiracy critics can unite in a common reading process, one that insists that they discovered, rather than fantasized, an underlying truth that only initiates can access. In this task, they resemble Michael Calvin McGee's account of critical rhetoric. Speakers, he writes, "make discourses from scraps and pieces of evidence. Critical rhetoric does not begin with a finished text in need of interpretation. . . . The apparently finished discourse is in fact a dense reconstruction of all the bits of other discourses from which it was made."[32] Conspiracy theorists go further: Beyond composing and decomposing texts, they assert the existence of a totality to which the fragments are epiphenomenal, disavowing the notion that what they produce is rhetorical at all in the sense that it is a compilation of readings that could only be made one way. Even where rhetorical techniques are deployed (e.g., figurative language, compositional choices) the key pillars of the discourse, its "quilting points," are not read or considered to be rhetorical.

The figure of the crisis actor is one of these quilting points for Sandy Hook denialists, reinforcing their resemblance to theater critics. "The most durable and entrenched trope for conspiracy," writes Carver, "is the stage."[33] Fetzer, in critiquing what he sees as a poor coverup by actors standing in for victims, is ultimately playing the role of a critic assessing both performances and plot.[34] Many theorists refer to "staging,"[35] and *We Need to Talk about Sandy Hook* uses the famous Shakespeare line "all the world's a stage." "The stage was a closed school in Newtown," says one conspiracy newsletter that criticizes the "bad" performances. "The story had scripted roles for highly paid crisis actors and professional performers who adopted fake identities . . . with the mainscream [*sic*] media cheering-leading in celebration of the naked Emperor's imaginary clothes."[36] Of course "stage" and "actors" are not really metaphors for denialists, who don't argue that Sandy Hook is *like* a stage but that it *is* a stage for a performance by paid actors, often ones who supposedly show up in repeat performances at various tragedies. While both dominant and conspiracy narratives are constructed from media fragments, that Sandy Hook conspiracists treat the latter as occult truths makes them analogous to delusional systems sometimes experienced in psychosis. They are not, however, deciphering some fundamental reality that underpins an illusory one. They are masquerading invention as discovery.

James Tracy, the former professor of communication at Florida Atlantic University, possibly originated the term *crisis actors* in conspiracy circles when he connected the events at Sandy Hook with ads for a company of professional actors who aid in emergency response simulations.[37] Since 2012 the theme has been consistently repeated with other public acts of violence such as the Boston Marathon bombing and school massacres at Parkland and Uvalde.[38] The idea that the same actor or actors stand in for a variety of different people has a close parallel with a specific delusion. In 1927, two French-speaking psychiatrists published a paper on a patient who was at times convinced that she was "the victim of enemies" that were *personae* of the same people, "of whom the main culprits are the actresses Robine and Sarah Bernhardt, whom she often went to see in the theatre." The patient's experience was described in reference to an Italian actor, Leopoldo Fregoli, famous for his skills as a quick-change artist. Various people that the patient knew or met she perceived as the Bernhardts in disguise as they were "capable of all types of transformation" and could "impose such transformations on others: they are Frégolis who can 'frégolify' any and everybody."[39] Today, the Fregoli delusion has mostly been absorbed into the broader category of "delusional misidentification syndromes." Although psychologists (as opposed to psychoanalysts) often consider these to be a primarily neurological disfunction, even they sometimes acknowledge the importance of attending to a patient's "psychosocial history, particularly their trauma history," to understand them.[40]

As socially shared phenomena, the collective delusions of Sandy Hook deniers resemble the Fregoli delusion but resist any exclusively neurological explanation. One would expect deniers with brain lesions to develop fantasies about those closest to them, not strangers whom they have sought out and studied, but there is little evidence that they harbor misidentifications with their friends and family. Further, while the individual delusion pattern is quite rare, the collective phenomenon seems far more common.[41] The clinical presentation of Fregoli delusion differs from the crisis actors theory in that it tends to express paranoia through fantasies of persecution by the impostors, while conspiracy theorists generally imagine their persecutors to be another party behind the actors—FEMA, Democratic elites, and/or the West's oldest scapegoats, the Jews. Finally, although it is notoriously difficult to disrupt conspiracy thinking, spontaneous recovery through persuasion is possible in ways that would be quite surprising in a neurological disorder. Therefore, I am not suggesting that conspiracy theorists experience the Fregoli delusion as identified by Courbon and Fail, but that they evince very similar patterns, which might be relevant if we believe (and we should) that the content and structure of the disorder is not fully reducible to biology.

The resemblances are striking. The Fregoli delusion, when expressed in media as something that forms the kernel of a communal belief, can be thought of as a non-rhetorical visual/linguistic device. For example, a popular conspiracy video by "citizen journalist" Barry Soetoro claims that an FBI sniper photographed at Sandy Hook is actually an actor who plays two parts in the staged hoax, the other being David Wheeler, father of a young boy who died in the massacre.[42] The FBI sniper is therefore *actually* this "Hollywood actor," who reappears multiple times. This is demonstrated by a visual juxtaposition of two images, one of Wheeler and another of the sniper, with lines highlighting some facial similarities. Wheeler is an actor, so the video claims, and his wife Francine is an entertainer too. Both play the parts of newly introduced figures: David Wheeler as "FBI Sniper" and "Grieving Father" and his wife as "Grieving Mother." This allegation is made about others based on similarities in photos and videos, including the claim that a family of actors (the Sexton-Greenbergs) played parents Nick and Laura Phelps and the family of murdered teacher Victoria Soto,[43] that H. Wayne Carver and purported hitman Richard Kuklinski were played by the same actor,[44] that Adam Lanza's father Peter was played by MADtv's Michael McDonald,[45] and so on. This "actor" accusation exists for nearly every victim at Sandy Hook, including the claim that children supposed to have died there performed at the Superbowl or never existed at all but were "played" by the children who were supposed to be their sibling (and, in real life, actually were).[46]

In contrast to the claim that family members were played by actors, it is sometimes alleged that Adam Lanza and the dead children at Sandy Hook were simply invented with manipulated records and photographs. A certain Dr. Eowyn[47] claimed that no birth or death records existed to confirm the massacre, and that therefore Lanza and his victims were fictional.[48] "Now here's the phony, fictional, computer-generated, Photoshop boy, the boogeyman Adam Lanza," Barry Soetoro claims. "Adam Lanza is fictional. He was manufactured in Photoshop on a computer in a cubicle at DHS [Department of Homeland Security] or the FEMA contractor that designed the Sandy Hook hoax." The analysis continues that the curls of Lanza's hair had to have been made with the Photoshop "clone" tool and that the lines of his face and neck are too straight to be authentic. "His bug eyes and his hair, all of this, the bowl cut, the kooky, autistic kid haircut was designed to terrorize families, terrorize parents, and terrorize children. He's not real."[49] These claims suggest a dynamic of recognition that is disrupted with the decline of symbolic efficiency. In *The Ticklish Subject*, Žižek explained that what allows an individual subject to exercise authority is partly that they are recognized as possessing it by the Other, a shorthand personification of the overall system of language, culture, and authority. Those vested with authority are affirmed by an "official" recognition, so that when they get a promotion, for example, but some functionary is not aware of their new position, they may have to appeal to the paperwork that represents the Other's bestowal of their status.[50] To say that the Sandy Hook dead do not have birth or death certificates is essentially to say that they are not authorized by the Other—they are fake, nothing but images that do not signify anything. To borrow from Daniel Paul Schreber's famous memoir of psychosis, they are "hastily-improvised-men,"[51] created hollow and incomplete, lacking real substance, and made only to serve some instrumental purpose in deception as Potemkin people. To believe that Adam Lanza is fake on the basis of one's untrained glance at a photograph is an excellent example of believing one's eyes, not the words produced by a Symbolic authority, and demonstrates again the erosion of order that leads Sandy Hook deniers to the brink of an abyss they cannot tolerate, requiring them to hastily improvise new coordinates of belief. The Fregoli delusion perhaps plays the same function, reducing complexity and uncertainty to a manageable (if frightening) sense that everything is the same underneath, allowing conspiracy theorists to return to order, however rigid.

The fact that documents are still affirmed as a kind of underlying proof demonstrates the fragility of this species of delusion, however. Documents could, from a paranoid perspective, always be fake, meaning that their presence would confirm nothing and therefore that their absence is hardly dispositive, although one might expect a high-quality conspiracy to produce them nonetheless. As in the allegation that the same child actors are used for different events, in this account the Other is taken to be shoddy, incompetent, and not fully real, but simultaneously all-powerful and calculating with global reach and apparently vast resources. For Sandy Hook denialism to be true, the federal government of the United States of America must be able to keep secrets held by thousands and orchestrate vast, closely coordinated events, and yet still be lazy about Photoshop. How are there so many mistakes? Conspiracist Vivian Lee suggests an answer. "Part of this ploy is the ridicule of the populace," she writes, "a 'macabre nose-thumbing at our complete indifference to our mental enslavement,' such as the smiling relatives and weird interviews . . . the myriad police photos providing no evidence, and—the ultimate joke on every sentient person—the students alive and well and singing at the Super Bowl. Such stunts are intentional, and are *not only fun for the perpetrators but are seen to enhance their power*."[52] Lee's assertion demonstrates the belief in an "Other of the Other," a secret force that coordinates everything from the shadows, typical of paranoid discourses. It also demonstrates how suppositions about what the Other wants and enjoys help to determine the shape of conspiracy beliefs. The conspiracy theorist masks their own enjoyment of their delusions by dissolving them in the enjoyment of the Other: It is the evil conspirators who enjoy our suffering, so the work of "citizen journalists" is simply what's necessary to survive and unmask this perverse pleasure.[53] The fact that conspiracy theorists enjoy the feeling of power that comes from unveiling mysteries or fantasizing about the Other's oppression cannot be openly admitted because doing so would disrupt their own sense of self. This is in line with Melanie Klein's notion of projective identification, in which something unacceptable in the self is attributed to an outside object or agent. "In psychotic disorders," Klein wrote, "identification of an object with the hated parts of the self contributes to the intensity of the hatred directed against other people" because excessive splitting of one's psyche weakens the sense of identity, representing a loss of "power, potency, strength, knowledge, and many other desired qualities."[54]

The fragility of the Fregoli delusion combined with the mechanism of projection may help to explain some of the more ghoulish aspects of Sandy Hook denial. Conspiracy theorists repeatedly insisted that they be shown the bodies of dead children. One message on Lenny Pozner's Google+ page said "Let's just dig up all the little bastards," while Oklahoma grandmother Kelley Watt (AKA "gr8mom") wrote "I want to hear the 'slaughter' and I won't be satisfied until the caskets are opened."[55] Fetzer, who shared Watt's comment, had previously demanded to see the bodies of 9/11 victims.[56] Wolfgang Halbig, an investigator who traveled to Connecticut himself and collaborated with others in the conspiracy community, threatened to dig up Noah Pozner's grave.[57] All of these examples nicely illustrate Žižek's use of Groucho Marx's line: "Whom do you believe, your eyes or my words?" For these Sandy Hook deniers, the answer is only their eyes—the decline of symbolic efficiency has left them with only what they directly see. They interpret the world through an unproblematic decoding of signs that can only have a single meaning, hence the refrain "do your own research," something that is said only because the theorist believes that theirs is the only possible honest conclusion. The same dynamic is at work in comparing "crisis actor" photos—it doesn't matter what others say about the identities of these people, because truth is revealed only by the eye and no alternative reading of the signs is possible.

Anti-Rhetorical Devices

Claims about crisis actors and hastily improvised gunmen demonstrate how signification always contains a hidden act of identification in that the signifier must be linked to what it signifies, perhaps what Lundberg describes as "affective labor" in his discussion of trope.[58] This work of connection is often conscious, especially when we use figure and trope, the two primary modes by which we tie signifiers to their referents, as opposed to literalism. Reading Cormac McCarthy's line "Fate ridden snake . . . little brother death with his quartz goat's eyes,"[59] some modicum of labor is required to connect signifiers ("little brother death," "quartz goat's eyes") with the signifiers they replace, and more to appreciate the associations that extend beyond lexical replacement. This work occurs in a field of multiple, ambiguous meanings, requiring that one experience or at least accept the possibility of polysemy, itself a metonym for the larger indeterminacy of our lives and experiences as it is mediated through language. Some labor may even be evident in clichés and dead metaphors. It is still performed in literal interpretations because the word must be accepted as a stand-in for a referent. Some formations of literal language, like unusual syntax or technical language, will demand yet more. If we think of this work as unevenly distributed across a discourse, then there is a kind of texture to communication, a rise and fall of linguistic intensity or force even when the tropes, figures, and styles of rhetoric are not (explicitly) employed.[60] This work is performed at the level of the *letter*—the "material medium [*support*] that concrete discourse borrows from language,"[61] or at the place where something is transfigured from the code of *langue* and deployed in the *parole* of everyday communication.

Some of the speech patterns typical of psychosis could be described in metonymic terms, as Lacan prefers, drawing connections purely at the level of the signifier through shared substance or proximity. Clanging, for example, which resembles the rhetorical figures of alliteration or assonance, is essentially a series of words linked only by similar sounds. Perhaps more significantly, psychotic speech also conflates signifier with signified, insisting on consubstantiality of the two.[62] An excellent example comes from a colleague of mine who is a practicing psychoanalyst. On a subway car in New York, she heard a man say, "a dime for a cup of coffee." Upon being presented with a dime, the man sat down, repeated the phrase, and swallowed the coin. This could be understood as a connection in which the dime, proximately connected to the coffee as something that could be literally traded for it, came to replace the coffee entirely so that the phrase "dime for a cup of coffee" should be interpreted so that the word *for* means "in place of" not "to be used towards."[63] The abstract principle of symbolic exchange mediated by money is gone and the connection is immediate and proximate instead, one of apparently shared substance or identity.[64] One fascinating detail reported by my colleague is the way that this man's concrete thinking drew her in. She recalled wondering how he would find coffee or afford it with just a dime in the subway, a line of inquiry that took his statement literally in a different way. She and her friend "got to live in this psychotic man's inner world of concrete/literal thinking—the land of lost metaphors and figurative language."[65] Perhaps nascent conspiracy theorists do, too—once we are exposed to others reading a logically coherent set of signifiers in a way that anchors them in a community, it becomes easier to let these discourses cushion us from the burden of interpretive work in a field of ambiguity. Over time, strategies of reading become inflexible when it comes to the key pillars of the discourse. The man on the New York subway and James Fetzer are united by their strategies of reading. Both insist that something they encounter in the world (a dime, a facial expression, a document) can only mean one thing, with no room for polysemy or even probability.

What is happening when Sandy Hook deniers interpret one person as undoubtedly another in disguise or insist on the absolutely certain, if occult, meaning of an investigative document or security camera image is a mode of interpretation distinct from either rhetoric or literalism. Rhetoric is distinct from literalism, but to read in one mode is not necessarily to deny the possibility of the other. As Hugh Bredin argues, because much figurative language has no effect on meaning we would be amiss to oppose rhetoric and literalism in every case. "A buzzard is a big bird" is figurative (alliterative), but simultaneously literal, not requiring an audience to choose from aporetic meanings. Syntactic figures such as these do not directly implicate meaning, but semantics involving the "transfer of names" (e.g., metaphor, metonymy, synecdoche—what I have labeled "trope," although Bredin does not make this distinction) might.[66] But as they are repeatedly used, tropes like "all hands on deck," "issued by the Crown," and "he's a teddy bear" operate as if they were literal because they are essentially univocal and conventional. For Bredin, metaphors like "night has fallen" are essentially literal, too, due to the principle of semantic hierarchy, in which a word like *fallen* is "felt" to have a "central or original meaning," the same reason that etymological and other "dead" metaphors (e.g., *bureaucrat*, or the word *metaphor* itself) do not produce new semantic meanings when they are used.[67] "The literal and the figurative," Bredin concludes, "are not contraries as such. Rather, figurativeness excludes literality only when it is of such a kind that it excludes univocacy and conventionality. If figures are not literal, this is not because they are figures. The true antonym of the literal is not the figurative, but the non-literal."[68] Rhetorical devices can thus be processed literally, and literal language read rhetorically.[69]

Rhetoric is undoubtedly a contested term, but its definitional least common denominator should include ambiguity, contingency, and polysemy. The reading strategy of Sandy Hook deniers is defined by an absolute foreclosure of these traits. Metonymy is not a precise enough term for this, even in Lacan's sense, which borrows more from linguistics than rhetoric. It is closer to literalism, but even that is inadequate since literalism and rhetoric overlap substantially, and even avowedly literal meanings do not have to render polysemy impossible as a condition for their own possibility; they merely need to choose an indexical interpretation over a figurative one. In conspiracy discourses, meaning is *sui generis* and incontestable because the key devices of these discourses serve no purpose other than to shield fragile subjects from the threatening void of formlessness produced by the decline of symbolic efficiency. The Fregoli delusion and hasty improvisation are kinds of linguistic devices, like figure and trope but explicitly in denial of them. I suggest that we think of them as anti-rhetorical or atropic devices,[70] significant, distinct formations in the topography of a discourse characterized by the disavowal of polysemy, ambiguity, and openness of meaning. They closely resemble psychotic speech but this parallel should serve to remind us that psychosis is a mode of experience broadly shared by many who would not be clinically diagnosed with it, not a pathologizing label for those who might be.

The concept of anti-rhetorical devices is not meant to replace metonymy as a description of psychotic speech, but to provide a new way of thinking about some instances of discourse—especially in relation to certainty—that are not captured by this concept borrowed from rhetoric and linguistics. The key attribute of anti-rhetorical readings is a common stance in relation to the identificatory aspect of signification: a refusal to accept the conventional connection of one signifier to another, instead insisting that the signifier is comingled with what it signifies in a nonarbitrary way. Here the Fregoli delusion is one device with possible analogues drawn from delusional misidentification syndromes[71] such as Capgras, subjective doubles (the "Golyadkin phenomenon"), intermetamorphosis, and reduplicative paramnesia.[72] Whereas trope performs the work of linking two signifiers through substitution (constituting metaphor, metonymy, catachresis, etc., depending on the procedure) and sparks new meaning, these devices actively sever identification: X *cannot* signify Y, because it *really* means only one thing, Z, and this is proven to be certain by the evidence of our eyes, not the words that situate X and Y together in the Symbolic and distinguish it from Z. X is a sign of Z, even if the Other of the Other tries to dupe us into thinking that X is a signifier of Y. Crossing media is often a key element, especially in terms of visuality: "I am supposed to believe official words about Adam Lanza, but I can see the truth in this visual image," or "They want me to think this shape is something else, but I *know* it represents the New World Order." Each figure condenses the sequence that I will argue characterizes every community discussed in this book: first, a foreclosure of received meaning (i.e., symbolic efficiency), then the vertigo that comes from exposure to the regime of language with no filter (i.e., to signification with no protocol for reading), and finally the assertion of some deep meaning to one scrap of discourse (i.e., a signifier) that shores up a new reality scar tissue covering a wound.

While rhetorical devices serve to connect signifiers in sometimes unexpected ways, anti-rhetorical devices undertake what Wilfred Bion called "attacks on linking." These are active efforts to sever connections between "objects" in the mind by refusing the labor of connection. Attacks on linking then lead to an "over-prominence in the psychotic part of the personality of links which appear to be logical, almost mathematical, but never emotionally reasonable. Consequently the links surviving are perverse, cruel, and sterile."[73] This "logical" but "perverse, cruel, and sterile" style of linkage fits Sandy Hook well: Extremely meticulous analyses of the photographs of dead children and supposed impostors are broken down by amateur sleuths, almost certainly incorrectly but with great attention to detail in establishing new connections, which serve to deny the emotional realities of grieving parents, dead children, and anything else that would demand an affective reaction from conspiracists. Those reactions still occur—demands to see the bodies, death threats, and so on—but only through a circuitous path after an initial refusal of the link authorized by the Other between signifier and signified. However much it might be comforting to some to call conspiracy theorists illogical (or even crazy), they almost never are. Conspiracy theories persist because of a powerful internal logic, which may begin from incorrect assumptions but tends to draw valid conclusions within its own coordinates, however divorced these are from cultural consensus or material reality.

This dynamic is distinct from "anti-rhetoric" in which a speaker says that they are not trying to persuade when they really are (they often say this precisely to persuade), and it is also distinct from efforts to deliberately avoid figurative language and simply "say what one means." These other moves acknowledge the possibility of rhetoric, but at best repress or deny it. Anti-rhetorical devices evince a certainty of conviction that is possible only when alternatives are rendered impossible, not just unlikely. When Sandy Hook deniers claim that Adam Lanza was "a work of fiction," they follow up immediately by clarifying that the matter is "resolved beyond any reasonable doubt. We have 50 photos. . . .

Doubt in this case would be reasonable were there a reasonable alternative explanation. But . . . there is none here."[74] This is especially remarkable given that the structure of conspiracy theories makes them logically precarious. If you say that the Freemasons are behind every tragedy and there's no evidence because they've covered it up (which proves the theory), you have few grounds to contest the hypothesis that any other group of conspirators is equally likely, which creates a problem like the "many gods" objection to Pascal's wager. Or perhaps the reptile aliens only want you to think that the Freemasons are behind everything, and the fact that you believe it is evidence that the plot worked—but of course, I may believe that the reptiles want us to blame the Freemasons because that is what the KGB wants me to think, and so on in an infinite regression. Versions of these problems regarding Sandy Hook include the mutually exclusive claims that mass shootings happen because of government mind control[75] and that the event was staged as a result of Jewish psyops,[76] both of which have essentially equally persuasive evidence. Tracy has claimed that conspiracy theories other than his own might be disinformation, and yet is confident in saying that the event never happened.[77] The assertion of certainty in a conspiracy theory happens within a logical structure where certainty is (literally) impossible because the attack is on a kind of linking, not just a specific link: Uncertainty (ambiguity, multiplicity, polyvalence) is precisely what is foreclosed, so the "cruel, sterile" link that replaces it is forged with absolute rigidity despite its inherent brittleness and perhaps in inverse proportion to it. The conspiracy theorist, in other words, alleges that powerful forces are deceiving nearly everyone, and yet it is impossible that they themselves are deceived by the signs they interpret: Their speech is not persuasive, but oracular.

Although much of the preceding discussion mentions speech, this mode of interpretation applies to mediation more generally. Part of Lacan's intervention in structural linguistics was to argue that signifiers refer to other signifiers, or that "no signification can be sustained except by reference to another signification."[78] The unconscious is ultimately the network of signifying associations that shape a particular instantiation of speech without being consciously observed by its subjects. Richard Serrano observes that Lacan "slides from rebus to sentence,"[79] mixing images and words in what amount to cross-media metaphors. Perhaps Lacan's formulation should be thought of more broadly, revised in light of McLuhan's claim that "the 'content' of any medium is always another medium."[80] Lacan did not argue that the unconscious *is* a language, but *like* a language it has a connective, referential structure. There is no reason to reduce the unconscious, or even Lacan's *letter*, simply to speech. The letter is the concrete mediation of something plucked from the larger structure of cultural connections, materially supported by media. The unconscious is the set of connections overshadowed by these instantiations yet still operative. The specificities of media are doubly important, because (to draw again on

McLuhan) the medium is (an element of) the message, and therefore meaning is not produced solely by signifiers but also the means by which they are summoned in a concrete discourse.

The importance of accounting for the media through which communities form after the decline of symbolic efficiency is demonstrated by the prominence of the Internet for Sandy Hook conspiracy theorists. On most forums, a user's identity is inherently uncertain. Any profile can be potentially doctored or simply invented, even leaving aside sites like 4chan where anonymity is a baked-in design feature. With the rise of bots, there is no guarantee that users are even human. There is a feeling of distance, perhaps, that things are both real and unreal at the same time, enabling both paranoia and extreme demands that might not be made face-to-face, such as the call to exhume children's corpses. The experience of navigating the World Wide Web led Kathleen Stewart to claim in 1999 that it "*is* a conspiracy theory: one thing leads to another, always another link leading you deeper into no thing and no place, floating through self-dividing and transmogrifying sites until you are awash in the sheer evidence that the Internet exists. The medium is the message again. Theory rules."[81] We should strive to avoid what Sarah Sharma called "a worldview of the singular effects of media upon a universal subject,"[82] recognizing instead that the multiplicity of subjectivity shapes and is shaped by the multiplicity of media, and as bots, algorithms, and humans mutually adapt, symbolic networks are both more inhuman and more personal than they have ever been. The discourse of Sandy Hook employs traditional media like books alongside edited videos, digitally manipulated images, and multimedia presentations designed to elicit affective responses beyond those called forth by speech alone. Ultimately, however, what flows through these mediated networks is not just information, but desire. Desire, always moving and obscure, is still the glue where humans are involved, and both particular forms of media and content persist because they do something for someone, or rather, a lot of someones. The next section analyzes the network of desire that runs on, and is partially determined by, the concrete media networks that serve to host it.[83]

Attack on Our Guns

Any discussion of the desiring structures underlying Sandy Hook denialism must necessarily be speculative. One theory that motivated this book is that it can be productive to think of signifiers as agents and the people who use them as media rather than the other way around. This is partly due to observations about the subjective experience of psychosis, in which words and phrases (the Other) seem to press in on the mind once the filters of symbolic efficiency are disrupted. Another premise—shared by rhetoric and psychoanalysis—is that we should attend to what people actually say rather than dismissing their speech as epiphenomenal to something else. People experiencing psychosis may speak in ways that seem incoherent or delusional but seeking out the internal logic of their worldviews, however alien, matters if we want to understand why some delusions occupy them and others don't. As a result, simply saying that Sandy Hook denialism bears a structural similarity to psychotic discourse is not enough. We should hypothesize about its contours as best we can. Because foreclosure kicks off the protocol of anti-rhetorical reading and desire sustains it, speculating about what is foreclosed and what is desired is a good place to start.

Several Sandy Hook denialists seem to have been involved in the traumatic deaths of children in accidents for which they may blame themselves.[84] While my mission here is not to psychoanalyze them individually, the death of a child forces a traumatic encounter with the Real and would be a logical impetus to foreclosure. The idea that this could *just happen* seems impossible, too random, too arbitrary. This sentiment shows up in Sandy Hook conspiracy theories that claim the tragedy could not have occurred because it is simply too awful. "Here's why this is a lie," writes Jon Rappoport for *Prison Planet*. "Killing your own mother, and then breaking into a school and killing 26 people, most of whom are very young children, doesn't, by any stretch of the imagination, resolve by assigning a motive. . . . There is no motive that can explain such a crime."[85] *Motive* is the key word here: Things can't just *happen*. There must be a reason. They insist that in fact the laws of the universe cannot have failed: Someone must be making this up. This is another example of psychotic subjects being the only ones who genuinely believe in an Other, that there really is a wee man behind the curtain. However sinister, a shadowy cabal pulling the strings reassures them that the Law always succeeds, even if we don't like its methods. Every individual piece of evidence in the "text" of their experience means exactly the same thing: The Sandy Hook massacre never happened.

This structure of foreclosure and replacement could apply to many conspiracy theories with little modification. Some key figures (Fetzer, for example) tend to believe not just one theory but many about different events—JFK's assassination, the September 11 attacks, Sandy Hook, and so on—or perhaps an ur-theory that explains them all, perhaps Jewish world domination or something QAnon-adjacent. One explanation might be that conspiracy theories logically resemble one another.[86] They may also involve a psychic need for consistency, order, and simplicity. In Lacanian terms, this corresponds with the belief in the wholeness of the Other. Hidden meaning must exist because the alternative is an unassimilable Real, something beyond our control and assimilation. In subjects with psychotic attachments, what ultimately breaks down is the filter that pares down, classifies, and orders experience to make it manageable. When the excess of incomprehensible reality bursts through unfiltered, new structures are created to plug the gap, while the broken-down filter is so thoroughly disavowed that even its memory does not remain. But what is foreclosed from the Symbolic returns in the Real, Lacan argues, which is why our perceptions (including hallucinations) become overwhelmingly meaningful.[87] Subjects seek a new kind of order in their delusions, but the foreclosed trauma of the Real is never quite eradicated. So, subjects traumatized by incomprehensible tragedies such as extreme weather, political assassinations, wars, and economic dislocation can avoid facing the cruel indifference of reality by reading these events as signs of order, not chaos.

The barriers formed against this intrusion of the Real constitute *defenses*. Readers of Lacan may look askance at this term based on his critiques of other psychoanalysts, but it remains a potentially helpful concept,[88] and this is where the French psychoanalyst turned to answer an important question. "What happens," Lacan asked, "when what is not symbolized reappears in the real? It wouldn't be useless here to bring forward the term *defense*."[89] Although Lacan claims that these defenses do not succeed in stabilizing psychotic subjects, if we understand psychosis as an anti-rhetorical pattern of discourse rather than only an individual structure, we might still expect defenses to operate as points of shared occupation around which communities can form and persist. For Sandy Hook deniers, as for many other American conspiracy theorists skeptical of government, guns are a major symbol of defense—literally, rhetorically, and anti-rhetorically. The notion that Sandy Hook was a ruse to justify government confiscation of private firearms is one of the most common motives advanced by conspiracy theorists.

The title of Fetzer and Palecek's book on Sandy Hook locates the role of guns as defenses that symbolize defense: *Nobody Died at Sandy Hook: It Was a FEMA Drill to Promote Gun Control*. In this fantasy, then-President Barack Obama wanted to confiscate guns from Americans, especially patriots and survivalists,[90] and so fake massacres like Sandy Hook were staged to provide the political capital necessary to finally disarm the population, sometimes by signing on to a United Nations ban on small arms,[91] making citizens unable to resist planned government tyranny.[92] The usual suspects (the UN, Agenda 21, the Jews)[93] are often accused of being behind this plot. Even theorists who claim not to be personally interested in guns sometimes ascribe this motive to conspirators.[94] Characteristic certainty is easy to find: "We already KNOW that this crisis will be used by this criminal government to begin the process of disarming the American people," reads an article in *SGT Report* immediately after the shooting.[95] Even the rapper Gunplay made a similar claim.[96]

Guns are special to Americans. National mythology attributes independence, identity, and power to them. In psychoanalytic circles, the lowest-hanging fruit relates guns to the phallus. *Phallus* and *penis* are not synonymous for Lacan, as the phallus is a structure of enjoyment, not the male genital, although the penis can be an example of something that fulfills this function. This distinction is often collapsed by commentators such as Stephen Marche, who argued that from a Lacanian perspective guns are "the world's most obvious phallic symbol" and that "[y]ou buy a gun because you're threatened that they're going to deny you one,"[97] a statement about castration anxiety. Marche relates this directly to male genitals. While the link may be exaggerated,[98] it is difficult to deny entirely, although this likely says more about the recursion of pop psychology concepts in American culture than it does about innate psychic structure. Besides (or perhaps because of) the many academics who have supported the parallel, we find gun enthusiasts aiming guns at their crotches online, buying "gun nuts," and even advancing their own dubious interpretations of Freud, who did in fact conflate guns and penises.[99] The 2016 meme "dicks out for Harambe," quickly coopted by the alt-right, supposedly conflated "dicks" and "guns" based on rap lyrics,[100] but doing so fit a prewritten script. Clearly, this equation exists, but it has reached the point of reflective humor, hackneyed enough that it perhaps doesn't tell us much that's new. Ending our analysis here would miss the specificity of guns in conspiracy theory discourse, where they are more than penis substitutes or even phalluses. As phallus, guns should provide access to enjoyment, which they clearly do for many, but for conspiracy theorists they also operate in a distinct role as defenses.

Marche and many others describe guns as "fetish" objects, a term with a fraught colonialist history, but the overall point that guns have been vested with some aura beyond their utilitarian function is worth considering. Physical items, especially weapons, have long played this role. Objects in English law were vilified for their parts in death (banes) or were surrendered ostensibly to God (deodands). Myriad weapons throughout history symbolize power, authority, or familial continuity, along with artefacts of myth such as Excalibur or Mjolnir. Familial or cultural continuity could be understood as metaphor—sometimes literally the Name of the Father, as in efficient symbols of authority like the British Ampulla or the Persian Kiani Crown. Objects are often understood in less abstract ways, however, when their signifying function is read more literally. E. P. Evans argued in 1906 that rioters burning a courthouse to protest decisions made by judge and jury demonstrate that the logic of the deodand "survives in schemes of expiation and vicarious sacrifice," lying "scarcely skin-deep under the polished surface of our civilization."[101] Courthouse-for-judge is a classic metonymic transfer, of course, based on principles of proximity rather than abstract connections of metaphor.

Evans's claim may sound dated (the broader passage certainly embodies the cruelties and ignorance of his time), but modern examples abound. The U.S. Department of Defense has this to say about the USS *New York*, an "instrument of freedom and peace": "'Strength forged through sacrifice. Never forget.' . . . Cutting through the water with a bow forged from 7.5 tons of World Trade Center steel, the USS *New York* carries much more than just the name of the Big Apple wherever it travels."[102] Here the violence of the September 11, 2001, terrorist attacks in New York is literally welded into a weapon of war—notably in "more than just name." A 2018 *Fox News* story reported on the "Holy Grail" of guns, two M1911 pistols forged from a 4.5-billion-year-old meteorite and priced at $4.5 million dollars. "Man [*sic*] has been crafting weapons since the dawn of time, it predates speech," said Rob Bianchin, the owner of the company that built these weapons. "I don't believe anything more outrageous or complex in a pistol can trump this."[103] Bianchin's claim may not be particularly self-reflexive, but his statement does suggest a kind of primal in-betweenness for weapons. Guns communicate. They convey threats, danger, reassurance, and authority. It is appropriate that in its military sense *communication* (as in "lines of communication") means nonlinguistic material transfer, like ammunition and supplies. Derrida called attention to the exclusive, violent aspects of its cousin-word *community*, perhaps recalling a walled city, with *munitions* in the same family.[104] Weapons are symbolic,[105] but in a particularly physical way that emphasizes a fantasy of shared material substance. This is not to say that all communication is not material—it is—but that this particular connection tends to rely on symbols that masquerade as extra-linguistic truths, much as they might in delusional fantasies.

The numinous importance of weapons signals how guns figure into conspiracy theories as a defense against the Other, in both the conventional and psychoanalytic senses. The materiality of guns makes them almost like an extension of the body, like cell phones or eyeglasses, something between self and Other that fades into the background. When the Other looms too close, guns act as a sign of separation and protection to help shore up the subject and prevent its absorption, seeming to act almost independently of their owners despite a certain well-worn NRA slogan. A close reading of Matt McCarson's language about Sandy Hook accidentally gives away the whole show: He describes Sandy Hook as "a staged false flag attack *against our guns*."[106] Note the phrasing: Gun owners are not the target, nor is the Second Amendment, but the guns themselves are, as if they were the real agents in this discourse. The frequent accusation that gun-control activists fetishize the weapons and misattribute agency to them ("guns don't kill people, people kill people," as if it were important to maintain the innocence of guns rather than treat them as tools) doesn't make sense rationally (everyone knows that it's the people, but the guns make killing easier), but it *does* make sense in this context, where the imbuement of agential qualities in guns is projected outwards then denied by the subject. The object relations school of psychoanalysis influential to Bion posits that subjects experiencing psychosis project bits of themselves onto external objects, only to perceive them as coming back from outside. Perhaps in this case guns are the failed defenses of the self, elements of order that have been cast out and introjected again as saviors and bulwarks of a fragile subject.

The gun-grabbing fantasy is so persistent because it represents a fear of the Other's total colonization. The threatening Other is racialized in many versions of the gun-grabbing fantasy, perhaps another example of projection and denial given the history of guns as weapons of American settler colonialism and racial subjugation.[107] For some reactionaries, the Jade Helm 15 military exercises were Obama "invading" Texas, making armed White patriotic conspiracy theorists the last bulwark against tyranny, a fantasy that ultimately felt "too Real" and became a spur to anxiety and violence.[108] Self-defense groups of various political persuasions and racial, sexual, and gender identities have supported gun rights in the United States, but the figure of Obama particularly galvanized White fear of persecution by a hostile government, something not totally reducible to policy positions but explicable by his racial otherness.[109] Guns have played a key part in anti-Black conspiracy fantasies,[110] not to mention the very real material histories of slave patrols, lynchings, and police violence. As we have seen, for many Sandy Hook conspiracy theorists the evil force staging the massacre and threatening to absorb them was the UN or "globalists," a common code word for "Jews," who are fantasized as disarming the American population to facilitate their domination. Denialists do not always center race, but their fantasies grow in a soil prepared by it already. This world is made from the accumulated remains of what has been staged in fantasy. It is marked by the paranoia and violence of historical Whiteness and its persistence in the imaginary of the American reactionaries, among others. Sandy Hook is no different. Who, exactly, does this largely White and economically secure community think it must protect itself against? Germans?

Anarchy features prominently in gun fantasies, where it is often lone gunslingers or homogenous cliques who must remake the law as vigilantes when the Other is revealed as corrupt, deficient, or too weak. This fits precisely with the demise of symbolic efficiency—the Other is no longer seen as authoritative and something else must be built in its place founded on absolute, unquestionable principles such as constitutional originalism or individual masculine sovereignty, both deployed as defenses against ambiguity and uncertainty.[111] These may coexist with more cynical (perverse) attempts to profit. As Gunn writes, a "key difference between psychotic and perverse rhetoric is self-awareness; in [perversion] symbolic authority is *knowingly* disavowed."[112] Influential figures in conspiracy circles promote fears about gun-grabbing to generate attention and revenue, but the fact that this ploy *works* suggests that others are genuinely ensnared in a manner closer to the anti-rhetorical structure of psychosis. In the context of Sandy Hook deniers who fixate on gun-grabbing as a motive for the conspiracy, guns are kind of psychotic media, munitions standing literally in the middle (Latin: *media*) of the community, a means of both separation and unity, like *metaxu* or the wall in Simone Weil's famous example that separates two prisoners who are brought closer by tapping on it to communicate. Guns defend against the Other, but they also tie subjects and communities inextricably to what they fear, because "[e]very separation is a link."[113]

Who Theorizes the Theorists?

This chapter has attempted to explain Sandy Hook denialism and related conspiracy theories in psychoanalytic terms, arguing that the model of psychosis might be the closest analogue for their anti-rhetorical discourse across various media. This protocol of anti-rhetorical reading and the atropic devices stemming from it describe the structural similarities between all communities covered in this book, which arise in the midst of the decline of symbolic efficiency and rebuild their shared worlds from the spolia left from its collapse. These communities are structurally equivalent, not ethically: Pro-ana forum users and God-fearing Pentecostals are not the same as neo-Nazis, Sandy Hook deniers, or anti-trans agitators. Their structural similarity advances the overall claims made in this book, but it should not flatten other differences between them.

Nonetheless, another structural resonance ate at the corners of my mind as I researched Sandy Hook. The term *conspiracy theorist* is likely to conjure images of tinfoil hats and beefy Texans frothing about gay frogs, or even anti-vax yoga moms and, increasingly, mainstream politicians. Those to whom we apply this label are, we tell ourselves, uninformed, credulous, uneducated where it counts. "Conspiracy theorist" is a "two-word counter-argument,"[114] if not quite a slur, at least a dismissive and loaded term, only rarely used as a label of self-identification. A conspiracy theorist is someone incapable of clear, rational thought, a sheep deluded by a false discourse—which of course is precisely what conspiracy theorists might say about those who disagree with them. Perhaps many who apply the label "conspiracy theorist" so confidently to others might enjoy what they're doing just a little too much.

As I was doing research that would ultimately inform this chapter, a former business school professor went on a shooting spree at the University of Nevada, Las Vegas. He had collected hundreds of links on his personal website about everything from "Powerful Organizations Bent on Global Domination!" (e.g., MIT's Department of Economics, the Rothschilds, reptilian aliens) to management cybernetics, cufflinks, card tricks, and bespoke tailoring.[115] He was, by all available evidence, both a former college professor and a current conspiracy theorist. How much should that surprise us? The opposite of "conspiracy theorist" in a lot of discussions is "expert." But what about James Tracy? Tracy, with a PhD from the University of Iowa, is a graduate of a well-respected university in a field closely adjacent to my own, where he was acquainted with several of my peers. Tracy taught a class called "Culture of Conspiracy" at Florida Atlantic University where he was a tenured professor in the School of

Communication and Multimedia Studies.[116] Maybe he is not an expert on school shootings in particular, but he *is* an expert on media. James Fetzer has a PhD in philosophy. Having published many articles on cognition and epistemology, he ultimately retired from the University of Minnesota Duluth, retaining the title of Distinguished McKnight University Professor Emeritus. He taught at excellent universities, including the University of North Carolina, where I did my doctoral work.[117] One might disagree with him about the epistemological validity of conspiracy theories, but if you believe the authority of the degree-granting, professor-hiring Other, he is unquestionably an expert on philosophical approaches to cognition. Sure, some conspiracy theorists who claim to have PhDs are anonymous and therefore cannot be evaluated as experts.[118] Some conspiracy theorists might suffer more profoundly with trauma and disorganization. Others might simply be gullible or already conditioned to read literally. Finally, there are trolls and hucksters. But the blanket dismissal of all conspiracy theorists as opportunists, idiots, or lunatics is unsustainable, even if you think this terminology is appropriate. There seem to be rational, incisive, sincere people who end up in these communities and people with all the negative stereotypes of conspiracy theorists who end up in academia. So why do academics become conspiracy theorists?

After a long immersion in both academia and conspiracy culture, I think a better question is why *more* academics aren't conspiracy theorists. Media scholars, myself included, argue that the news is doctored, public opinion is manipulated, and technology is used to spy on users to maximize corporate profits and sell them things they don't need. None of that is controversial, yet it overlaps at least superficially with elements of nearly every conspiracy theory. There is an academic career path that essentially amounts to repeatedly finding the same root cause beneath many different things. Like the *Scooby-Doo* gang at the climax of an episode, it is tempting to just keep ripping off the mask and declaring that it was neoliberalism (or whatever) all along. Psychoanalysis is parodied in popular culture for doing just this—look, repressed sexual urges again! This is not to say that grand concepts are not helpful and even true, but they do seem to filter a complex reality much as conspiracy theories do and even provide anchors for the repeated enjoyment of unmasking. Some of us might over-rely on the "hermeneutics of suspicion," even if we have read Eve Sedgwick's brilliant work and should know better.[119] Academic terminology might even seem to mirror delusional speech. Rhetoricians can be particular about their exhaustive Greek and Latin lexicons, but there's no faster way to produce an angry red glow between a black turtleneck and black beret than to confuse "the Name-of-the-Father" with "the Father-of-the-Name" at a Lacan conference.

To be clear, I am not suggesting that academic work in the humanities necessarily employs conspiracy thinking. The standards and processes of research are more rigorous. The same set of social forces really do seem to underpin many phenomena, even if we are sometimes prone to overdetermination, and we know this because we have spent years researching, debating, and revising. While we may take our jargon too seriously, we rarely confuse label and concept or read anti-rhetorically to the same degree. We may sometimes reify socially constructed categories, but we often do so as a product of their deep instantiation in our cultures that requires that we acknowledge their power to order material reality. Even in humanistic fields where ideas are difficult to conclusively falsify, most academics cannot fully shelter themselves from those who disagree and must sometimes defend their beliefs against spirited inquiries at conferences, department colloquiums, or the dreaded external review. And of course, even if we *were* psychotic, that wouldn't make us wrong: Even paranoids have enemies, as they say.[120]

They key difference between widely entertained academic concepts and conspiracy theories is the tolerance for uncertainty and ambiguity they reflect. Most of us are not like Fetzer, Tracy, or Tony Polito even though paranoia, unwarranted certainty, and the trauma of foreclosure probably characterize *some* relation with *some* signifiers for *every* subject. As my colleague realized after her experience in the New York subway, these modes of thinking might pull us in without warning, if only for a moment. Seeing our own methods reflected in the funhouse mirror of conspiracy theorizing should give us academics occasion to cultivate our rhetorical reading sensibilities, especially openness to ambiguity, contingency, and uncertainty. There is a difference between theory serving humanity and humanity serving theory. As Lee Edelman writes, "accounts of structures can never access the structures they analyze . . . in trying to resist the temptation of acceding to the world as it merely appears, they depend on models of reading drawn from the very world they read."[121] Those who forget this lesson sometimes might miss the serpent in the tall grass until the time comes when it is too late to avoid its venom.

2

Serpent Handlers

Snakebites and Sadists

I found out that my uncle was afraid of snakes one July afternoon while hiking in the Scottish Highlands. Exhausted, he sat down on a thick patch of gorse and announced that he didn't even care if an adder bit him on the arse; this Scottish heatwave was too much. But even in that sweltering sixty-five-degree Fahrenheit weather, the prospect of a fatal arsebite clearly bothered my uncle, so we got to talking about snakes. I learned that my Gaelic-speaking great-grandfather had learned English from the King James Bible and as a result sometimes used archaic-sounding words. His grandchildren were raised in Glasgow, filled with quite secular and religious perils of another kind, ignorant of what dangers might be slithering in the heather. My uncle was warned away from one hill in particular: "On that hill, boy," his grandfather exclaimed, "there are *serpents*!" His impressionable grandson never forgot, hence this lingering fear many decades after my uncle had learned to take Highland stories with a grain of salt which even Donald Dinnie couldn't lift.

As a rhetorician with Lacanian leanings, what fascinates me about my uncle's story is how it displays the centrality of the signifier. Snakes of all sorts are fairly rare in Scotland, and he has never actually seen one in the wild (European adders are Scotland's only venomous reptile and not particularly dangerous). He was already aware of snakes, and this significant memory of his youth was not associated with ever encountering one. It was the word *serpent* that struck so powerfully. "Serpent" is likely to conjure many associations more starkly than does "snake" to a native English speaker living in a society heavily conditioned by Christian symbolic networks, or even "adder," a word that does appear in the King James Bible. The Bible is full of serpents. One tempted Eve in the Garden, and from this association might come others (wisdom, corruption, knowledge, hubris, sensuality) that are themselves quite potent nodes of meaning. Moses throws down his staff in front of Pharaoh in an act of defiance, and the menace of his action is that the staff becomes a serpent. As the bronze figure Nehushtan, the serpent becomes a false idol, redoubling its associations with deceit and deception. Leviathan, the dragon of the sea, is also "the piercing serpent" and "that crooked serpent." In Revelation, "that old serpent" is the Devil or Satan, one of the most consequential symbolic figures in the history of the world.

A significant and contentious appearance of "serpents" in the King James Bible occurs in Mark 16:17–18, which reads as follows:

> And these signs shall follow them that believe; In my name shall they cast out devils; they shall speak with new tongues;
>
> They shall take up serpents; and if they drink any deadly thing, it shall not hurt them; they shall lay hands on the sick, and they shall recover.

Some Biblical scholars argue that this ending to the Book of Mark is not authentic, but the Gospel of Luke 10:19 corroborates the key passage: "Behold, I give unto you power to tread on serpents and scorpions, and over all the power of the enemy: and nothing shall by any means hurt you." Romans 15:19–21 can be summarized as a command to show these signs of "them that believe" for the benefit of those who don't:

> Through mighty signs and wonders, by the power of the Spirit of God; so that from Jerusalem, and round about unto Illyricum, I have fully preached the gospel of Christ.
>
> Yea, so have I strived to preach the gospel, not where Christ was named, lest I should build upon another man's foundation:
>
> But as it is written, To whom he was not spoken of, they shall see: and they that have not heard shall understand.

Taken together, these lines can be read as an injunction to take up serpents in the name of Jesus to show His works to unbelievers, and some Christians do precisely that. "Signs followers" are inspired by Holiness and Pentecostal traditions to believe that all five signs of Mark 16 are alive today. Although they do not preach that any individual failing to exhibit the signs will be damned, when they meet to worship in homes or small churches, primarily in Appalachia, and are moved upon by the Holy Spirit, they take up in their hands venomous snakes like timber rattlers and copperheads. They might also "drink the deadly thing," which means drinking lye, strychnine, or other poisons. Sometimes, the faithful die in the signs, publicly and painfully.

Much of the attention earned by the serpent-handling community—academic and otherwise—focuses on the snakes as exotic spectacle, made meaningful by an available network of negative Appalachian signifiers—ignorance, fundamentalism, inbreeding, poverty, and monstrous physicality. The whole faith is reduced to the serpents, and its practices are presented as having grown from supposedly immutable cultural traits, economic despair, and so on, perhaps used as a parable about the exploitation accompanying capital's movement through this wrecked mountain region. Excepting dedicated contemporary studies such as those done by Ralph Hood and Paul Williamson (probably the world's foremost academic experts on serpent handling), many discussions of serpent-handling minimize or discount the theology of the church while trying to discover deeper factors that "explain" why Appalachian believers practice in such unorthodox ways.[1]

My twofold interest in serpent handlers is somewhat different. First, I seek to describe the shared rituals that bind their community together, focusing on how they find meaning in symbols. Far from illiterate superstition, I will argue that serpent handling is evidence of a clear and valid set of reading practices arguably more consistent than mainstream versions of Pentecostalism. I do not presume to "explain" serpent handling, and as an outsider, some of my work must be speculative. I hypothesize about the structure of desire pinning together the community as it is revealed in their approach to language, without claiming that this study exhausts the possibilities for academic work on serpent-handling Christians. Second, I seek to understand how serpent-handling communities have become the targets of sadistic derision in popular and academic contexts. Serpent-handling pastors have been highly visible in the last few decades, sparking a flurry of documentaries, books, and news stories. Particularly as they maim and kill Holiness pastors, serpents are the key signifier around which media audiences congeal—no snakes, no story. Popular stories often dishonor these believers so thoroughly that they mock and celebrate their deaths.

These two topics—biblical fundamentalism and media sadism—may seem unrelated, but I propose that they represent opposite kinds of symbolic engagement: one that is exceedingly "close" or literal, and one that operates at such an ironic distance that people who suffer and die are treated essentially as literary figures unworthy of compassion. Taken together, alongside rare supportive media from outside the church, these reactions demonstrate the complexity of social links and the multivalent results of reading the same signifiers in different ways that still cohere around similar structures of desire. Serpent handlers' belief in direct contact with a transcendent power is hard to dismiss as artifice when one observes a serpent held aloft. This authenticity is precisely what is disavowed and perhaps envied by those who persecute them through a strategy of ironic distance. One thread we will examine here, then, is how serpent handling's aura of authenticity may be simultaneously alluring and repellent for outsiders, suggesting that ironically detached discourses, just like psychotic ones, may seek an encounter with the truth of the Real much like serpent handlers do and simply mask it more thoroughly.

This chapter begins with a brief presentation of the history and practices of serpent handling before moving into a discussion of the signifying practices of "them that believe," focusing on their literal readings of Mark 16. Next, I will summarize some of the prolific media coverage earned by—or inflicted upon—these churches, including books, documentaries, and news stories. While several narrative strands can be followed from this coverage, I will concentrate on those that celebrate or mock the deaths of serpent-handling preachers, arguing that this reaction demonstrates a sadistic reading practice that suggests an underlying structure of desire closer than one might expect to that which inspires serpent handling itself, distinguished primarily by its tropological defenses rather than its self-proclaimed intellectual and ethical superiority. Finally, I will suggest a few implications of this example for the relationship between symbolic efficiency and psychosis as a cultural phenomenon.

Serpent-Handling Practice

Serpent handling is now widely considered a fringe ritual, but it arose from larger movements. Pentecostalism and the Holiness movement were major influences, and serpent handlers still have much in common with other more mainstream churches in Appalachia, including songs, styles of dress, speech patterns, beliefs, and customs. While external attention has encouraged serpent handlers to foreground their belief in Mark 16 in response to critics,[2] snakes are not actually being held throughout most of any given serpent-handling service, often being handled for only a short time in a multi-hour worship event and sometimes never appearing at all. Congregants at these churches are not required to handle serpents and many do not. Serpent-handling services differ little from their Holiness Pentecostal cousins, and the chief theological debate within the serpent-handling tradition itself is over trinitarianism versus "Jesus only" belief, something unrelated to the key passage in Mark 16 (although argued from similar literalist grounds). They are a small sect today, disavowed by the traditions from which they arose and often misunderstood.

Hood and Williamson note that the practice was once far more common than is now acknowledged, accepted at least in principle by some early Pentecostal leaders. A. J. Tomlinson, the first General Overseer of the Church of God, said in 1922, "I would hate to be in the shoes of some who are so bitter against taking up serpents,"[3] reflecting the fact that many Pentecostals realized that the biblical literalism they espoused made it difficult to practice some of the signs of salvation, such as laying on hands or speaking in tongues, while arbitrarily excluding the most daunting instruction from the resurrected Jesus. Concerned about how the unregulated emotional expressions of the movement would be seen by the White middle class, however, church leaders increasingly distanced themselves from worship that might threaten the movement's respectability[4] and, at the same time, disavowed the largely Black origin of Pentecostalism demonstrated by the Azusa Street Revival.[5] Serpent handling, in particular, has been underplayed in the historiography of Pentecostalism.[6] As Hood and Williamson document, however, these established historical narratives overlook the degree to which serpent handling was once discussed in mainstream circles and the threat it posed to the coherence of these beliefs.

The challenge of serpent handling began in the early twentieth century in the figure of George Went Hensley, founder of the Church of God with Signs Following and considered by many to be "the Saint Paul of serpent handling." Climbing White Oak Mountain in Tennessee around 1908, Hensley is supposed to have asked God for a sign directing him in his interpretation of Mark 16, whereupon he saw a large rattlesnake. Hensley picked up the snake and brought it down to Grasshopper Church of God, where it was handled by other congregants who followed his example.[7] It has been suggested, however, that the practice arose spontaneously more than once, and Hensley's first wife disputed the claim that it originated with him.[8] Williamson and Hood note that conversations in early Pentecostalism suggest that the practice might have already existed, and that it fit with traditions in the Appalachians and Ozarks involving snakes.[9] Serpent-handling pastor Jimmy Morrow claims that Hensley saw serpents handled near Stone Gap, Virginia, by the prophetess Nancy Younger Kleinieck, decades before he experienced his revelation at White Oak. Morrow also relates that a Jesus Name preacher called Oscar Hutton handled serpents in the 1890s, and that Kleinieck's families by birth and marriage both preceded her in the practice.[10] Over the decades since, the practice has also apparently appeared spontaneously amongst those who had no previous contact with serpent-handling churches.[11] As "long as people read the King James Bible," Hood and Williamson predict, "there will be some who will take the plain meaning of Mark 16:17–18 to heart."[12] This statement, combined with the apparently multiple origins of serpent-handling practice, nicely demonstrates Lacan's notion that the signifier speaks through the subject: The injunctions of Mark, not simply the actions of one modern evangelist, have insisted on the ritual. It spread throughout the Southeast, waxing and waning but reaching as far as the urban areas of Pennsylvania, Ohio, Michigan, the West Coast, and Canada.

The actual practices of these churches vary, but all involve venomous snakes. Believers inspired by Luke 10:19 also sometimes "walk" on the serpents, placing them on the floor and putting their feet upon them (although they do not seem to "trample" them violently), and in rare cases are reported to handle scorpions as well.[13] Photographs and videos of serpent handlers frequently show serpents draped around the necks of worshippers, held in bunches above their heads, and passed from hand to hand. Serpents are brought to church in specially designed boxes, often with relevant Bible verses marked on them. The snakes used in these services are predominantly native to the regions in which the faithful congregate, including copperheads, cottonmouths, and various eastern rattlesnakes.[14] Snakes from outside the region are also sometimes used, including western diamondback rattlesnakes, coral snakes, and even cobras.[15] Believers will sometimes also drink poison, typically strychnine or other substances that can be fairly easily obtained. The notion that the snakes are defanged, torpid, or even rubber fakes, or that the deadly poisons are actually harmless substances, is clearly false. As a student writer sardonically noted in *Foxfire*, "We can now lay those rumors to rest . . . the preachers that have been bitten and have died weren't gummed to death."[16] Indeed, there have been at least a hundred or so deaths "in the signs" over the last hundred years.[17]

Serpent handlers pick up serpents either under the "anointing" of the Holy Spirit or "on faith." Those handling under the anointing have felt the Holy Spirit "move on" them, enabling them to perform the signs. Those handling on faith have not necessarily felt the Holy Spirit at the time in which they are handling and therefore are perhaps not fully protected from venomous bites, although their faith in God is still understood by practitioners to provide some level of insurance. An experience of faith is one in which the person believes that God has made it *possible* to handle serpents, while the anointing involves a "felt connection with God" and "exuberant feelings of victory and protection from danger," signaled by affective and bodily sensations.[18] Being anointed does not necessarily mean handling serpents, as it has a role in Mark 16's other signs as well. Different members of a congregation may have different gifts, such as prophecy, handling fire, healing the sick, speaking in tongues, or translating for those who do. Serpent handling is, therefore, one sign embedded in a broader theory of signification through which these Holiness people encounter the world.

While one should avoid asserting with confidence that serpent handling was "determined" by an identifiable set of clear historical factors, it may still be worth noting that many accounts of its early origins revolve around cultural and economic change. David Kimbrough wrote that serpent handling emerged "in response to the social anomie that resulted from industrialization."[19] These changes included the exploitation of Appalachia for coal and timber, mill towns, sharecropping, and related industries. In this interpretation, "One way to adjust to threatening new values was to reject them, and the snake handling group demonstrated the tension of people . . . thrust into the modern world."[20]

Weston La Barre agreed, claiming that serpent handling "is a crisis cult of the acculturating poor whites" who rejected the new values of industrial capitalism in favor of "miracle and mastery" through their dangerous rituals.[21] Tidball and Toumey even suggest, with a notable paucity of evidence, that serpent-handling rituals are deliberately "bizarre" to prevent them from being stolen from disadvantaged practitioners by their more capitalist oppressors, against whom their worship is directed.[22]

These descriptions sound much like the decline of symbolic efficiency described in the Introduction—dominant ideas of authority are rejected and meaning is found in another set of signifiers that become defining for a group. Walter Hollenweger describes biblical literalism as a kind of ritual motivated by the need to have an "assured point of reference" in "a world of the transvaluation of all values, in which what yesterday was good is today bad."[23] What makes serpent handling a particularly interesting case is that this rejection happened as the new ideas were taking root in disrupted Appalachian communities, not after decades of decline, and the timeline is much earlier, beginning around the turn of the twentieth century, making signs followers both exploited outcasts ground down by coal companies and simultaneously canaries in the coalmine for the demise of symbolic efficiency. Where serpent handlers resemble every other group analyzed in this book is that what they reject (foreclose) is ambiguity itself, in this case, the shifting uncertainties of new economic and social mores, which probably undergirds their rejection of ambiguity in the Word of God. La Barre's commentary—problematic in many ways, as discussed below—even links serpent handling to a larger decline in public bonds in Vietnam War–era America. The "numbed anomie, helpless puzzlement and directionless acedia" of the era recounts the "Hellenistic despair" of Athens.[24] Rapid technological advancement is "alike in kind, psychologically, to the acculturative stress and culture shock felt by primitive societies when they are overwhelmed by the juggernaut of change."[25] The result is "a time ripe for vast and violent, mindless and blindly anti-adaptive social movements" such as, presumably, the serpent handling "'crisis cult.'"[26] Dramatic tone aside, La Barre's invocation of 1960s America and the "moral death" of Athens is a useful reminder that concerns over the decline of symbolic efficiency are not new. Wayne Flynt (who unfortunately follows La Barre in his use of the term "cult") offers a similar account dating back to George Went Hensley himself, arguing that serpent handling was a rejection of both new social values imposed from outside and traditional Appalachian practices that could be deemed "worldly." Believers are "otherworldly and ascetic," he writes, "rejecting the existing social order as corrupt and beyond redemption. . . . One way to adjust to threatening new values was to reject them," with results that "isolated them as completely from twentieth-century values as their remote hollows had cut them off geographically."[27]

This account of cultural change enables a new perspective on foreclosure that could be helpful in applying Lacanian models to groups—foreclosure may include active rejection, but there is also an element of being rejected oneself by a larger social order. Lacan's use of the English word "foreclosure" might be yet more evocative than it appears. If the subject is the "borrower" taking signifiers from the "bank" of a larger social order, it is the bank that forecloses on *them* and denies the use of some signifier, not the other way around. Serpent handlers certainly reject the secular world, but their doing so is only part of a process in which social structures, meanings, and mores (broadly, the Symbolic) change around them, leaving them stranded. When they in turn develop a system of belief that restores meaning to the world, the possibility of their authentic experience is again rejected, not only by a mocking culture, as demonstrated later in this chapter, but also by that ultimate Symbolic authority, the law, which criminalizes their practice everywhere except West Virginia.[28] Serpent handling was at one time even punishable by death in Georgia.[29] Some legal experts still advocate for its prohibition,[30] while another who grudgingly accepts its legal argument still mocks it, feeling the need to claim that preacher Andrew Hamblin "resembles a character from a Flannery O'Connor story with a Facebook page and a D-list reality TV show,"[31] an invocation of Appalachian inferiority discussed at much greater length below.

Sign, Signifier, Serpent

Any researcher of serpent-handling congregations will repeatedly encounter an ominous phrase spoken by its preachers: "There is death in that box."[32] The presence of snakes is a constant reminder of death and the promise that God will grant the faithful victory over it.[33] Attitudes toward potential death reflect a belief that the time and manner of one's passing is "predestined before the foundation of this world."[34] One common misinterpretation of this practice is that it is a "test of faith" and that serpent handlers touch snakes primarily to show that they are chosen by God, believing that the unholy will be killed while the righteous are protected. Carden and Pelton described this as the "most universally misunderstood aspect" of serpent-handling religion.[35] In fact, serpent handling is not a test of faith but a demonstration to unbelievers (often simply called "sinners" by Holiness adherents) that the word of God is true. As serpent handler John Brown put it, "We are not trying to prove our faith when we take up serpents . . . [it] is a sign unto the unbeliever that the Word of God is right."[36] Congregant Mary Bailey argued that this demonstrative role explained why bites were necessary. A sinner "could be sitting there thinking, 'Well, those serpents have had the poison drained out of them.' . . . Maybe if someone [was bitten by] the serpent, then this would prove to that unbeliever that *was* God."[37] Serpent handlers seem to understand their potential envenomation more like early-Church martyrdom than the judgment of an angry Old Testament God. Death in the signs only signals God's will, not necessarily that the decedent was unholy or unworthy.

Theories of communication are indispensable to the study (and practice) of serpent handling. The sect has its own reading protocols—implicit and explicit—that govern its understanding of the Bible and help members to interpret experiences within their communities as well as relations to the outside world. Serpent handlers communicate with one another but also attempt to signal God and read a response, a practice called *fleecing* based on a story in Judges 6:36–40 in which Gideon laid out a fleece and asked for God's sign that Israel would be saved by his hand.[38] This practice noticeably disavows any ambiguity: One asks a question and reads God's sign, which bears a powerful meaning in excess of the symbols employed to mediate it. This sense of certainty is also present in speaking in tongues. The languages so spoken are meaningful and inspired directly by God, even if that meaning is impenetrable to those who lack the gift of understanding them. The concept of Holy Ghost anointing and the often heard belief that serpent handling is a type of religion "better felt than told"[39] suggest that for adherents these services include communication that extends beyond the power of words, which may also partially account for the emotionally resonant, powerful music central to so many churches.[40] There is no escape from language: Jesus is still the Word, and even the physical and emotional sensation of the anointing is sometimes called "the word of knowledge;"[41] and of course only protocols for reading the *text* of the Bible make this faith tradition possible. These examples (fleecing, serpent bites, the KJV text of Mark 16, and so on) have nonarbitrary, concrete meanings for serpent-handling believers, making them signs, not signifiers. Lacan's explanation of the difference is that a sign is essentially code, a signal that means something present and direct, without ambiguity, like the rattle of a snake communicating danger. A signifier is a symbol that refers to an absent referent, making it an arbitrary part of a larger symbolic order, not an inherently meaningful thing in and of itself.[42] Signs followers are not signifiers followers. In their theory of communication, there are many words, things, and actions that signal, rather than signify.

The key difference between serpent handlers and mainstream Pentecostals who have disowned them is the insistence that *all* of the signs must be followed, including the injunction "They shall take up serpents." This is why serpent handlers may describe themselves as "full Gospel" believers: One either follows the full Gospel, or one does not.[43] There is no à la carte Christian faith. As believers are wont to mention, Revelation 22:19 reads: "And if any man shall take away from the words of the book of this prophecy, God shall take away his part out of the book of life, and out of the holy city, and from the things which are written in this book." The Bible provides its own protocols of reading ("plain meaning"), and no other text is necessary for its literal interpretation. Intertextual refutation is therefore irrelevant if one accepts the Bible's *sui generis* engine of meaning, and refutation based on the text of the Bible itself makes it very difficult to dismiss serpent handling while retaining the text's authority in other areas. As Hood and Williamson put it, "Appalachian serpent handlers can no more conceive of Pentecostalism without this practice than Catholic believers could conceive of Catholicism without the Eucharist."[44] The prior assumption for this position as a theory of communication is a refusal of figurative meaning: Mark 16 is not allegorical and cannot be interpreted as metaphor.[45] In other words, it is not *ironic* in the broad sense of having a potential to mean other than what its signifiers most frequently indicate, and the divine inspiration of the English translation supersedes any ambiguity in the Greek term *airō* (αἴρω), which could mean pick up, remove, destroy, or kill, among other things.[46]

In Lacanian terms, the refusal of metaphor defines foreclosure. There can be little doubt that serpent-handling believers are sincere and certain that the word of God is true, as they risk grave injury and death in the practice of a faith that serves only to isolate and impoverish them relative to the broader Christian community. The faith of serpent handlers is metamorphic,[47] not metaphoric. The alternative to the kind of faith that results in following the signs is damnation, something that cannot be confronted, meaning that to accept the ambiguity of Mark 16 is to court a literally unthinkable fate. As a result, serpent handlers foreclose rhetorical readings of the Bible and replace them with their own structure, one in which the letter of God's word is directly inspired by the Holy Ghost, certain, realer than earthly real, and absolutely meaningful, even if the will behind those words remains inscrutable. The condition of possibility for these communities is their structure of engagement with the signifiers of the Bible, while the snake rituals attracting so much outsider attention are only a result or symptom of their reading practice, although a rejection of rhetorical ambiguity in favor of literalism alone is probably not the most fundamental level of this foreclosure.

Pastor Jimmy Morrow's response to Weston La Barre's Freudian interpretation of serpent handling illustrates how believers relate to the letter of the Bible, and how this relation sustains their communities: "Academics like LaBarre [*sic*] and believers . . . will forever be at odds. If one will not accept the Word of God, they must seek elsewhere for explanations. But we who believe and know God's word have the only answer we need."[48] The heart of the serpent-handling tradition is entirely dependent on a practice of reading that is so unshakably faithful to the text that death and mutilation can have no victory over it. Even Holiness people who cannot actually read written words have cleaved to the Word with absolute certainty in its literal truth.

Their reading seeks zero-degree literalism so closely that serpents and poison are not treated in the same way: Mark says they *shall* take up serpents, but only that *if* they drink the "deadly thing," it shall not harm them, and this conditional is interpreted just as literally as any other part of the text.[49] There are disputes among different factions, including over media exposure and baptism (Trinitarian or Jesus Name)—as one serpent handler reported, these people "are the most organized unorganized people you'll find . . . split among themselves," while "the slightest thing separates them."[50] In other words, in a movement divided by various factors both unique and general, fidelity to the literal Word emerges as the primary, or perhaps sole, adhesive. As Andrea Shan Johnson puts it, serpent handling serves "as a bridge across what is a wide theological divide for most other Pentecostals. It is as if the common practice is more significant for them than the basic theological differences that would typically keep Pentecostals from fellowshipping together."[51] But like Sandy Hook deniers, to whom they bear no ethical or political resemblance, serpent handlers are anti-rhetorical about the Bible (or at least Mark 16) because their practice of encountering the text forswears the possibility of alternate readings altogether, defending against the possibility of uncertainty in God's word in ways that exceed garden-variety literalism as a mode of interpretation. "There is death in that box" could therefore be read as trope, but a more accurate interpretation might be as an anti-trope: What is in that box is *only death* in that having victory over the serpent means life everlasting, and the failure to agree (at least in principle) that we are commanded to take up serpents is absolutely to swear off immortality in Heaven, because "take up serpents" cannot have any other meaning but this.

Serpent-handling believers are thus profoundly literate in their sense of univocal fidelity to the Bible's letter, especially to the signs of Mark 16 as this passage demands the most and is followed the least, encouraging the faithful to double down in their commitment. This reading forms the basis of a bond resulting in, not founded by, the ritual of snake handling, which also contradicts the notion (at least for communities) that psychotic readings cannot sustain social links. In fact, this connection is turned outwards as a sign to unbelievers that they should change their ways and follow God's will in fellowship with the faithful. Their interpretation of the Word might be disputed by other Christians, but it is hard to imagine a criticism that doesn't rely on them reading *too much* or *too strictly*. This is not the prevailing image in media, pop culture, or even among many academics, however. According to one attendee at a signs-following homecoming, gawkers turned up to "prove [serpent handlers] were illiterate," echoing a common derision against the poor generally and Appalachian people specifically.[52] This is only a mild insult—the persecution and cruelty visited on this community by outsiders can be so intense that some occluded structure of desire must be at work beneath the surface. Just as serpents bind the faithful together by symbolizing their shared practices of reading, so do they galvanize audiences who consume media mocking and denigrating them to the point of celebrating their deaths. Understanding the duality of the serpent signifier and the contradictory modes of symbolic engagement upon which it relies requires a closer look at how others have mediated snake handling from the outside.

Enantiodromia horridus

Few religious practices are so thoroughly dishonored by mainstream society as Holiness Pentecostal serpent handling. The ritual and its practitioners pose a challenge to a supposedly inclusive, multicultural, and tolerant society that celebrates difference—a self-image shared by many academics as well as educated, liberal Americans more generally. According to Jim Birckhead, the common image of serpent handlers as White, Appalachian (or more generally Southern), poor, isolated, Protestant fundamentalists may even stigmatize researchers interested in them.[53] Birckhead reports students laughing during a documentary when a serpent handler who survived a bite was reported to have died from drinking poison.[54] YouTube videos of Holiness worshippers handling serpents are often sites of great vitriol and derision. Clips of Pastor Jamie Coots, a well-respected and charismatic serpent-handling preacher featured on the National Geographic show *Snake Salvation*, elicited viewer comments such as "I hope [Coots will] suffer. . . . People like this, who believe in such ridiculous scriptures and form a cult do not deserve any form of sympathy. They deserve to receive agony for their ignorance. Nature > Man." After his death from a snakebite in church, others wrote "Stupidity can kill. . . . Hooray for the snakes," "The snake did a great job," "I only wish more of those idiots would get bitten. . . . Those snakes are doing society a great service."[55] The last video of Coots worshipping with his family and fellow parishioners has almost one million views and six thousand comments at the time of writing. A few are supportive, but many are not. Some include: "This is hilarious! Especially the time he got bit in the face!" "Give that snake a medal," "It's the funniest when he gets bit by the snake" (accompanied by a "crying laughing" emoji), and "It actually pleases me to learn about someone so incredibly ignorant dying such a horrible, painful death."[56] Nearly every video related to serpent handling includes comments about inbreeding, the film *Deliverance*, the perceived obesity of church members, and many references to the Darwin Awards or natural selection, alongside mixed reactions to the unruliness, emotionalism, and movements of serpent-handling worship.

Surely, it is known that the internet is cruel, and YouTube comments are the worst humanity has to offer. Similar cruelty appears in other media, however, especially in comedic formats. In the 1990s, British-American comedian Ruby

Wax visited serpent handlers for her pseudo-documentary series *Ruby Wax Meets . . .* , interacting with some well-known believers like Dewey Chafin in an obviously mocking way.[57] An old spoken-word comedy bit from gospel singer Wendy Bagwell resonates with later comedians in the vein of Jeff Foxworthy and Larry the Cable Guy. Bagwell, although not entirely unsympathetic, describes his fear as an observer upon watching a serpent-handling service.[58] Comedian Anthony Davis is less playful. Sitting in a Holiness church, Davis decides "it would be hilarious if somebody got bit by a snake." His response when the preacher was bitten was to "laugh [his] ass off. . . . Irony!" He describes the preacher falling to the floor ("It's so great") and "freaking out," with parishioners "trying to save his life, I don't know why." Eventually, "He died in the hospital, so, f-ck the guy." Acknowledging the sadism of the joke, Davis says, "I love telling this joke, but everyone pulls back at this point. Alright? It's fine, okay. It's fine. He was shaking the shit out of f-cking snakes, everybody."[59] The crowd laughs throughout.

Other media can be equally unkind.[60] *TMZ on TV* mocked Jamie Coots and his son Cody in the wake of Jamie's death by snakebite, complete with zany sounds, jokes, animation, and mockery of their Eastern Kentucky dialect.[61] The Young Turks aired a direct address to Cody Coots in slow, condescending tones, asserting that his father was dead "because he was wrong" with a graphic reading "like father like dumb." "Was your dad a sinner, and hence deserved to die, because he was not pure enough, or is your God a malicious jerk who killed your great dad, what, out of spite? . . . Have at it, hoss, but you're an idiot," said Cenk Uygur, suggesting that Cody might end up "like his dad and his grandfather."[62] Leaving aside that Greg Coots, Cody's grandfather, was alive and well and that the Coots family does not live in Texas, as Uygur seemed to believe, the statement misunderstands serpent-handling theology. A later episode from the same outlet was similarly condescending, as well as apparently unaware that Cody Coots received medical care for a subsequent bite.[63] All of these videos serve as points for commenters to share commonplace calumnies about Holiness Pentecostals. While probably not unique, the venom with which some attacks are made and the joy apparently inspired by the deaths of these strangers is striking. Why does it happen?

Popular perceptions of serpent handling shape and are shaped by a media economy fascinated by Appalachian people as atavistic, grotesque, violent, unruly, and simply evil. Birckhead suggests that cruelty and disgust toward serpent handlers may be explained in part by the convergence between ostensibly factual media and fiction, in which the news constructs snake-handling stories to fit the generic conventions of some genres of entertainment, leading them to be read as fiction.[64] With the addition of self-promotion on social media, what Paul Vance wrote fifty years ago still rings true: These churches are only "brought to the attention of the general public on the occasions when one of the believers suffers a fatal serpent bite or when some extra enthusiastic reporter exploits the religious practices of the sect for a sensational article."[65] And yet, defined by a constellation of interconnected stereotypes, the small sect of Holiness Pentecostal serpent handlers has come to influence overall perceptions of the region as the most visible representatives of Appalachian religion.[66]

The film *Deliverance* is an easy example that helped to popularize what Isabel Machado calls the "redneck nightmare" genre of stories set in the U.S. South, in which outsiders must contend with brutish, inbred natives who are often deformed, racially impure "White trash."[67] Humming a few bars of the famous banjo duel is enough to signal disdain for "hicks," "hillbillies," inbreeding, or Southerners even for many who have never seen the film. The poor, deformed hillbilly shows up in *The Simpsons* as Cletus Spuckler, who sports a snake tattoo, is missing a toe, and is marked by allusions to incest and bestiality, in line with the conflation of monstrosity, poverty, and disability often projected on the Appalachian South (*The Simpsons* also establishes that Moe Szyslak is a religious snake handler). A Pittsburgh casting agency generated backlash in a call for "deformed" people with "physical abnormalities" constituting the "look" of "literal inbreeding" in a West Virginia "holler" for the Julianne Moore film *Shelter*.[68] The physical grotesqueness of these Appalachian imaginaries is then recalled by emphasis on the lingering injuries of serpent handlers—Jamie Coots's missing finger in *Snake Salvation*, for example. News accounts of serpent handling grow from such a poisoned garden, and most are intertextually linked through the comments sections of serpent-handling media online.

The film and book *Night of the Hunter* extended this demonization to Appalachian Christianity, evoking a mad, hypocritical religiosity in the figure of Reverend Harry Powell that the nonfiction *Salvation on Sand Mountain* would echo in connection to serpent handler Glenn Summerford, accused of trying to kill his wife via rattlesnake. Malicious serpent handlers show up in a number of novels of varying quality and distribution, perhaps most notably Wiley Cash's *New York Times*–bestseller debut novel *A Land More Kind Than Home*, which begins with a Pentecostal Holiness preacher covering up snakebite deaths in his church and escalates from there.[69] The 2019 film *Them That Follow* includes a terribly miscast Jim Gaffigan removing the arm of his snakebitten son with an electric carving knife to prevent authorities from cracking down on his church, led by a pastor played by Walton Goggins.[70] At a minimum, the serpent handlers of the political comedy *The Campaign* are gullible and naïve zealots, deceived by a corrupt politician (Will Ferrell).[71]

Some documentary films following the generic conventions of fiction include the National Geographic television series *Snake Salvation*, which followed the Coots family and Andrew Hamblin, a charismatic young serpent-handling preacher in Tennessee. Producers apparently goaded their subjects into taking part in snake hunts in other parts of the South in ways that they would not normally do and, following other reality television, edited and arranged footage for dramatic effect. Some of this is asserted in Julia Duin's *In the House of the Serpent Handler*, a book that itself veers uncomfortably toward supercilious self-aggrandizement, and perhaps even exploitation, while still successfully documenting some of the ways that modern serpent handlers use news agencies and social media to spread their messages.[72] The 1967 documentary *Holy Ghost People* did much to establish iconic images of serpent handling in the popular imagination.[73] Its intertextual influence and potential to blur into fiction is evident from the fact that a serpent-handling thriller released in 2013 bears the same name (although with a considerably less even touch).[74]

Contemporary academic treatments tend to adopt a more neutral attitude and focus on recounting the rituals, beliefs, and experiences of Holiness Pentecostals without sanction. This has not always been the case, however. In 1941, Richard F. Day recounted a young pastor as a "brute" with "wild-eyed followers" including "foul-breathed, stubble-chinned, grimy-necked louts," all while repeatedly misstating George Went Hensley's middle name.[75] This dehumanization may have extended as far as sexual predation in the case of one lab assistant in Durham, who reportedly sought after snake-handling women who were in a state of emotional vulnerability after their services.[76] The only major psychoanalytic study, written by Weston La Barre and first published in 1962, contains the word "cult" in its title. The "forgotten people of backwoods Appalachia, last stronghold of country innocence and archaic religiosity," La Barre writes, were "naïve bucolic folk" who developed their "zany and dangerous snake-handling cult" in the 1940s and 50s.[77] In a chapter on the psychology of the "poor Whites" comprising much of the serpent-handling faith, La Barre asserts that they are "puritanical, fanatic, narrow, and fundamentalist. Fate seems to have preordained [them] to be . . . textile worker[s]."[78] La Barre references works of fiction like *Tobacco Road*, *Baby Doll*, and *The Ponder Heart*, declaring that their writers "know exactly what they are talking about," and, while careful to note that not all Southerners fit the label, is happy to riff on the dangers of "poor White trash."[79] This latter epithet has a particularly rich history, calling up mental infirmity, racial deficiencies, and disease.[80] La Barre's psychoanalytic approach, which tends to reduce serpent handling to phallic representation, has also been rightly criticized as pathologizing, oversimplifying, and demeaning.[81] Jim Birckhead reported much later that presentations on serpent handling sometimes drew laughs and prurient questions about inbreeding, *Deliverance*, and snake lore even from educated social scientists at academic conferences. Noted biblical scholar Bart Ehrman concludes a blog post on serpent handlers (in which he demonstrates unfamiliarity with their actual rituals) by writing, "I've always thought that someone in the ambulance on the way to the hospital ought to tell one of those snake handlers, 'You know, that verse wasn't originally in the Bible.'"[82]

Serpent handlers are aware of this scorn. Barbara Coleman told an oral historian that "Some people think we are crazy to handle serpents.... We are always portrayed as poor, dumb hillbillies."[83] This observation echoes similar ones from as far back as the 1940s, such as Archie Robertson's interlocutor, who claimed that another writer had portrayed them as "poor and ignorant."[84] Jimmy Morrow, a prominent serpent-handling pastor, was acutely aware of La Barre himself, as noted above. Morrow described La Barre's affirmation that "serpent handlers provide an example of primitive religion" as "LaBarre [*sic*] characteriz[ing] the followers of our tradition as backward, impressionable, intellectually-deprived people."[85] Even the fact that many academics (and, presumably, media creators) do not seem to expect serpent handlers to be media literate might reflect an underlying assumption of isolation from the modern world and primitive naivete. In fact, contrary to this expectation, because serpent handlers are abnormally targeted by media attention they may have been more critically reflexive about media issues for decades than many members of contemporary American society.[86] Serpent handlers are certainly aware of legal judgments as well given that, as previously noted, the practice is illegal in most Appalachian states.

Taken together, the experience of Internet mockery, academic condescension, legal discrimination, and media caricature suggests that for this sect of Holiness believers, Carden and Pelton's title of "persecuted prophets" might not be far off. Even if one supports the notion that their practices should be regulated for safety reasons, the fact that this tiny, politically irrelevant and socially harmless sect should be openly mocked to the extent that their deaths are celebrated seems extreme. This opprobrium might be described as a sadistic practice of reading. By priming audiences to figure serpent handlers as semifictional characters in heavily edited formats advertised as authentic, media producers have transformed them into acceptable targets of dislike in the mold of Paris Hilton, Kim Kardashian, or the cast of *Jersey Shore*, but without the social and financial power that results from celebrity. A certain degree of distance permits spectators to characterize their enjoyment as ironic meta-enjoyment while still becoming emotionally occupied by the media they consume: It is permissible to watch "bad" television as long as one declares that they are "hate-watching" it or that it is "so bad it's good," much like the titular "irony bribe" in Dana Cloud's work.[87] This distance prevents identification on the terms of one human subject with another, but still permits empathy in the sense that audiences can imagine something about how serpent handlers desire, feel, and think, much in the same way that audiences can sustain fantasy identifications with explicitly fictional characters in novels or film. Sadism operates in this environment by creating a fantasy in which the audience imagines that some object is particularly important to a targeted other and enjoys the prospect that it could be lost to them.[88]

Snakes are this object, despite their very different place in the imaginary world of serpent handlers. La Barre argues that snakes are a phallic symbol to their handlers and the ecstasy of handling them constitutes "public orgasm." For La Barre and others, the key to understanding the sect's belief is not literal reading practices but the snake itself, representing deity, danger, and death. Serpent handlers are frequently charged with worshipping snakes, which they do not do, and of kissing, "fondling," or otherwise coddling them (which in fairness is sometimes, albeit rarely, done),[89] suggesting that their public fantasy image includes the notion that the snakes symbolize desire for the handlers. The danger and wildness of the ritual is in keeping with stereotypes of Appalachian people as moonshine-drinking illiterate outlaws, living without the constraints of propriety.

The tie binding sadistic audiences together is not immediately apparent to them, however. Sadistic media consumption can be described in Lacanian terms as a species of "hainamoration," an admixture of hate and enamored jealousy that comes from a conviction that the object of sadism has access to a kind of enjoyment that is prohibited to the sadist.[90] The emotionalism, stomping, shouting, testifying, loud music, and ecstatic trances in the Holy Spirit may violate propriety when done by others who are denigrated as "holy rollers," but the serpent handlers' direct encounter with death and apparent freedom from social norms can be read as enjoyment so joyful that it transcends any limit. Serpent handlers seem to dissolve as individual subjects into what Georges Bataille called *continuity*—the desired state of union to which all rituals point and all subjects aspire through sex and death, but which paradoxically has as its condition the abolition of discrete individual identity.[91] The continuity these subjects seem to access is the Real, a condition beyond language and mediation to which they are totally and unironically devoted, which is denied to their critics and therefore must be disavowed by them. According to Bataille, individuals are drawn toward excess and abandon because it abolishes the separation from the world we experience as unfulfilled lack. Societal prohibitions (i.e., propriety) both create and frustrate desire while simultaneously permitting the minor enjoyment of transgression, such as when audiences vicariously experience serpent handling before condemning, and perhaps even enjoying, the indecorousness of mocking handlers' deaths. Mockery maintains the prohibition, but the prohibition wouldn't exist if there was no drive to violate it. Hostility also lets the critics pull back from the engulfing, ego-destroying nature of their own desires to experience the Real. By criticizing what they subconsciously interpret as the desire for continuity, they can retain the myth of their own discrete subjectivity.

This is where the communicative theories of the serpent handlers and their enemies converge. The literalism of serpent handling asserts a hidden truth that signs don't gesture toward but directly constitute. In other words, it is a proximity between signifier, signified, and Real so intense that it denies the distinctions between them. Sadistic readings, on the other hand, happen at the opposite extreme of irony, in which the signifiers of the church (e.g., serpents) are essentially arbitrary and have no inherent truth—they are empty metaphors. This distance is a disavowal or repression, however, of a desire for contact with the Real that is deemed unacceptable, meaning that the ultimate driver for both serpent handler and sadist is the desire for continuity and what separates them is primarily the degree of artifice with which they conceal it. Sadists react to what they cannot have (and do not acknowledge that they want) by denigrating it: mocking the rituals of serpent handlers, declaring them foolish, and even belittling their supposedly desired objects by declaring that the snakes are defanged or drugged. There is even a literary example: In Harry Crews's *A Feast of Snakes*, Joe Lon reacts to talk about a serpent-handling preacher's obedience to God by despairing about the lack of meaning and direction in his own life. When Joe Lon finally reaches his homicidal breaking point at the novel's conclusion, the serpent handler is his first victim.[92] Joe Lon cannot tolerate the preacher's power of belief, and therefore must destroy it.

This coincidence is further supported by serpent-handling media on the opposite pole of admiration. Burton explains these contradictory reactions nicely:

> [I]t is easy to view one aspect of serpent handling rather than the whole and, consequently, either to romanticize or brutalize the people and the practice. One can feel after attending a service that it is completely irrational, wild—people running around, falling down, quivering, uttering strange sounds; taking venomous serpents . . . and staring at them nose to nose . . . petting them. . . . On the other hand, one can . . . feel completely awed by the faith, sincerity, and mysterious power manifested by these people—sensing somehow they know, feel, have something in their lives that is redeeming amidst a lost world. . . . The integrity of serpent handlers strikes one as something real in the omnipresence of appearances, an inspiring breath in the mists of "mouth honor."[93]

The differences between supportive and hostile reactions are real and consequential, but both are structurally resonant with each other and with the communicative theories of serpent handlers themselves, because both desire an unmediated encounter with reality, one that is frustrated by our immersion in language, the very condition that makes us human subjects.[94] Supportive reactions get to transgress enough to enjoy some vicarious contact with continuity through death, but not enough to actually be bitten by it, although some observers end up taking up serpents themselves. Dennis Covington's *Salvation on Sand Mountain* is probably the single most famous work produced about the sect. In it, Covington, who initially intended to simply report on church meetings as a journalist, describes being moved to handle a rattlesnake:

> I'd always been drawn to danger . . . as low as [the snake] was, as repulsive, if I took it, I'd be possessing the sacred. . . . Nothing had to be given up except my own will. . . . I felt no fear. The snake seemed to be an extension of myself. And suddenly there seemed to be nothing in the room but me and the snake. . . . And I realized that I, too, was fading into the white. . . . I knew then why the handlers took up serpents. There is power in the act of disappearing; there is victory in the loss of self. It must be close to our conception of paradise, what it's like before you're born or after you die.[95]

The language used here clearly evokes Bataille's concept of continuity with the dissolution of the subject into an unbounded universe through religious rituals of ecstasy and death. Less dramatically, researcher David Kimbrough included photographs of himself holding serpents in his study of Eastern Kentucky churches.[96] Colleen Sexton, who does not claim to have handled serpents herself, still reported that she was attracted to the sect because she wanted to believe, even to have God speak to her. Seeing the faithful, she wrote "I realize that I, at no time in my life, have ever had that kind of faith. Now, with a desire beyond longing, I want to return to Jolo to be a witness in the congregation of the Church of the Lord Jesus Christ with Signs Following."[97] Jim Birckhead reflected that, in retrospect, he was "attracted to serpent handling, like a moth to a flame, as an arena in which to confront and play out long-term existential obsessions and unresolved . . . needs."[98] Julia Duin, who is somewhat more critical of serpent handlers that she met, still makes a point of claiming proximity to them by saying that her coverage "put [Andrew Hamblin] on the map," that God sent her to Tennessee to report on the sect, and by implying some distance between herself and less enlightened journalists who "expected to meet some inbred hayseed."[99] Even musician Abe Partridge, probably the popular-media interpreter of serpent handling currently most worthy of respect, invokes the rituals of death and exaltation by using Jamie Coot's rattlesnake-skin guitar strap, given to him by Cody Coots.[100]

Taken at the level of the discourse itself, rather than the subjects speaking it, the two extremes of outsider perspectives represent a kind of enantiodromia, a repeated inversion of hate and love, both intense and based on a desire for transcendent, continuous experience. "Serpent lovers" may acknowledge this, even if they don't see it directly, and flirt with unmediated contact, although they maintain a separate identity and do not fully give themselves over to dissolution in religious ritual. "Serpent haters" bar themselves from this experience due to their own notions of propriety, burying this denial beneath avowed hostility and mockery toward those they may actually envy. At their deepest level, these two discourses bear a strange but unmistakable structural affinity to the serpent handlers themselves: All are pulled toward unmediated contact, but each negotiates a different discursive structure through which to approach it with varying degrees of humanity and grace. So, this investigation started with a tiny outcast sect of American Holiness Pentecostalism and concludes that while the contents of its belief system mark it as exceptional, the underlying structure of its desire could be much more typical than its practitioners, partners, and persecutors might realize. What might we learn about how communities form in the wake of symbolic efficiency?

On Snakes That Are Not Serpents

Where outsiders differ from the discursive theories of serpent handlers is their acceptance of artifice, as noted. For their critics, the serpent handlers and their snakes are manifest content that *represent* unmediated experience, standing in metaphorically for something latent—precisely what Lacan described as the function of a signifier. For serpent handlers, however, serpents are imbued with inherent, mysterious, transcendental meaning by the word of God conveyed in the King James Bible. No substitution is possible. These mark structural differences, but it could also be said that serpent handlers and their sadistic audiences are reading different signifiers: "serpent" on the one hand and "snake" on the other. Indeed, this distinction is sometimes made by serpent handlers themselves: Every serpent is a snake, but not every snake is a serpent.[101] This reaffirms part of Lacan's argument about how different words, not the things they represent, can organize our identities and unconscious affiliations. He illustrates this with a story about a boy and girl facing each other in a train that pulls up to a station. When the boy announces that they are at "Ladies," the girl replies that they are at "Gentlemen," both reading different signs for identical restrooms. Both insist on being right, although both are surely wrong about the station's name. Through these "incomplete significations" reflected through the darkness will arise "the immeasurable power of ideological warfare.... Gentlemen and Ladies will henceforth be two homelands toward which each of their souls will take flight on divergent wings." The children will never reach agreement because "being in fact the same homeland, neither can give ground regarding the one's unsurpassed excellence without detracting from the other's glory."[102] Gentlemen, Ladies; so too serpent and snake: The serpent handlers are exalted by taking up serpents, while their enemies deride them for picking up snakes. Both are the same animal split asunder by signification.

The serpent-handling mode of reading lines up with the notion of psychosis as foreclosure of metaphor, but it is important to note that serpent handlers are still capable of using metaphor in everyday speech. "There is death in that box" or "take up serpents" might be interpreted univocally, but probably none of these biblical literalists believe that St. Peter was actually a rock (Matthew 16:18) or that Jesus was a loaf of bread (John 6:32–41). This suggests psychosis, at least as a shared discourse, is not a deficit in metaphor globally but an anti-rhetorical relationship to particular signifiers. Although serpent handlers engage rigidly with the King James Bible, this does not extend to a general fixation on written text per se, as evidenced by the extreme paucity of writings by serpent handlers themselves defending or propagating the faith, as opposed to other media like Facebook, gospel singing, and speech.[103] The degree to which different signifiers seize on different subjects determines how influential they are in forming communities. Signifiers that animate some may fail to engage others, evidenced by the fact that not everyone who becomes aware of serpent handling is fascinated by the subject. Since the interpretive impulse for all three modes of relation to the serpent for those whom it does capture (haters, handlers, lovers) have an encounter with the Real at their core, and all are organized around particular signifiers, we should acknowledge that if the underlying structure of serpent handling is extreme, it is only in degree, and therefore remember the potential importance of this drive for unmediated experience as a binding agent for other groups. It should also support the conclusion that individual serpent handlers are not necessarily psychotic, as Kimbrough argues and as (admittedly quite limited) psychological evaluations support.[104] Their mode of attachment to the serpent simply lies outside the bounds of socially accepted practice.

Classical Lacanian interpretations of individual psychosis tend to depict psychotic subjects as totally isolated from society. Foreclosure, the condition of "*knowing nothing of the thing, even in the sense of the repressed,*"[105] implies a complete break from whatever is rejected. Serpent handlers may completely refuse the possibility of ambiguous (i.e., rhetorical) readings of the Bible, but despite their denunciations of "the world,"[106] handlers are conversant in modern electronic media and capable of informed, critical engagement with it. Birckhead reports a "comical and critical" reading by serpent handlers of media about themselves.[107] Tidball and Toumey note that some preachers became minor celebrities as far back as 2001,[108] a condition that has been much accelerated in the past decade or so after *Snake Salvation* and various popular books.[109] The willingness of some serpent handlers to invite media attention and interact with "sinners" suggests a continued commitment to life in the world. Their cognizance of larger society is also reflected in the decisions of some churches to cease cooperation with the media after feeling betrayed, as Duin notes with some frustration,[110] and is evident in the relative obscurity with which many once-prominent young serpent handlers choose to live.[111] Jim Birckhead claims that "media coverage . . . is not an epiphenomenon in serpent handling communities but is integral to how people dialectically construct themselves within and against the reflections of popular commodified representations," resulting in a situation where some "became media celebrities and lost their souls," while others capable of "critically reading their parodically constructed selves in media became decentered serpent handlers, no longer able to continue the practice in a nonironic way."[112] We should, therefore, not assume that communities developing their own systems of propriety, even in radical opposition to what they perceive as a dominant society, do not continue to interact with that society in complex ways. This highlights one difference between communities based on anti-rhetorical reading and the individual experience of psychosis and should serve as a reminder that psychosis is a concept useful in understanding this discourse, which does not make serpent handlers "psychotic."

Finally, the contrasts between serpent handlers and their sadistic readers might influence how we think about irony in relation to anti-rhetorical readings. The zero-degree literalism of serpent handlers and their willingness to engage in dangerous rituals in the name of faith can be read in simple terms as sincerity. As will be discussed more fully toward the end of this book, we might see irony as a potential response to the fanatical worldviews of some communities founded on psychotic engagements with their signifiers. However, the case of serpent handlers shows that a community organized by a rejection of rhetoric is not inherently dangerous, as most serpent-handling sects do not seem any more violent or exclusive than other comparable groups (even though their organization around these particular encounters with text limits their capacity to blend with larger communities they see as fallen). Nor are ironic, rhetorical readings necessarily better than literal ones in an ethical sense. Ironic distance may be partly what enables sadistic audiences to treat serpent handlers as fictional characters to the point of cheering on their suffering and laughing at their deaths. It may be that we always interact not with others but with our internalized images of who they are. Still, a certain kind of abstraction allows us to imagine that they don't *really* suffer the way we do, but we can still imagine what they want enough to rejoice when it is destroyed.

The hundred-year history of serpent handling, its explicit foundation in a mode of reading, and the intense coverage it has evinced from outsiders makes it a particularly fruitful example for the study of how misfit groups break out and hold themselves together as the myth of a mainstream increasingly weakens. Signification is at the center of this story. Like the serpent itself, signifiers twist and writhe, bite and latch on, injecting sometimes inscrutable meaning into the bodies of communities. A thorough analysis of serpent-handling believers demonstrates that they are pathologized, not pathological: It's not that they are literal readers and others aren't, it's that their brand of literalism isn't accepted like other kinds of unquestioning attachment might be. The language of this sect and the outsiders that engage with it demonstrates that seemingly opposite structures of language may still bear structural similarities, often in ways that the traditional Lacanian theory of psychosis cannot fully explain. Signifiers may swallow us whole. But as another community demonstrates, we may swallow them too, consuming them relentlessly, even when they signify nothing.

3

Pro-Ana

Wanting Nothing

Hunger is sometimes presented as inimical to speech, and by extension, community itself. Nathan Stormer has eloquently summarized this view as "a brute, destructive relation where want of food blankets and suffocates civil discourse . . . hunger . . . takes over the desire to persist in being (conatus)." "Starvation," he writes, "is a potent, wordless appetite that supersedes the normalized rhetorics of national and international politics, an incredible motive force whose danger lies in the fact that it smothers other strains of rhetoric that may forestall such violence."[1] Starvation draws the limit of rhetoric. Hunger is inexhaustible: Humans, inescapably embodied and doomed to rot, must constantly keep eating lest they die and decompose even faster. Metaphorically, they hunger for everything, and this is the basis for all communication: If we didn't want some kind of satisfaction or change from speaking, then we wouldn't speak. Desire intrudes in the enjoyment surplus to need: They want not just to eat, but to eat some things rather than others. We would expect communities to form around (literal) tastes and the needs of hunger: The entire march of our history can be seen through this lens, from the development of agriculture to *Top Chef.* Starvation, on the other hand, should be silent, the durable center of no bond, for as Elaine Scarry has argued, this kind of bodily suffering does not translate easily into symbolic speech but is instead communicated through less signifying means.[2] But the psychoanalytic insistence of the presence of absence should teach us to know better.

This chapter explores pro-anorexia ("pro-ana") communities, founded on hunger at the paradoxical intersection of asceticism and gluttony. Since the early days of the Internet, people identifying as anorexic have come together online to share tips, aspirations, photos, and stories defending and promoting anorexia as a lifestyle. These communities were the subject of brief moral panic in the 2000s and 2010s, largely fading into obscurity as a result of deplatforming before experiencing a renaissance on social media. While platforms and content have shifted over time, the celebration of "cyberspace" as a disembodied realm independent from "meatspace" certainly helps to produce the conditions for these communities, which are founded to some degree on a denial of the body. Katherine Dee argues that this disavowal makes anorexia the "nexus of all online communities" and finds in pro-ana communities the perfect exemplar of how identities form through the circulation of online media.[3] The repression of the material body is followed by its (materially) mediated return in the hyperfocus on bodily sensation, body parts, and appearance evident in pro-ana discourses, all subject to intense hermeneutical scrutiny. The body remains central in this discourse but is rendered into text: Pro-ana posters may (or may not) have similar bodily experiences, but they are ultimately bonding over shared signifiers. Nonetheless, the body stubbornly remains in its surplus physicality, intruding sometimes as Real limit to discourse. Pro-ana communities are so heavily dependent on shared media that Emma Seaber called anorexia a "reading disorder."[4] The reading protocols of this community, like others in this book, are hyperliteral to the point of being anti-rhetorical: Anorexia is figured as an agent in itself and often personified, skeletal thinness is coded with discipline and obscure piety, and food becomes deeply meaningful as contamination, filth, and weakness. Written texts, such as memoirs, self-help books, as well as images of starvation, take on univocal meanings and are read in the same way as inspiration and instruction. Pro-ana communities are formed by and around these practices of reading. Attention to the discursive aspects of pro-ana experience, therefore, is more than a "dangerous Gallic fascination with the signifier."[5]

Emmanuelle Desbordes has linked pro-ana discourse to the demise of symbolic efficiency, or as she puts it, in "contemporary times, the faltering Symbolic no longer suffices to organize the relationship of each subject to the world that surrounds her [*sic*] and to claim her singularity."[6] This engagement with signifiers closely resembles that of other communities studied in this book. Like Sandy Hook denialists, pro-ana subjects come together around images and texts, although the "true" meanings they see beneath the surface tend to involve moral judgments and self-discipline rather than conspiracy theories. Like the reactionary pseudoscientists discussed in the next chapter, they fixate on bodily markers to provide structure to their worldviews. Like serpent handlers, anorexics have a persistent, complex relationship to death, with anorexia being frequently cited in mainstream literature as the most deadly of all psychiatric disorders.[7] Serpent handlers seek to encounter and overcome death through their devotion to biblical scripture, while anorexics sometimes run toward it while simultaneously disavowing it,[8] making a relation to the promise of nothingness a fundamental element of their community. Perhaps more so than any other group, however, pro-ana communities demonstrate the preponderance of the something/nothing at the heart of desire, beyond words and eternally unobtainable. As Lacanian analysts have said, anorexia is not primarily a refusal to eat; it is instead an attempt to *eat nothing*, with "nothing" occupying the structural place of the object of desire. Following the psychoanalytic complication of presence and absence, anorexics are actually gluttons for a "nothing" that would unmake them as subjects were they ever to experience it directly.

This chapter explores the reading practices common in pro-ana communities to explain how they sustain communal ties in what Kelsey Osgood describes as "a kind of nebulous death cult in which every member is his or her own personal and omnipresent demagogue"[9] and "a disembodied culture of people conspiring on how to kill themselves and one another . . . getting as high off the collaborative aspect of it as they do from the starvation or disordered eating itself."[10] There is an implicit theory of reading in much existing work on eating disorder communities, one that casts their members as naïve readers who fall victim to patriarchal media. Here I will argue that pro-ana communities do bond together in anti-rhetorical readings that find hidden meaning in symbols, but they are not passive victims. Participants in pro-ana sites are often active readers who articulate desire and identity in surprising ways that are not reducible to conventional notions of sex and the male gaze but conform with the psychoanalytic concept of *Other jouissance* as a mode of desire. Pro-ana communities are not about the refusal of food so much as the desire to eat nothing, a key distinction that inverts conventional wisdom. While psychoanalytic concepts are helpful in this case, pro-ana identities and discourses also offer an opportunity to think differently about some of the problematic assumptions and categories often deployed in this area of scholarship. Psychoanalysis has too often defaulted to binary concepts of sex and gender and privileged sexuality as the locus of all desire. But pro-ana communities defy this binary and hunger is not just a euphemism: It is an alternative means of theorizing desire itself, one that is truly ubiquitous and perhaps equally complex. The expansive vocabulary of hunger and want might provide an opportunity to rethink the hegemonic role of sexuality in psychoanalytic theories of desire, permitting us to talk about identities and attachments in other terms that rely less on the unfortunate tendency of psychoanalytic thinkers to read culturally specific normative expectations about sex, gender, and sexuality as if they were universal, contrary to the implications of their own theories.

To get a better sense of pro-ana communities, I spent months reading posts on Tumblr,[11] one of the social media/microblogging platforms where pro-ana content is still relatively easy to find, along with more obscure groups and archived sites that no longer produce content (e.g., My Fading Obsession, ED Support Forum), and a host of subreddits that disguise their pro-ana leanings to varying degrees. Individual pages also exist, many of them on blogging platforms readily discoverable with search engines. Learning the terminology of pro-ana sites makes searches more productive, as some pages avoid obvious tags (e.g., "pro-anorexia") but use insider argot as an algorithmic shibboleth. The same holds true for pro-ana and adjacent accounts on X (Twitter), Instagram, and Tik Tok, all of which have hosted a substantial amount of content. This experience, colored by periodic encounters with pro-ana Internet media over the last twenty years or so and substantial time with both academic studies and popular journalism suggests that many common representations of pro-ana communities formed during the moral panic of the 2000s and 2010s may need revision. Perhaps most noticeably, these communities are not as young, White, cis, and femme as they are often made out to be.

What this chapter will not do is attempt to "explain" anorexia as a clinically diagnosed condition experienced by individuals. My interest is in the discourse of pro-ana communities, so "anorexic" here means simply those who identify with that label as part of a community and not necessarily subjects clinically diagnosed with anorexia nervosa, unless indicated otherwise. It is possible to meet the criteria for anorexia without belonging to a pro-ana community and possible to belong to a pro-ana community without meeting the criteria for anorexia. It is also possible to dispute "anorexia" as a valid diagnostic category, or dispute the validity of diagnostic categories more generally, but this is beyond the scope of this chapter. Further, while they are sometimes used as a cover for pro-ana discourses, there are also nonjudgmental recovery and support groups for eating disorders. These are not the object of this chapter and should not be grouped together with communities that actively valorize anorexia or its aesthetics. I hope to show how pro-ana groups reveal something about how hunger, sex, desire, and reading function more broadly, not to analyze anorexia per se. To the extent that pro-ana groups are pathological, therefore, it is because *everything* is pathological, which is not the same as "bad" in a normative sense. Pro-ana discourses are not founded on the violent negation of otherness found in some of the groups I explicitly criticize in the next chapter. So, although it's not my place to insist that you don't judge them, I'm not out to help you do it, either.

How to Starve Online

As many memoirs of anorexia relate, communities formed around this shared diagnosis before the Internet. Residential programs, clinics, and mental hospitals all had patients, usually cis women, who read the same books, shared tips, and often competed against one another to appear sickest or thinnest. The multimedia affordances of the Internet expanded the potential for communities to form around anorexia, but outside of managed care, institutions, or industries focused on women's bodies. New technology magnified the "influential potential" of pro-ana messaging, as Seaber notes: "Whereas a simple text can only go so far, websites can couple text and image, and use video, even music, to promote anorexia to readers."[12] Online availability also magnifies the reach of text, as the huge proliferation of anorexia memoirs on Amazon attests. Many self-help books and personal stories are available for instant download, often for free. If the Internet did not kindle pro-ana communities, it did serve as the "crucible."[13] Once more common on Yahoo, LiveJournal, and Pinterest,[14] pro-ana communities remain extant today on Discord, Kik, WhatsApp, Tumblr, and on their own dedicated pages visible on the clear web. The nature of the World Wide Web as a simultaneously time-binding and space-binding medium makes online communities persistent, sometimes ready to sprout again when fed with new attention. Pro-ana discourse may even be experiencing a revival on Twitter,[15] Instagram,[16] YouTube,[17] Quora, Reddit, and especially Tik Tok.[18] YouTuber Eugenia Cooney, who does not make explicitly pro-ana content but is generally coded as anorexic,[19] has millions of followers for her makeup and fashion videos, many of whom are highly engaged commenters.

Wise to censorship, pro-ana sites are often indistinguishable from support and recovery groups, especially now, or exist as crypto-communities and subdiscourses within those spaces. Deplatforming may have suppressed some of these groups, but more spring up to replace them,[20] and their need to be more subtle may make their messages more difficult to identify. Pro-ana sensibilities and media may show up in places that claim to be against the practice or simply don't engage it, advancing a subtext even when they do not dominate a platform. Photographs of thin women ostensibly shown as warnings might be read as inspiration instead,[21] operating as a kind of accismus in the same way that stories of child abuse seem to engage QAnon adherents a bit *too* much.[22] What distinguishes pro-ana communities is their support for anorexia as an aesthetic or lifestyle choice, and as such they are not the same as simply the sum total of people who might be classified as anorexic in contact with one another online or those who bond over conventionally therapeutic attitudes about recovery, management, and mutual aid. As one would expect, members are often conflicted, sometimes drifting toward treatment and at other times defiant in their efforts to contain and control deep, perhaps unbearable, ambivalence about their own identities.

Although images and other media play important roles in the social life and cohesion of pro-anorexia communities, writing has long been a significant adhesive.[23] Before the Internet, anorexics shared memoirs and even clinical works alongside common fictional touchpoints (*Alice in Wonderland* seems particularly popular).[24] Beyond the contents of any specific text, pro-anorexia groups are tied together by a "special relationship between particular writing and reading practices and anorexia identity formation," with many narratives evincing "peculiar ways of approaching, producing, and consuming written texts . . . modes of reading—interpreting, understanding, and responding to—social and cultural texts that are highly distinctive."[25] Seaber suggests that anorexia is a "textually transmitted disease" and that it is characterized by "disordered modes of reading" alongside its classic symptoms involving food.[26] More specifically, the characteristic mode of anorexic reading is one that "teases out arcane, profound, perhaps broadly bewildering meaning," not just inverting memoirs and cautionary literature by mining them for weight loss tips, but actually transforming them into "scripture," insisting on a single, unitary meaning and refusing any alternatives.[27]

Starting from a quantitative perspective, Emily Troscianko came to a similar conclusion, discovering in her survey results that eating disorder memoirs in particular were both widely read and reported to reinforce symptoms.[28] Whether reading practices are actually a central part of anorexic identities for most individuals and particularly those who are inclined to write anyway is hard to establish, but Troscianko's work supports this case. She argues that metaphor, narrative, and literary perception all support a notion of eating disorders as "in part illnesses of interpretation."[29] Further, she suggests that self-identified anorexics swing between hypermeaningful (and potentially psychotic) encounters with certain signifiers—much like anti-rhetorical readings adopted by conspiracy theorists—and shallow encounters with others such that abstract notions like control over hunger may eclipse the actual bodily experience of starvation, again suggesting the importance of signification as a bond. Online interaction produces much more evidence about how people communicate than it does about how they actually eat, which cannot generally be verified, and not everyone who identifies with pro-ana communities would be diagnosed as anorexic in a clinical setting. In any case, because pro-ana Internet communities are necessarily mediated by writing and other technologies, the case that they are shaped by practices of interpretation is hard to dispute and does not require any conclusion about writing and anorexia per se.

Pro-ana identities come with distinctive rhetorical habits, including a specialized argot. Some of this, such as a common set of acronyms (e.g., GW for "goal weight," CW for "current weight"), enables brevity. A series of euphemisms or circumlocutions highly relevant but not unique to those experiencing anorexia attempt to find humor in mental health experiences (e.g., "grippy sock jail" for psychiatric facilities) or evade social media censorship (e.g., in relation to suicide: "unalive," "kms," "kill mice elf"). Because pro-ana content is now monitored more closely, evasive language specific to eating disorders also exists (e.g., star emojis replacing the first four letters of "starving," or various misspellings, allusions, and letter substitutions to avoid filters). This particular variety of linguistic change again demonstrates the importance of medium: While subjects coming together around pro-ana media may forge connections in their discourses, some of this work is performed by or in response to social media company policing that creates the need for adaptation. In this case, the belief in a persecuting Other characteristic of some psychoses is literally true: As in the case of conspiracy theorists, the Internet actualizes fantasies of persecution. Inhuman algorithms really do read what users say and punish them, perhaps even erasing their (digital) identities. Evasive language is also evidence that anorexic subjects are not incapable of linguistic figuration,[30] even if some of the devices and attachments that occupy them are ultimately anti-rhetorical. Anorexic readings, like others sharing this structure, are selective, characterized by anti-rhetorical attachments to their key "quilting points" but also including rhetorical and literal interpretations of other signifiers.

Personification is a particularly common device. Michele Mason stages a conversation with Anorexia throughout her memoir.[31] Jen Dixon fears that even in recovery her eating disorder "lurks around every corner waiting to grab me by the throat and pull me back into its vortex."[32] Keller, writing in a creative nonfiction format, describes her eating disorder as a complete character. "I pictured him as an attractive GQ businessman," she writes, "complete with a strong jaw and an expensive suit. . . . I relied on the voice of ED to coach me throughout my illness, motivating me to keep pushing myself when I wanted to give up."[33] Brittany Burgunder signals her recovery with a shift in her figurative language, addressing a letter to her eating disorder but insisting that she no longer thinks of it as a separate entity.[34] Ana (anorexia), Mia (bulimia), and Ed (eating disorder) are all common examples, sometimes further adapted to mask their referents, such as when an anorexic is called a "friend of Ed" or when a surname is added, such as Ed Sheeran. These personifications sometimes bleed into a religious context in which Ana is treated as a "goddess,"[35] well-known pro-ana maxims are treated as "Thin Commandments,"[36] and various food rituals (such as cutting into tiny pieces or overchewing) can be understood as rites, furthering the links between anorexia, religion, and psychosis. Melissa Espinoza writes of four "secrets" to thinness that became her "scripture" and the gym as a place where she went to "pray to the gods of slender" with other "congregants." The fifth secret, so "powerful" that it could someday "come alive" is that "the first four secrets have a name, and her name is Anorexia."[37] Espinoza figures Anorexia as the agent of her story in the title of her book and includes imaginary dialogue with "Ana," as many memoirists in this subgenre do.

Personification is an apt form for the pro-ana community. Lacan's "mirror stage" described subjective development as a process of identification with a signifier, which permits the entry into language at the expense of an unmediated connection to the world. This signifier of the self is authorized by the Other, or the larger system of the Symbolic, and in a sense is metaphorical: It stands in as a unified symbol for an absent, impossible, divided unity. It is defined in contact with other metaphors, key linguistic nodes that tend to condense an array of conscious and unconscious meanings in a graspable form ("American," "woman," "worker," and so on). These metaphors might be agential themselves, but they are not generally understood as such. For hyperliteral readers like anorexics, however, personification better describes the way that signifiers like "hunger," "anorexia," and "thinness" seem to act on the subject as if it was passive, persecuting and defining it oppositionally. The result is a rigid but brittle subject, and yet one that differs from others largely in its awareness of external definition, not in some categorical way.

Many memoirs of anorexia suggest that personification helps to anchor subjects and grant them stability in the face of disorientation. While individuals may do this, those participating in pro-ana communities can have their attachments reflected and magnified by others. Sharing photographs, goal weights, and diet plans creates the conditions under which one can demonstrate fidelity to "anorexic" as an identity. Burgunder wrote that she "felt safe" with her eating disorder. "It was a best friend and an authority figure to me, a parent—someone I could always depend on to accept me and be there for me. . . . I thought ED was holding me together."[38] "Authority figure," repeated later in the book, is telling in the context of the diminished norms of symbolic efficiency—pro-ana communities bind not only with texts, videos, and other media objects, but with the signifier of Anorexia itself, an automatic defense against dissolution. Pro-ana social media posts mention the desire to disappear often, to waste away, even to die, as do many memoirs directly in their titles, such as *Shameful Vanished* and *How to Disappear Completely*. These are fragile identities, ones that embrace the possibility of fading away and remain rooted largely due to their collective identification with anorexia as figured through shared texts.[39]

Much written pro-ana content is fragmentary. It often takes the form of short aphorisms about eating, easily circulated by social media or microblogging sites. These statements tend to be written in such a way that they don't emphasize the writer's voice but derive from some external source or injunction of the Other. Common ones include: "What you eat in private you wear in public," "A moment on the lips, a lifetime on the hips," "Empty is pure, starving is the cure," "Nothing tastes as good as skinny feels" (popularized by model Kate Moss). Many of these slogans overlap heavily with mainstream diet culture and weight loss sites, which is partly why pro-ana content can be difficult to root out. Along with photographs, drawings, and videos of skeletally thin people (often, but not always, young women), these slogans serve as "thinspiration" or "thinspo" and comprise a large part of online pro-ana discourse, including variants like "meanspo," "bonespo," and so on. The original context is unimportant; part of what makes this style of interpretation distinctive is its willingness to lift images and phrases from anywhere, including recovery materials, and redeploy them in the service of an anorexic ideal. Artificial intelligence may even be increasing the production of pro-ana materials by generating images and providing extreme weight loss advice.[40] Sharing this content contributes to a sense of community. Pro-ana groups might be the some of the most cohesive online communities organized around eating disorders, redoubling identity through shares, likes, and the provision of a space to (temporarily) escape stigma and pain.[41] Memoirist Brittany Burgunder writes that the "ED world, as artificial and Internet-based as it was [in her time participating there], certainly was a way to feel competitive, have company, and occupy my time," concluding that it was a "toxically addicting" bubble.[42]

Some time spent in this bubble suggested to me that three main stereotypes need to be revised. First, although anorexia has been traditionally depicted as a disease of relatively affluent White American women, online communities demonstrate significantly more diversity. Although images and users still appear to be disproportionately White, content by and depicting people who would likely be coded by most as Hispanic, Black, and Asian anorexics is readily apparent, and not exclusively in English. Clinical evidence suggests that trans people may be disproportionately diagnosed with eating disorders.[43] Many trans or nonbinary pro-ana group members relate the bodily changes of starvation to the process of transitioning or altering the appearance of their bodies to better fit their sexual identities. This is evident on Tumblr, where there is a substantial amount of pro-ana trans content, including the occasional use of hashtags that facilitate encounters between these accounts (e.g., *transpo, trans ana*).[44] The same appears to be true on other pro-ana forums that are still active. Accounts linked by these tabs often mention a desire to become androgynous or erase their sexual identities altogether. For some (especially transmen), adopting anorexic practices may even be a reaction to the lack of gender-affirming care, both to change the shape of their bodies and to exercise control when denied it in other contexts.[45]

Second, popular accounts of pro-ana communities overemphasize visuality.[46] Journalistic coverage of eating disorders almost always contains either extended discussion of thinspo or simply includes the images directly. Some academic treatments emphasize the role of visuality and the gaze to the exclusion of other factors. Text is everywhere in pro-ana communities, however. Posters contextualize images with hashtags, which readers can follow or simply click to find more content and more accounts, allowing them to build their own community interactions through words and labels. Many posts are nothing but short statements, often including various weight-related numbers, although photos are still common. Visuality is important, but hardly dominating to the exclusion of textual communication, and various forms of media presentation are far more likely to influence and enhance one another than they are to operate alone, if such a thing is ever possible.[47] The significance of text is also evident on more specialized, contemporary pro-ana forums that foreground diet and health information, perhaps to avoid easy detection. On ED Support Forum, a still-active community where users publicly post diets, exercise plans, and other information that would clearly constitute disordered eating by *DSM-5* (*Diagnostic and Statistical Manual of Mental Disorders, Fifth Edition*) criteria, photographs are limited to a members-only section requiring a certain number of previous forum posts to access.[48] Eating disorder groups on Reddit, too, including those that are more or less openly pro-ana, tend to be dominated by text.

Third, and perhaps relatedly, pro-ana subjectivity is not explicable solely by pressure for young women to be thin and attractive to men. As Carrie Arnold and Spectrum put it, "people with anorexia are commonly thought of as oversensitive young girls hell-bent on fulfilling cultural ideals of thinness."[49] Gender normativity and patriarchal sexualization are certainly powerful forces—to ignore their role would be a mistake. However, it would also be a mistake to interpret pro-ana discourses simply as an epiphenomenon of them. ED communities are disproportionately queer, are not solely composed of young women, and do not form exclusively around body images in advertising or celebrity-focused media. Although some thinspo includes famous models and celebrities (e.g., Kate Moss), much of it depicts lesser-known or private figures.[50] Burgunder reports telling her therapist that she wanted to destroy her body until it became undesirable,[51] a sentiment echoed by some Tumblr users who claim that they want to look sick, not pretty. Others identify erasing markers of sexual attraction as an important motive, suggesting that although the male gaze clearly influences some members of this community directly, their reception is far more complex than a simple media effects narrative can describe. Thinness is often discussed, but so are less conventional aesthetics. This is not to say that media images are not major factors for some or that body image is never important, but taking it as the sole explanation for anorexia would miss many dimensions of these communities. This is in line with Su Holmes's research on anorexics as active participants, rather than passive victims, of media.[52] Holmes, who identifies as having been anorexic for two decades while teaching university courses on television and media, is hardly a naïve consumer of popular culture.[53] Media may have more influence on how eating disorders are perceived by outsiders than on how they are understood by those diagnosed as having them.[54] In describing their own motives, many anorexics reflecting on their condition ultimately emphasize the need for control above all other factors.[55]

In short, pro-ana communities demonstrate much more diversity in terms of identity, aesthetics, and outlook than is captured in popular media representations of lily-white upper-middle-class teenage waifs. And yet, these diverse subjects end up in the same places, bound together around the same media. So what thread stitches these communities together? What discourse speaks through them? What is it that they attach to and find in each other? The answer I will propose is: Nothing.

Passion for the Symptom

Nothing—or rather the complex relationship between nothing and something—is the heart of psychoanalysis. In the *fort-da* game described by Freud, an infant that is periodically left alone throws a toy away and hauls it back, simulating control over presence and absence that it does not have in regards to its caregivers and learning to enjoy this surrogate instead. The absence of the toy exemplifies the false binary between something and nothing—"nothing" is really "no-thing," a hole where a toy should be, and therefore a place where the toy is present in its absence. What the infant enjoys is not so much the toy or its absence as a fantasy of agency. A second example, from Alenka Zupančič: If one looks at a set of numbered encyclopedia volumes on a shelf, and a narrow space exists between 16 and 18, there is something missing, the hypothetical 17. A third, from Homer Simpson: The hole exists because of the donut around it; it is made significant because it is a presence of an absence, not simply an empty space. Gaps, holes, and lacks are significant partly because, by being legible only through expectations primed by the larger order of a system, they reveal its logic in unexpected ways. This logic appears in an old Soviet joke about shortages: A man walks into a shop and asks, "Do you have any fish?" The clerk responds, "Comrade, this is a butcher. We don't have any meat. The shop across the lane is a fishmonger. *They* don't have any fish." The inverse of this principle is to say that "nothing is there" is to assert the paradoxical presence of an absence. This is something like the figure of zero—inserting "0" is different than simply not writing.

Desire is possible only because of lack. In the simplest sense, if we did not perceive (at least unconsciously) that we were missing something, there would be no motive force to seek it. The sense that we are missing something, however, is a byproduct of the conditions that make it possible for us to exist as subjects in the first place. Every subject is forged on a negation, a separation from everything else. This creates the conditions for us to be unique individuals in a world full of signifiers defined in negation of one another—here, Lacan, Bataille, and Kenneth Burke unexpectedly converge. Negation has a price, though. We lose the "oceanic feeling" or continuity with everything else and become aware of what we don't have. There is a lack at the center of our being that can never be filled because it is inherent to the Faustian bargain of subjectivity: To be ourselves, we can never truly be one with everything else. When we seek objects of desire, we are really trying to fill that void, the nothingness that can never be consummated because doing so would entail dissolving the border between self and other such that we would seek to exist as subjects. Never being able to fill our central nothing, we desire endlessly, substituting one object for another (metonymically, Lacan says) but finding them all wanting. There is a nothing (lack), a place where something should be, what Lacan calls *objet petit a* ("little object a," so called because it has no specific identity), which could never really exist but is missing all the same.

This understanding of presence, absence, and desire is the basis of Lacan's novel take on anorexia. Anorexics don't refuse to consume or lack desire, as the etymology of the term would suggest. In fact, the anorexic *does* consume, but what they consume is *nothing*. As Domenico Cosenza puts it, "the anorexic is not, in reality, the one who refuses to eat," but rather is the one who "eats an unheard-of object: the nothing." In doing so, the anorexic subject attempts to access "a full and limitless enjoyment," which they are "not willing to give up for anything in the world."[56] Nothing is a perfect object, and food is an inevitably corrupt one, which is why the anorexic subject "takes the bread out of their mouth to continue devouring their nothing."[57] In this sense, anorexia is more akin to gluttony than temperance. Rather than direct their attachments toward an object, anorexics organize themselves around something of impossible purity, which could never be fully absorbed because it has no end.[58] A variety of symptoms cover this impossible lack—dietary, perhaps, for individuals, but organized primarily around shared media for pro-ana communities. Anorexia, in this understanding, is not a structure of its own equivalent to neurosis, psychosis, or perversion, but an orientation of desire that can be found across these subjective positions. It reflects "the intensity of our desires and ambitions, our *hunger*," as Kate Taylor observed in getting to know other anorexic patients in treatment.[59]

We should be careful not to oversell this idea. Because every anorexic subject is a unique product of discourses, life experiences, and predispositions, there cannot be a universal explanation of the condition—the same behaviors may signify very different things. Contingency plays a vital role in psychoanalysis (and rhetoric), so we should tread carefully in generalizing about individual subjects lest we essentially reproduce the deficiencies of the *DSM-5* classification approach. These insights do capture something about pro-ana communities, however, and are potentially more helpful in understanding these heavily mediated identities than anorexia per se. Cosenza suggests that anorexics have "a progressive tendency . . . to leave the social bond," but that they may replace it in pro-ana groups with "narcissistic-specular relationships that reinforce the identity of the jouissance linked to the symptom."[60] Selfies ("body check" content) and thinspo are examples of these relationships in which images are shared and enjoyed as symptoms, which does not mean that thin bodies are the goal so much as a result that can anchor *jouissance*, an outward sign of control and discipline.[61] The "narcissistic-specular" aspect of this social link can be seen in the ways in which anorexics compete with one another to be the thinnest and the sickest, as noted in nearly every autobiographical account of the condition. Far from being inert, pro-ana identities are immensely passionate about their symptoms.

For a discourse to create community among subjects it must have signifiers available for collective attachment and a shared protocol for reading them, otherwise called a *social link*. The demise of symbolic efficiency is essentially the loss of a social link in that a shared sense of symbolic propriety has begun to unravel. All kinds of words, images, concepts, and injunctions continue to exist, but subjects are left at the mercy of their signifiers without the sensibility that makes them malleable symbols, not oracular signs. The Other does not disappear, but our accustomed modes of navigating it do, leaving us to face the world with a new uncertainty about what we are supposed to do (or be) to have a place. For Cosenza, this erosion may explain why some people become anorexic. The concern their starvation evokes in their families and friends proves that the Other loves them, reassuring them in a time of uncertainty that they are wanted.[62] Osgood recalls wanting to be "sick enough for someone to love me back to health," while Cosenza comes to a similar but more general conclusion through theory and clinical data.[63] This dynamic is an even better explanation of pro-ana communities, however, because they are explicit efforts to forge new social links, ones that offer meaning and stability in the face of ambiguity. "Ana" or some other personification concretizes the Other, creating a new "authority figure," in Burgunder's terms. Pro-ana sites teach online anorexics how to read and provide shared language and practices. The goddess Ana personified becomes a source for new rules and norms. The discipline, denial, and purity of anorexic lifestyles become signs of virtue and devotion to her. Food is corrupt and invasive. Cosenza argues that pro-ana groups are engaged in "active and militant propagandizing of the symptom and represent . . . an internal trend in contemporary social discourse: the construction of social ties around identificatory signs, not correlated to one's own subjective history but to generic identities, often expressing themselves in a symptomatic condition denied as such and, rather, glorified as a way of life." Pro-ana sites are a "self-segregationist agent" such that there is a "collective and exclusive reinforcement of the passion for the symptom as an alternative way to the social bond."[64] The fact that every memoir and scrap of recovery literature is bent in service of the symptom is evidence that this style of reading, like others in this book, is essentially about the reassuring certainty of seeing hidden truth revealed, not the contingent interpretations of rhetoric or even more constrained literalism.

Anna Shechtman writes that anorexics do "flirt with literalism—The culture tells me to be thin; here you go, I've done it!," but also claims that they "practice a highly creative misreading of cultural cues, as I did when I took my textbook's cautionary tale as aspirational."[65] This second relationship is close to what I have described as hyperliteral or anti-rhetorical. The ambiguity of images of starvation is erased in favor of a reading that inverts their significance. Describing how images of starving bodies from the Nazi genocides in Europe are read as inspirational by some anorexics, Shechtman argues that this "symptom" of a "reading disorder" is "a more structural condition of the starving mind: one that is rooted in obsessive fixation and decontextualization, allowing a single feature of the human body to stand in for the totality of one's self-worth, like a synecdoche. Or one that lets the signs of starvation . . . stand in for one another, like a metonymy."[66] The degree to which these connections become immutable suggest that they are only *like* synecdoche and metonymy since they permit no flexibility. The anorexic knows that they "really" mean something else, something hidden but absolute. In fact, this truth is so overwhelming that it is worth suffering and dying for.

The hidden truth of anorexia as an identity in pro-ana communities is ultimately the impossibility of any object to fulfill desire. The meaning that anorexics validate for each other is that one can never be too thin or too sick, or abstain from eating too much. Food is an object of need so basic that it credibly stands in for everything that one might desire, but like any surrogate object, it cannot fill the constitutive lack that causes us to want in the first place.[67] In pro-ana discourses, food represents the intrusion of the world, something that threatens the integrity of the self. This is not a metaphorical relationship but an anti-rhetorical one: Food can *only* be this contaminating danger, and hunger can *only* be a mark of purity. It is, in fact, the only means to experience jouissance, what Cosenza identifies as the "counterintuitive paradox embodied in the anorexic relationship with food: at the basis of this refusal [is] something other than an absence of hunger, but rather an 'orgasm of hunger' where 'pleasure is concentrated in the silent intoxication of hunger, sought, chased, and found.'"[68] Refusal of food is not a metaphor for anything, but a defense against a kind of paranoid threat from the Other, and hunger is not an absence of desire but the apotheosis of it. Pro-ana readings of shared signifiers and texts reject the possibility of any alternative and are "anti-metaphorical,"[69] or more properly anti-rhetorical, perhaps not in every self-aware personification or euphemism, but in regards to the dominant signifiers of the discourse (hunger, food, starvation, thinness, etc.).

The object (nothing) that anorexics consume transcends any other, breaking dependence on a threatening other by paradoxically eating what it can never give. This act is not about being desired by a specific other, but instead possessing (consuming) the engine of desire itself. Most subjects want to be wanted by the Other, which is taken to a radical extreme in the structure of perversion.[70] But in pro-ana circles, no amount of being desired—either through racist and patriarchal beauty standards[71] or the envy of other anorexics—is ever enough. Pro-ana communities seem to intuit the impossibility of desire's completion and the nonexistence of the *objet petit a*. While some recoil from this void, pro-ana communities attempt to swallow the very source of desire embodied in the lack that they project onto the Other. Not only do pro-ana subjects seek independence from the Other's demands, they refuse anything but the lack that it cannot give, the obscure origin of its seeming desire to invade them. Perhaps "rotten with perfection" in a Burkean sense,[72] they endlessly share rituals, inspiration, and texts meant to give meaning to their desire and push each other toward an unattainable goal that promises to erase them more and more as they approach it.

Other Jouissance

For Leslie Heywood, the anorexic body is a literalization of a modernist desire to not desire.[73] From a psychoanalytic perspective, it is the literalization of a desire for nothing. Pro-ana communities are strong candidates for what Lacan calls "Other jouissance," a movement of desire that he figured as one of two orientations in feminine jouissance. The remainder of this chapter will critique the notion and language of "masculine" and "feminine" sexual enjoyment with the aim of salvaging its revolutionary insights along with those provided by its critics. Psychoanalysis, long steeped in heteronormativity and patriarchy, has transformed itself under the weight of critique, often from inside. And yet the implications of a critique of sexual binarism in psychoanalysis—a project in motion but far from completed—have yet to be seriously absorbed.[74] There is even less to say about the limits of sexuality as a metaphor given the existence of asexual and aromantic people. Pro-ana movements illustrate these critiques even as they demonstrate the utility of psychoanalytic concepts like Other jouissance, but before we choose what *spolia* will make it to the next iteration of the structure it is necessary to describe the theories from which this debris is generated.

For Lacan, all subjects are affected by castration, his characterization of the subject's entry into language through a paternal "no" that separates mother and child, an operation that Freud described as Oedipal. The "no" is part of the paternal law that organizes the Symbolic register of experience (language), embodied in the "Name of the Father," Lacan's term for the structuring metaphors that make a discourse intelligible for neurotics and are rejected (foreclosed) by psychotics. This organization of the Symbolic permits subjects to exist as discrete entities and participate in language, but the "cut" of their separation also creates a "lack," the condition for desire that can never be fulfilled, as explained above. That desire is expressed in masculine or feminine modes. Masculine desire involves the possession of an object, the reduction of an other to something that can be grasped and possessed. Men enjoying in this mode treat women as serial objects,[75] all ultimately reducible to signifiers that could be exchanged for one another. This is "phallic" jouissance, in which the subject is really enjoying *themselves*, not the object they seem to seek, since the object of their desire is simply one metonym in an endless chain. In the *fort-da* game, the child doesn't enjoy its toy so much as the feeling of control over it: its own subjectivity; masculine enjoyment, Lacan argues, is similar. Feminine enjoyment involves a double move. On the one hand, feminine subjects want to possess the desire of another, which is distinct from being the object of another's desire. They express feminine identity in a way that is always performative and fluid, a "veil," not convinced of its own rigidity in the way that masculine subjects can be. Doing so allows them to express the qualities of ambiguity and incompletion that are the cause of masculine desire, not its object in the sense that men reduce women to metonymic objects in the chain of desire. On the other hand, feminine subjects also seek access to something that exceeds the limits of our Symbolic order altogether and approaches the Real—namely, Other jouissance. While the veil acknowledges the artifice and mutability of subjectivity, the pull toward the void embodied in Other jouissance threatens the subject more fundamentally with the possibility of death and dissolution. In its existence beyond the limits of language, Other jouissance is unobtainable without undoing the conditions that make discrete subjects possible, and as such represents the impossible beyond of eroticism and death.[76] Colette Soler elaborates the role of death in feminine jouissance in her discussion of Ysé, a character in Paul Claudel's *Break of Noon*. What "reigns over" Ysé is "the mortal aspiration that breaks every human bond," effacing her would-be lovers "in the name of a wish for the abyss, a vertigo for the absolute for which love and death are only the most common names, and for which 'jouissance would not be inappropriate.'" For Soler, this "quasi-sacrificial trait of annihilation is the specific mark that designates the threshold, the border" of desire that is not phallic, not masculine, but geared toward "the absolute Other."[77]

The lure of Other jouissance helps to explain how desire operates in pro-ana communities. In eating nothing, anorexic subjects epitomize both aspects of "feminine jouissance" by consuming the lack that is generative of desire while seeking this external Other. The former function does not have to be read in relation to masculine enjoyment—anorexic subjects are not epiphenomenal of masculine desire, but rather suggest impossible striving toward perfection defined as something that cannot be reduced to any set of concrete symbols, despite their constant efforts to do so. The drive for self-destroying transcendence links pro-ana advocates with the Western saints of the Middle Ages, who fasted unto death in a mystical pursuit of God's love. What they sought was a kind of transcendence that Georges Bataille described as continuity, a state of unity that is promised through erotic melding with another but also through death, the limit point of both *Eros* and *Thanatos* where the desires of a subject are paradoxically fulfilled only in its ultimate dissolution.[78] This helps explain the signifiers of death in pro-ana communities, including deathspo, bonespo, skeletal imagery, and the oft-expressed wish to disappear. Kelly Osgood described pro-ana communities as a "disembodied culture of people conspiring on how to kill themselves and one another, many smirking while they do it, getting as high off the collaborative aspect of it as they do from the starvation or disordered eating itself."[79] Some anorexia researchers worry that recognizing it as a terminal condition might encourage patients to seek the diagnosis as a path toward assisted suicide.[80] The turn toward death might break human bonds, but the circulation of content in pro-ana communities and the common bond of the object nothing permit something new to grow in their place. The argot of these communities gives name to something nameless and permits members to anchor themselves in something that allows access to the void while simultaneously keeping it at bay. Whatever the structures of anorexia in general, in the context of pro-ana sites, the community serves as a new social bond that still retains the orientation toward death. Although we should be cautious not to valorize these communities or instrumentalize them as lessons, the structural orientation toward death in pro-ana discourses can be read as a particularly open demonstration of a relation constitutive of many, if not all, communities—certainly all of those covered in this book.

Studies of anorexia have often used the language of male and female, feminine and masculine. Cosenza, for example, identifies feminine jouissance as the reason so many anorexics are women.[81] Often, these studies describe anorexia exclusively in terms of women's experience (read ciswomen's experience), with only the occasional passing reference to men and almost never any move to consider those who defy hegemonic gender categories. The discourses and identities of pro-ana communities suggest, however, that this sexual binarism is at best antiquated. Many pro-ana site users are trans, nonbinary, and queer, as the studies cited above suggest.[82] Even those who identify as women do not necessarily seek to change their bodies to better fulfill the masquerade of feminine desire—some might, but to reduce the phenomenon of pro-ana discourse solely to the male gaze would miss much of its complexity and character. The dynamic of Other jouissance is a compelling frame from which to understand pro-ana discourse, its patterns of desire, and its orientation toward death and language. But to label this as necessarily "feminine" might say more about the hangups of psychoanalysis than the communities we are discussing, many members of which actively refuse gender binarism. So what is to be done with the concepts derived from this binary in which we might still find value?

Pretending that the problem does not exist is not an adequate response. Addressing an audience of psychoanalysts, Paul Preciado declared that one "can no longer continue to assert the universality of sex and gender difference . . . in a society where it is legal to change gender or identify as gender non-binary. . . . To continue to practice psychoanalysis with clinical tools like the Oedipus complex is as absurd as . . . claiming the earth is flat."[83] While some Lacanians stubbornly refuse to confront their shortcomings, even doubling down on their transphobia,[84] others are more thoughtful. Psychoanalysts from Lacan forward, including Zupančič and Soler, are quick to note that "masculine" and "feminine" describe structural positions, not biology. They are patterns of desire that the same subject might even demonstrate at different times. This explanation—while in many ways productive—still begs the question of why "masculine" and "feminine" remain the habitual signifiers if they are essentially nothing more than metaphors for modes of desire that could be called otherwise. Any rhetorician will remind you that metaphors are more than decoration. They organize our thinking, and the more powerfully invested they are with cultural meaning the more they do so. Instead of using male and female as organizing signifiers, perhaps we should ask Preciado's question: "What if the epistemology of sex, gender and sexual difference in itself were a pathology of the signifier?"[85]

Annie Rogers moves toward an answer in her discussion of the Name of the Father. Traditional Lacanian theory relies heavily on this concept to explain the formation of subjects through their entry into language and to describe what is foreclosed in psychosis. The demise of symbolic efficiency is essentially a translation of this concept from the domain of individual subjects to that of discursive communities. And yet, it seems like a blatant relic of patriarchal thinking. We might be tempted, following Preciado, to reject the notion of the Name of the Father altogether. But Rogers suggests that *acknowledging* it is an even more radical gesture, if done with a twist. The Name of the Father is a perfectly appropriate term for this ordering function in modern societies, but instead of being the thing *rejected* in psychosis, it is an *example* of psychosis. Patriarchal societies believe in it with implicit certainty just like any other psychotic delusion, but it is just that: a way of foreclosing the encounter with radical ambiguity and uncertainty by creating a rigid protocol to cover it up. The Oedipus complex is real, too, at least in some contexts, but instead of a (near) universal mechanism of desire, it is a symptom that results from the Name of the Father.[86] The Name of the Father is another name for patriarchal heteronormativity, one that recognizes that it is essentially pathological even as it exercises its hegemonic privilege to label feminists, gender nonconformists, anorexics, and all manner of dissenters "crazy" for challenging its premises.

Rogers's claim that the Name of the Father should be read as a psychotic fixation permits a rethinking of traditional psychoanalytic theories of sex and gender categories. Here Zupančič's work supports a theory that establishes these identities as performative, not essential, while still recognizing them as anchors for durable, even hegemonic, investment by a patriarchal signifying order. Zupančič sees radical potential in Lacan's infamous claim that "Woman does not exist." Lacan, ever the provocateur, no doubt intended this statement to be both incendiary and opaque. Zupančič argues that because patriarchal violence is organized by the imposition of fixed identities for women (housewife, Jezebel, mother, waif...), to say that Woman does not exist is to return to a more ambiguous and protean view of identity more in line with Freudian "polymorphous perversity" than the rigid normativity critiqued by Preciado. Without the existence of Woman as an a priori identity, no binary is possible. In this view masculinity is distinguished only by its psychotic insistence on itself: It is simply a defense against the inherent fluidity and ambiguity of sex and gender by a discourse that cannot bear to acknowledge them.[87] Hence the plus sign often appended at the end of LGBTQIA and its variants: No scheme of classification, however comprehensive, can ever map the landscape of possibility without remainder.[88] The alternative is not to ignore sex and gender identities, but to fully internalize the knowledge that they are (often unconsciously) performative, arbitrary, and culturally forged, not transcendent structural inevitabilities. The result of establishing a psychoanalytic path to the performativity of gender and sex should be greater nuance and sensitivity in the study of pro-ana communities. They may be organized around "Other jouissance" and possessing the lack, but to insist that these two modes of desire should always coincide and be called "feminine" is counterproductive.

Oedipus and Erysichthon

"Feminine" and "masculine" might be due for more limited applications. What about sexuality? For Zupančič, the sexual is an imperfect name for a negativity that cannot be captured in language. It is the constitutive absence that makes a subject possible, the inevitable failure of relation onto which we script various kinds of interactions, ties, and connections. There is nothing natural about sexuality: It is the "*operator of the inhuman*, the operator of dehumanization," something that marks disorientation and instability.[89] Sexualities are identities that we use to grasp this unspeakable absence, but they are essentially catachrestic. Sexual enjoyment can be understood as derived from any surplus, including speech. Zupančič acknowledges, however, that "sex" in the quotidian understanding of this term is at best metaphorical because the sexual is really just a name for an irresolvable contradiction, another of these famous negations and lacks, and enjoyment extends to many (all?) things not usually considered sexual. Saying that sexual desire is a metaphor, however, opens up the possibility for other terms. Both rhetoricians and psychoanalysts must acknowledge that metaphors both shape and reflect thought. So what other possibilities might exist, and how could they influence our understandings of desire generally and pro-ana communities in particular?

As a longing caused by lack that involves the potential for surplus enjoyment and can never be extinguished, hunger is an obvious alternative. Indeed, hunger is frequently used as an everyday metaphor for desire. Everyone hungers; while asexuality and aromanticism are problems for the sexual metaphor,[90] anorexia does not play the same role for a theory centering hunger. In his "Three Essays on Sexual Theory," Freud himself relied on parallels with hunger to explain libido. Biologists, he wrote, "assume the existence of a 'sexual drive', following the analogy of the drive to seek food—hunger. The vernacular lacks a term corresponding to the word 'hunger'; for this purpose, science uses the word 'libido.'"[91] Orgasm is "a satisfaction analogous to the sating of hunger," he claimed.[92] The chief difference for Freud is that libido "permits so much variation and such debasement of its object, something that hunger, which is far more energetic in its retention of its object, would only permit in extreme cases."[93] Anorexia and the notion of an "object nothing" complicate this assertion, as we have seen above. So does a theory of desire that moves beyond Freud's quite specific characterization in this passage, which would fall under Lacan's "masculine" pattern of enjoyment and fail to reach universal applicability even in a binary theory.

In another age, perhaps hunger would not have the resonance that it does at this moment in history. But given the validation of rapacious desire and overconsumption in neoliberal economic conditions, it might be said that we live in an age of subjective hunger and objective gluttony. Humans are metaphorically treated like food: used as resources, chewed up, consumed, excreted, or simply spat out. The applicability of these metaphors to industrial racial capitalism, various forms of human trafficking, gender-based exploitation, and settler colonialism should be clear. For Freud, the superego's embargo on some sources of (sexual) pleasure was a major function in human psychology, and while it is not necessary to declare this insight fully obsolete, the Lacanian notion that the superego now orders us to enjoy perhaps better matches our modern pattern of surplus consumption and excess. Eating always has an economy and ecology to it, a system of material transformation and exchange that both produces and is driven by the surplus enjoyment of taste. It has an element of enjoyment surplus to need in that people like some foods more than others and, as we know, often eat simply for pleasure. It has powerful taboos—cannibalism is perhaps equal to incest in terms of its prohibition and behaviors like pica and coprophagia are also stigmatized. The inevitable byproduct of eating—shit, to use the good old Anglo-Saxon term—represents a disavowed aspect of the drive that has itself been an enduring topic in psychoanalysis.[94]

Freud was ever fond of myth to situate his concepts. Oedipus embodies themes of sex, prohibition, and self-destructive drives. Even if we don't think that referring to this myth is equivalent to believing that the Earth is flat, it cannot possibly be a window on universal patterns of desire. And yet, myth is nothing if not durable, so I propose that we might add another ancient Greek myth to our allegorical compendium.[95] As told in versions by Ovid, Callimachus, and others, there is a story of Hunger personified (Limos) who breathed her lack into Erysichthon, a nobleman of Thebes. Eryischthon cut down a tree sacred to Demeter, goddess of heath, grain, and the harvest, killing the nymph inside along with one of his own companions who intervened to stop his desecration. Demeter responded by sending an Oread messenger to her inverse figure, Limos. The messenger entreated Limos to infect the sacrilegious Erysichthon such that no plenty could ever extinguish his craving. Limos, so emaciated that her bones and organs are visible beneath the skin, crept onto Erysichthon while he was asleep and breathed her emptiness into him, cursing him with insatiable hunger. He dreamt of food and eating and was ravenous upon waking. The cursed apostate then consumed every morsel of food he could get his hands on, demanding more even as he desperately ate. He bankrupted himself and his household to satisfy his cravings, but to no avail. Soon, Erysichthon's only asset of any value was his daughter Mestra. He traded her away so that he might eat yet more, but each time she was bartered off to some new suitor, Mestra changed her shape and escaped, just to be exchanged by her father again. Eventually Erysichthon was overcome by his own hunger and gnawed on his own limbs, eating himself to death in a final act of autocannibalism.[96]

What are the affordances of such a myth for our understanding of drive, desire, and jouissance in pro-ana communities, and perhaps more broadly? The changeability of sexual identity is a prominent feature of the story. Mestra changes sex and even species to escape the men who buy her. Across various sources, Limos has no fixed sex, being rendered as female by Ovid, male by Callimachus, and sometimes ambiguously by others. Among other things, anorexia involves the interpretation of various bodily markers: the protuberance of bones, the erasure of secondary sexual characteristics, the mutability of shape that accommodates new clothing. Limos, described as a skeletal figure with "wasted jaw" whose bones and organs are available beneath parchmentlike skin, shares these markers: Insatiable yet famished, she is an apt figure for anorexia as it is idolized in pro-ana communities and also desire writ large. Erysichthon, the one filled with a lack (Limos), can be a metaphor for the emptiness and insatiability of a drive that is not reducible to masculine or feminine formations. Erysichthon's exchange of Mestra to various men for food equates hunger, sex, and death, capturing Lacan's observation that the drives for sex and death are aspects of the same drive for continuity (an argument also made by Bataille, midcentury's greatest edgelord) and discussed above as a key element of pro-ana discourses. Erysichthon eventually disappears, as anorexic subjects often fantasize that they might, having found that there is no food that can satisfy the lack inside him. That lack—the hunger that Limos breathes into him—is an excellent example of the object nothing, both an absence and a presence, impossible to understand by reducing it to either. Like phallic jouissance, eating can be read as a means of possessing an Other, but the metaphor offers more expansive possibilities—unlike Lacan's account of serial philandering, the Limos myth has much to say about the desire to incorporate or absorb the Other.

The orality of hunger creates an obvious parallel to speech, but it is the figure of Mestra that best serves as a mythological allegory for the function of the signifier. Like Lacan's "letter,"[97] she is exchanged in a symbolic/material economy for the fulfillment of desire, but she "means" something different to everyone. Mestra mutates, only reliably finding her way back to the subject who produced her, the starving father Erysichthon, perhaps in parallel to the letter "always finding its destination" and returning in "inverted form" to the speaker as Mestra returns changed each time. This could suggest the arbitrariness of the signifier, but also potentially the hyperliteralism of bodies circulated by pro-ana circles. Thin bodies of others are always aspirational no matter how starved, and one's own body is always too large. The forms may change, but they always mean the same thing: yearning when presented by the shapes of others but disappointment and disgust with one's own lack of discipline. Propriety is doubly represented in the Erysichthon/Mestra myth by sacrilege committed against Demeter and the implication (at least in Ovid) that Erysichthon is reduced to eating unclean foods, finally including his own body. Again, there is the disappearance of a subject, combined with the notion that hunger is unseemly and food is contaminating or abject.

While much of the hunger metaphor seems geared toward explaining acquisitive desire and the object nothing, it also accommodates the notion of Other jouissance. The collective desire for a something that exceeds the limits of language altogether highlights the similarities between pro-ana communities and the religious ascetics they sometimes reference.[98] The Desert Father Evagrios the Solitary identified gluttony as one of the three demons on the "front lines" of sin. Hunger, he wrote, was an antidote to sin, even as he compared prayer and holiness to food.[99] John Cassian, a student of Evagrios whose work formed the basis for the Seven Deadly Sins in the Western church, named gluttony first in his listing of the eight temptations, praising the virtues of hunger and arguing that Sodom was destroyed due to a "surfeit of bread."[100] The attitude of these early ascetics, repeated throughout the ensuing centuries, was an orientation of desire toward hunger, not simply a failure to eat. "Spiritual food" stands in for the object nothing, something pure and otherworldly that has no analogue here on Earth. Perhaps others are right to point out the religious aspects of pro-ana communities, including their reverence of texts, personification of the unseen, and personal asceticism. Structurally, this similarity is about a relation to an unknowable, impossible Other that is present in its absence, like the unspeakable God of negative theology. This resonates with Osgood's "death cult" label in that pro-ana subjects, like religious ascetics, strive to leave the fallen, corrupting world altogether. The focus on the world to come and life everlasting is an orientation toward death that figures it as a signifier for transcendence and continuity.

Mystics, fundamentalists, conspiracy theorists, and anorexics all read their key symbols with an (often implicit) assumption that the world surrounding them is illusory and deeper meaning is hidden but accessible to initiates. Sometimes, however, those who have taken comfort in illusion are faced with intolerable vertigo when their beliefs are questioned, requiring them to seek out a new basis of truth. As the next chapter demonstrates, various groups organize under the banner of "science" to ward off the threat of ambiguous otherness when their supposedly unshakeable assumptions about identity are revealed to be the products of systemic inequality rather than its cause. While the anguish of those who identify as anorexics sometimes turns them inward to strike against themselves, it does not typically spill over into hatred of others. Would only the new acolytes of pseudoscientific elitism remain so insular.

4

Reactionary Science

Agents and Alibis

Rick Sanchez, one of the titular main characters of *Rick and Morty*, is the center of a fan base often considered "toxic," or at least pretentious in a specifically masculine way.[1] An ironic aspect of the show is that the titular Rick, idolized by some fans, is himself miserable and in many ways pathetic, available to be read as a critique of "toxic" masculine fantasies of control, independence, and hyperrationality. Rick is "the smartest man in the universe," but the insights of his science are bleak, depersonalizing, and depressing. He seems to be a pessimistic nihilist, concluding from his vast knowledge of the universe that nothing means anything beyond hedonistic pleasure, as summarized by his grandson Morty: "Nobody exists on purpose, nobody belongs anywhere, everybody's gonna die. Come watch TV." Rick has godlike power, but he uses it to insulate himself against all the universes where he is *not* the smartest being in existence. He is insecure, emotionally disconnected, and fragile, prone to suicidal depression and subject to base human feelings even when he should know better.[2] Ultimately, science is not an impenetrable armor for Rick but the means by which he attempts to bury his trauma, sometimes literally, but rarely with any lasting success. For all his talk about "rising above," science doesn't make Rick any better than those he despises.

Rick and Morty's notion that idolizing science could be a failed disavowal of underlying trauma hints toward a broader cultural phenomenon. Of all Babel's spolia, the term *Science* is among the most revered, signaling a kind of objectivity that is hard to find once we've lost our bearings in the Tower's rubble.[3] The decline of symbolic efficiency also means the weakening of collective beliefs that gave us purpose and shielded us from the starkest implications of the void. New communities may compensate by clinging to Science as a signifier of extralinguistic authority to deal with the trauma of collapse, especially if they once belonged to a privileged caste that did not need to defend its claims against those they subjugated. When the erstwhile immutable categories of race, sex, and gender are revealed to be arbitrary, their adherents may become unhinged from the structures that unjustly elevated them. Science becomes attractive because it allows one to dismiss claims for recognition and justice. It is supposed to be objective, an aspect of nature rather than human culture, but Science as a signifier and science as a mode of knowledge production do not coincide exactly. The notion that superiority is scientific can serve as a new catalyst for community, lending some sense of stability and legitimacy to beliefs that fall well outside mainstream propriety. This new function is ironic given that the challenges to racial and gender hierarchies that produce this anxiety often grow out of scientific knowledge that debunks social categories. Part of its promise is an escape from agency because if the social order is determined by something beyond human control, then those who profit are blameless and those who suffer are simply doomed.

This chapter examines how different communities shore up their identities around the signifier of Science. Whereas previous chapters of this book each focus on a single community formed around literal readings of a small number of signifiers, this chapter studies how several communities mirror one another in their anti-rhetorical readings of one signifier, highlighting the ways that signifiers may act as agents, but also demonstrating the limits of that conception through the study of this one in particular. "Involuntary celibates," or incels, preach a council of despair based on studies of mating strategies. What they call the "blackpill" is a realization that their romantic and sexual fantasies are made impossible by genetics, acting at the individual level to make incels undesirable and at the social level to code for mate-selective behaviors that doom them to solitude. Racial realists also claim that inequality is inevitable due to population genetics. Racism and race both precede their "scientific" justifications temporally and logically, but Science has given a particular kind of coherence to these beliefs, allowing these communities to cast them as neutral or even tragic truths that provide alibis for inequality. Transinvestigators are a newly emerging community of conspiracy theorists who argue that almost every celebrity figure is secretly transgender but can be easily unmasked by scientific knowledge. This nascent community, so far sustained almost completely by social media, demonstrates how mutable Science has become in the intersection of transphobia and conspiracy thinking. All three of these groups fixate on bodies, and especially bones, seeing in them the literal structures of difference and truth. All of them overlap in some ways, but in their structural relationship to Science they resemble each other more profoundly than it may initially seem.

The resonance of Science for these overlapping but disparate groups is a path to evaluating Lacan's claim that signifiers are the real agents of discourse, while subjects are largely epiphenomenal functions of these basically inhuman operations of language. While scholars of communication often fret over how we misuse science to provoke an unwarranted uncertainty,[4] this perspective draws attention to the ways that the signifier Science misuses *us* to instill an impossible *certainty*. Doing so should help us think through some of the main themes of this book, particularly how modes of reading help determine the character of communities that form around particular signifiers in new ways made possible by the affordances of contemporary media, and how central those signifiers are to founding new patterns of social linkage in the wreckage of our (imaginary) cultural consensus. The common denominator, as always, is desire: Each of the three communities examined in this chapter is the result of an affective fixation on something that gives a sense of meaning and importance, promising fulfillment while only delivering the painful enjoyment of jouissance.

Science is a particularly interesting case of a signifier gone rogue because its aura of authority seems to have survived the decline of trust in those who used to invoke it. For example, while vaccine skeptics impugn Dr. Anthony Fauci as a symbol of scientific authority, they often do so while still appealing to Science. The focus of some debates over the legitimacy of science on individual scientists (rather than, say, evaluations of competing scientific methodologies using broadly shared metrics) highlights this distinction between Science as a signifier and science as a mode of inquiry focused on particular standards of evidence, revision, probabilistic claims, and so on.[5] Science in the latter sense should (at least in theory) be a corrective against unthinking reliance on authority because it elevates observable evidence and repeatable experiments above stature and reputation, and although it will never be objective due its status as a human activity, its standards reside in agreed-upon protocols, not only the (imaginary) passions of particularly avid subjects.[6]

For the most part, this chapter tracks how Science as a signifier is invoked as a defense against ambiguity and not a social practice or mode of inquiry, but Lacan also had something to say about the social function of science more generally. In "Science and Truth," Lacan argued that the "prodigious fecundity" of science is possible only because it "does-not-want-to-know-anything about the truth as a cause."[7] This is a reference to his notion of foreclosure, a defining attribute of psychosis in which something is not just repressed but totally refused because the subject does not "*want to know anything about* [it], *even in the sense of repression*."[8] It is unscientific to even ask some questions (e.g., about ultimate cause), not just to pursue answers in ways that don't match scientific conventions for evidence. For the communities analyzed here, the not-knowing of this foreclosure becomes intolerable and something fills in, demonstrating how "a successful paranoia might just as well seem to constitute the closure of science."[9]

I hope to demonstrate that what fills in for the foreclosure of cause in science *as a discourse* is Science *as a signifier*. Faced with an essentially traumatic absence in their encounter with the world, these groups assert access to a hidden truth derived from Science, an absolute that permits no place for chance or social construction. White supremacists do not have to acknowledge that their privilege results from a legacy of systematic violence and oppression, let alone that their identity is fluid and ambiguous, instead declaring that their social position is the inevitable result of immutable biology. Transvestigators do not have to acknowledge that both gender and sex are porous categories that exist by consensus, declaring instead that physiology can demonstrate that binary sex is *true* in an absolute sense. Incels do not have to face the uncertainties inherent in romance, the instability of patriarchal privilege, or the limits that their ideologies impose on their lives but can instead believe that nature has determined in advance how humans ought to live, claiming that feminists are the only ones with an ideology. In every case, there are no ambiguities and no accidents: Science makes the outcome inevitable, and the world reassuringly predictable and stable, even when the revealed truths are unpleasant ones.

This chapter begins with a discussion of signifiers as agents, (hopefully) clarifying Lacan's arguments about the relationship between language and subjectivity. Next, I will explore ways that Science is deployed by so-called racial realists (concentrating on the White supremacist site Stormfront), incels (primarily on incels.is), and Transvestigators (largely on Facebook and TikTok). I have chosen to focus on a small range of Internet sites for each group based on their centrality to the larger discourse and persistence over time, although, in recognition that these communities are fluid, I view these as starting points for discussion rather than strict limits. The conclusion of this chapter summarizes the implications of this study for how we theorize discursive phenomena, especially in the context of agency and responsibility.

Two notes about terminology are necessary. First, *incels* (a portmanteau of "involuntary celibates") refers to men who identify as such in a particular discursive mode characterized by the "blackpill," extrapolating from it that mainstream feminism is the proximate cause of their inability to find fulfilling relationships with women, while iron laws of genetics, ethology, and evolutionary biology are the ultimate cause. Many of the men who frequent incel forums are racialized, disabled, "neurologically" divergent, or otherwise marginalized. "Incel" has become a label frequently applied by others as a term of abuse, sometimes intersecting with the kind of left-sadism encountered by serpent handlers,[10] and sometimes apparently with an eye toward deradicalization. Not all people so labeled necessarily fit the definition I have given, and not everyone who is involuntarily celibate identifies as an incel or shares these radical orientations. My use of the term in this chapter is in reference to those who do.

Second, I have chosen to capitalize "White" when referring to the identity category. There are good reasons to take pause at this decision, perhaps most significantly that the racists I analyze here tend to favor the same capitalization. Having considered the opposing case, I have chosen to capitalize it not to mark it as exceptional but because it is a demonym like any other. Whiteness operates in part through invisibility as an unstated norm against which everything else is distinguished, which is a function perhaps magnified by treating it differently than equivalent terms, even permitting it to recede (uncapitalized) into the background. I am usually referring to a group that identifies as "White" in a specific sense, not to an objective category or even to all people who might be coded as "White" in various circumstances since its referent is contested. Like the concept of race in general, Whiteness exists as a social force but is not "real" in any natural sense.[11] It is part of a larger Symbolic machinery maintained by desire, identification, and affective investment, a fantasy with material consequences like the signs "Ladies" and "Gentlemen" adorning public restroom doors and sorting who is sanctioned to be where.[12] The capitalization of the demonym "White" is therefore meant to mark its artificiality, as opposed to the object-quality descriptor "white." A bleached skeleton in the College of Physicians of Philadelphia is white, but a person who thinks they can use its measurements to prove their innate superiority is White.[13]

Subjects and Signifiers

A classic dispute exists in social theory about the relative importance of structure and agency. This is very much an issue for scholars of media and technology who grapple with determinism. Rhetoric has traditionally fallen on the side of individual agency even though concepts like the rhetorical situation exist to describe the interaction between speakers and their environments. Psychoanalysis, characteristically, has a convoluted and self-negating position. Freud posited that human agency largely originates outside the conscious mind, operating in response to trauma along rails firmly laid down by the Oedipus complex, repetition compulsion, libido, and castration anxiety. At the same time, however, psychoanalysis is distinguished from many other traditions by its focus on the particularity of individual subjects who suffer from their traumas, which is why it tends to eschew the categorizing impulse of the *DSM-5* and its ilk.[14] The issue of agency is complicated, therefore, because it involves not just the interaction of an individual with their social environment (as internalized in the superego), but also the question of where agency is located *within* an individual.

Lacan's application of structural linguistics to Freudian theory complicated this situation even more. At first glance, it appears that he sided with the determinists. One of his most frequently paraphrased teachings is that the signifier speaks through the subject, and therefore signifiers, not subjects, are the agents of language. In the title of his essay "The Instance of the Letter in the Unconscious," the word "instance" (*L'instance*) condenses several important associations. Any act of speech is an "instance" where the letter ("the material medium [*support*] that concrete discourse borrows from language") appears.[15] The letter also *insists*: it presses upon a subject, determining in part what is sayable for them and pushing its way seemingly unbidden into everyday discourses through parapraxes and unconscious associations.[16] Other translations replace "instance" with "agency" in the essay's title, stressing that human subjects are essentially media, while the signifier they create ends up communicating through them. In "Seminar on the Purloined Letter," Lacan uses Edgar Allan Poe's story to demonstrate how their differing positions relative to a letter—the contents of which are never precisely known—define various subjects in relation to one another in an ephemeral but intricate social structure. For Lacan, the letter is the "*true subject* of the tale" in every sense of that noun, and it is the "signifier's displacement" that "determines subjects' acts, destiny, refusals, blindnesses, success, and fate, regardless of their innate gifts and instruction, and irregardless [*sic*] of their character or sex . . . everything . . . follows willy-nilly the signifier's train, like weapons and baggage."[17]

The signifier in this account is not a static thing, a word printed or spoken in isolation neatly tied to a conceptual signified. Signifiers are always deployed within a network of other signifiers, instantiated concretely in a particular place and time as a "letter."[18] Important signifiers act metaphorically by accreting or making meaning, more like a protocol for navigating a network than a lexical reference to a dictionary. When operating metaphorically, one signifier (as a word, say) takes the place of others, referenced but not spoken, which are invoked even if they are not directly perceived. Signifiers used like this tend to accrete meanings like crossroads lead to human settlements, gathering only because important paths of transfer cross in one place.[19] Though they are not explicitly present, signifiers that operate to condition a concrete discourse event constitute the unconscious as a situational, embedded thing for a particular subject or group of subjects who are organized around a text or media object where the signifier is made manifest as a "letter." The signifiers active in a discourse are therefore more than just the ones used. Those that are unspoken but influential constitute the unconscious. It might be better to think of signifiers as knots composed of many tangled threads, all participating in a discursive formation without any of them constituting it alone. Thus, the signifier *Science* may refer to a cluster of related terms that rely on and reference it even when the word itself is not legible on the surface of a discourse.

Based on this reading, one could make the case that psychoanalysis does very much preserve a place for agency—but the agent *is* the structure in the form of the signifier. The issue is not so much that individuals don't have agency as there *are* no individuals; what we understand as the subject is largely a placeholder for the negativity of lack around which conflicting forces of drive, desire, language, culture, and fantasy endlessly circulate. This is what Lacan meant by the "metaphor of the subject," his reading of Freud's phrase "Wo Es war, soll Ich warden" (where it [the Id] was, I [the Ego] shall be), in response to Heidegger.[20] A signifier, like a name, stands in to create something that operates in language where there is essentially nothing—another of the *fort-da* presence/absence paradoxes of psychoanalysis. Recognizing that the subject is a metaphor does not make it any less important. It is a fundamental fantasy that provides an anchor for one's participation in language, because the signifier of the subject becomes a transferable commodity in the economy of discourse, allowing a speaker to recognize themself at a remove like any other object.[21] The battery of signifiers taken together is the Other, and from this resource subjects are made through usually unconscious associations. National identity is important to some people, for example, but they don't invent the concept of "American" or they (often) freely choose it but are defined by it in advance. This is how the signifier "speaks though" the subject: What we take to be "ours" is a mediated discourse that we channel to others. And yet, the meaning that grows up around signifiers does so as a result of their repeated use and invocation. Letters may insist, but the frequency and manner by which they do so is not constant. Some kind of choice must inhere outside the structure of language, even if it is difficult to locate, and even the most forceful signifiers shift their unconscious associations.

In many ways, subjects are simply media. Words flow through us that we did not forge, dragging with them all sorts of meanings and associations that we cannot control. Even if we were perfectly free agents deliberately assembling our discourses, the reservoir of signifiers from which we can draw preexists us and cannot completely be refigured by us. This is akin to Kenneth Burke's "unending conversation," a discussion that we join while it is already in progress and are forced to leave before any conclusion is in sight.[22] Subjects are not agents, but metaphors for agents, placeholders for something that we feel must exist but cannot precisely locate. This is why Lacanians tend to cling to this notion: There is some excess to signification that acts as an agent, consciously or not, but it cannot be directly located precisely because it is excess to signification. Particularly invested signifiers may help subjects shirk whatever agency they have by creating the impression that strong influence is the same as determination.

This has been the role of Science for many. In terms of the metaphor of this book's Introduction, Science was a particularly imposing part of the Tower's construction: It was not just a recognizable piece of the façade, but a major load-bearing element, something that helped to support the whole edifice of our always-already-lost consensus. Invoking it lent powerful authority—"studies find," "scientists have determined," "it is a law of nature that." Proper names can be invoked to conjure the whole discourse metonymically—Curie, Oppenheimer, Newton. Einstein came to represent the very concept of intelligence, while Darwin has been most troubling in the hands of reactionaries. White lab coats exercise such symbolic power that they are only allowed in American drug advertising under certain conditions.[23] In this cluster of associations, Science can be thought of as the central metaphor, with a range of other terms connected to it in a metonymic web, but it is also mutable. This explains the ironic inversions in how Science is regarded. Once subject to academic leftist suspicion, the population-level management by Big Pharma was lauded by the center-left during the COVID-19 pandemic, while the authority of doctors and scientists was trashed by conservatives, who paradoxically leaned into all kinds of technological development and declared that "facts don't care about your feelings." Scientists, especially mainstream virologists and climate scientists, are often ridiculed by reactionary communities, but these same communities tend still to endorse rogue researchers and charlatans under the banner of Science. The next three sections provide examples of Science operating to cohere communities through which it speaks.

Involuntary Celibates

The portmanteau "incel" for "involuntary celibate" seems to have been coined (at least on the Internet) by a young Canadian woman in the mid-1990s.[24] The term became an identity unmoored from its original community and is now situated among pickup artists, so-called men's rights groups, masculinity-focused religious traditionalists, Andrew Tate adherents, and Men Going Their Own Way as part of the broader "manosphere." Incel content often shares aesthetics, memes, and references with other Internet groups, particularly in the alt-right and its successors. This includes antisemitic and racist language, including biological racism, although in various self-reports incels are not overwhelmingly White and the performance of bigotry in Internet forums should not be interpreted unambiguously.[25] Following an increasingly strident web presence and connections to a large number of spree killings and other hate crimes, the primary incel subreddits have been banned and many older forums no longer exist.[26] Deplatforming has been at best marginally successful. The community remains active, and incel discourse has become fairly normalized across the Internet, a situation perhaps enabled by media exposure and persistent mockery among those hostile to incel identity. An extensive lexicon exists, including some terms that are now broadly legible (e.g., the hypermasculine figure of "Chad"), and others of which remain more niche (e.g., LDAR for "lie down and rot," "looksmatch" for an appropriate mate, "rope" for suicide).[27]

The scientific discourse of the "blackpill" seems to be a major reason for its acceptance, as the prevalence of scientific (including social scientific) terminology in its exposition testifies.[28] Incels claim that evolutionary psychology has revealed hard rules of mate selection in human beings and that one's "sexual market value" is largely a product of biology, with some men being so objectively ugly that their hopes of "ascending" or finding a desirable long-term mate are perhaps literally zero. Women, they believe, want to mate with the most attractive, dominant, and aggressive men and will happily cheat on their long-term mates, whom they select only for financial stability ("betabuxx").[29] What determines a man's market value is largely his appearance, which incels analyze in incredible detail. In a discourse partly shared with pickup artist and "looksmaxxing" sites, incels have assembled a vast set of terms, many anatomical, which are used to distinguish between "Chad" and "incel" appearances, which are hierarchized by number (1–10) or with categorical descriptors (Gigachad, Chadlite, normie, failed normie, subhuman, etc.). The conclusion of inevitable destiny that the blackpill authorizes for incels gives rise to one of the most openly misogynistic of their tenets, namely that access to sex must be "redistributed," perhaps by force, since the Pareto principle otherwise dictates that eighty percent of women will mate only with twenty percent of men.[30]

While scientific and anatomical jargon is everywhere, bone features particularly prominently in incel accounts of natural attraction. One of the most visible incel memes is a digitally altered comparison of an ostensibly ugly face into an ostensibly attractive one with a more prominent jaw, downward-slanting eyes, and a stronger brow. The original version was captioned "The difference between Chad and non-Chad (incel) is literally a few millimeters of bone."[31] Another oft-repeated incel phrase is "jaw is law," suggesting the immutable social and sexual destiny of any man based on this particular facial structure. As it is summed up in a quasi-academic pro-incel book, "all paths, for the most part, are already determined by bone."[32] Incel.tech is a website appearing in 2024 that allows users to upload photos for instant analysis. The results are far from scientific: I was told that I had a "perfect" palpebral fissure length, although I was also informed in subsequent iterations that my eyes are both too far apart and too close together. The algorithm is clearly subjective, and image results are heavily dependent on the angle of photos—it rates me generally better than Brad Pitt, for example, which is a conclusion unlikely to be sustained by a broad sample of the public other than my mom, and only then if she knew I was listening.

The certainty with which many incels seem to attach to their belief system is stunning. Already imbued with some religious themes (prominent incels, for example, are called "saints"), inceldom has a rigid, if perhaps inconsistent, fatalism. The mantra "it's over for" one group or another—sub-5, sub-8s, "ethnicels," White incels, short men, etc.—is a repeated element of the discourse, as is the statement that one should or must "lie down and rot." Factors such as height, race, facial structure, disability, and many more identified as central by incel communities are largely unchangeable, and the defining characteristic of the blackpill is the inevitability of "lookism" and female sexual dominance at a societal level, even when individual incels might ascend through prostitution or other means. Science permits incel discourse to plug the holes of its normative judgments—women are mercenaries who owe men sex—with supposedly objective foundations and thereby retain its conviction.

White Supremacists

For centuries, scientific research has had a symbiotic relationship with slavery, colonialism, and racism, both borrowing from and contributing to conceptions of race in wide-ranging areas of (post-)Enlightenment thought.[33] Early speculation took the superiority of White Europeans for granted and attempted to explain it, focusing on various theories of African "degeneration" due to climate or positing multiple origins and/or species for humanity. Later efforts sought to respond to the thesis of human equality by proving White superiority or at least Black inferiority, as Samuel George Morton's (perhaps unconscious) falsification of data about skull volume exemplifies.[34] These efforts persist, albeit in a more marginal relationship with scientific discourse, combining new tools such as genetic analysis and intelligence testing with older ones such as craniometry and early twentieth-century racist anthropology despite overwhelming evidence that race does not exist as a natural phenomenon despite its persistence as a social one.[35] The primary contemporary move in White supremacy is to claim that the illusion is not race itself, but the evidence purporting to disprove it. Inverting the process of social construction, contemporary racists claim that human equality is a social fiction while race is inescapable biological reality, which is why no efforts to improve the lot of marginalized peoples can succeed. This view is called *racial realism* by its adherents and is somewhat distinct from older concepts of race based on religion or simply visceral hatred of human difference.

Stormfront, an early locus of White supremacy on the Internet, remains a key forum for the discussion of race and constitutes a community in itself. As it is popular, persistent, and still widely used,[36] discussions of scientific racism on Stormfront can be inferred to reflect some beliefs among White nationalists and White supremacists generally, although variations exist and are important in mapping these discourses. Stormfront's proclamation of racial realism is sometimes further euphemized and made scientific-sounding with the label "human biodiversity,"[37] a term used by the small group of scientists still clinging to biological notions of race and declaring Black Americans and Africans inferior. Much of this research with a more anthropological bent appears in *Mankind Quarterly* and forms a distinct academic community where authors tend to primarily cite each other and a few central figures such as J. Phillipe Rushton.[38] Along with the authors of *The Bell Curve*, Nobel laureate James Watson, once described as the "Caligula of biology,"[39] also shows up often—the anniversary of his co-description of DNA was celebrated by a banner on Stormfront during the period of my research.

Genes and bones are both fixations among biological White supremacists. Jonathan Marks notes that physical anthropology was founded on a "fetish" for skulls,[40] which is evident in their continuing significance in racist discourse. Carleton Coon was an American anthropologist who measured craniofacial features to classify races, including sub-races of Europe, an occasionally divisive topic amongst White supremacists who may see some (e.g., Nordic, Anglo-Saxon) as superior to others (e.g., Slavic, Mediterranean). Although Coon wrote in the early twentieth century, skull-focused racists claim that his work is still current as research in this area has been discouraged.[41] Stormfront's "Anthropology Enthusiasts" group includes assertions about the truth of phrenology, self-reported head measurements and CT scans, discussion of Coon and others, and even the claim that Black people are distinct from Whites because they have more teeth.[42] Books and other resources are quickly found by reading comments and clicking on shared links, expanding outward from a site like Stormfront by following an essentially metonymic logic: this connected to this. For ideologues committed to Science as an authorizing principle, the result is exposure to many low-effort ephemeral posts, but also articles in *Mankind Quarterly* and elsewhere alongside books from Arthur de Gobineau through Coon and to contemporary meditations on race and physical anthropology, not always written by authors with extensive scientific training.[43] In some ways, genes are the new bones: White supremacists also assert the biological fact of race (and, inevitably, racial hierarchy) with reference to genetic variation, often advanced through inexact deployment of the term "haplogroup" as a first link in the metonymic chain to genetics and Science as signifiers.[44]

The White supremacist fixation on physical difference has produced spectacles covered by popular media outside their own communities. One that demonstrates the contradictory operation of desire involves, of all things, milk. A number of videos appeared in 2017 of White supremacists drinking milk after a protest involving the dairy product at an anti-Trump art installation.[45] Prominent members of the alt-right included milk emojis in social media profiles as the phenomenon went viral. Part of its appeal was the denigration of "soy boys" as weak liberals in opposition to masculine consumers of animal products, but milk also has a long racial history in that the genes coding for lactose tolerance have historically been associated with Whiteness.[46] While much of the Internet display of milk drinking was clownish and may have been simply trolling,[47] the use of "cute" or absurdist displays to convey a more sinister or violent "true" meaning hidden beneath the surface is common in reactionary Internet content, such as the silly name and Hawaiian shirts of the Boogaloo Bois (accelerationists dreaming of a second American Civil War), Pepe the Frog memes on "Frogtwitter" (especially those with childlike renderings of the character and I-Can-Has-Cheezburger-esque misspellings like "fren" for "friend"), and the insider gags of White supremacist trolls, such as the intertextual references of Andrew Auernheimer's GNAA and Goatse Security. In the case of milk, scenes of milk chugging and emojis added to social media handles coexisted with suggestions that lactose intolerant people be deported, clearly signifying the more threatening undertone of the performance. The ambiguity of these symbols demonstrates intentionality that is nonliteral and deliberately difficult to parse, but still contains what creators might understand as immutable, hidden truths: Ultimately, despite the playfulness, White supremacy is still the point.

Milk drinking suggests a kind of semiotic theory of the body among White supremacists that resembles other anti-rhetorical readings discussed in earlier chapters. Performative milk drinking indicates that the subject has a lactose-tolerant phenotype, which means a lactose-tolerant genotype, which means European ancestry, which means White. This chain is interpreted as a series of signs, not signifiers, meaning that to the White supremacist subject these are not arbitrary associations but inevitable, objective channels of meaning not susceptible to rhetoric. Like the Fregoli delusions of Sandy Hook deniers, they are supposed to be refutations of ambiguity: Each step in the chain can only mean one thing and must mean that thing. There is a difference, however, between this chain of reasoning that employs Science as a guarantor of truth and the employment of widely accepted scientific methods. Leaving aside the inaccuracies of White supremacist understandings of genetics and anthropology,[48] science as a mode of inquiry revolves around doubt—evidence is gathered for probabilistic conclusions, and rarely (if ever) for programmatic, unshakeable convictions about nature as such. The signifier of Science serves to retroactively affirm what White supremacists "know" to be true, not asking questions but refusing them.

The insistence on Science as a justifying signifier for White supremacy rather than a mode of inquiry is also evident in controversy over DNA tests. The expanding availability of testing from companies such as 23andMe led a number of racists to have their genes tested. Several, including some prominent leaders in White supremacist organizations, received results suggesting that they had African, Asian, Jewish, and/or Indigenous American ancestry. While some used these results as ammunition to question the Whiteness of others within the community, the overall response was one of justification and inclusion. Instead of declaring that race isn't scientific or that the science of genetics proved that these people were not White,[49] both strategies that could still accommodate racist beliefs, most White supremacists on Stormfront instead claimed that the results were manipulated by Jews or otherwise discounted them.[50] These strategies may be read as responses to the anxiety produced by the precarity of Whiteness, a category that must be continually shored up but by its nature can never be conclusively delimited.[51] Significantly, the signifying power of Science was not challenged—Jews were simply blamed for infiltration, consistent with other White supremacist conspiracy theories, or other modes of "scientific" thought were given prominence. One, noted by Panofsky and Donovan, is the "mirror test"—white supremacists insist that they can objectively "see" race, or crowdsource their appearances to be judged by others using protocols in line with Coon's craniofacial measures of European race.[52] This shows clear parallels to Žižek's Groucho Marx line, mentioned in the Introduction, about trusting one's eyes.

Transvestigators

"Transvestigators," a portmanteau of "transgender" and "investigators," describes a "transvestigation" community currently forming around the conspiracy theory that all or almost all public figures are secretly transgender. At the time of writing, this group is relatively new and has yet to reach the media prominence of incels or various White supremacists. The factchecking website Snopes.com reports that as early as 2008 it received repeated inquiries into the "true" identity of Michelle Obama on the basis that she may have been born biologically male and is merely pretending to be a woman. Subsidiary beliefs of these questioners are that she may not be the biological mother of her children, Sasha and Malia; that her husband, President Barack Obama, may be homosexual; and that she may have once been named Michael Lavaughn Robinson, a fact since concealed by the Obamas.[53] This complex of theories was subsequently amplified by Alex Jones, then America's premier conspiracy theorist,[54] and given further weight when comedian Joan Rivers died shortly after asserting that Michelle Obama was a trans woman, an event that conspiracy theorists took as evidence of a plot to conceal the truth by any means necessary.[55] Allegations about Obama's sex overlapped with similar claims about Serena and Venus Williams,[56] demonstrating the intersection of misogynoir and transphobia in the notion that Black women, especially rich, famous, and powerful ones, are inherently masculine.

Although female athletes and celebrities such as Jamie Lee Curtis have been subject to sex-related allegations for decades, Obama conspiracy theorists seem to have been the most proximate catalyst of the contemporary transvestigation movement. The movement has now broadened its focus to nearly every major celebrity, including hypermasculine actors like Jason Momoa, The Rock, Vin Diesel, and Russell Crowe and classically feminine models and actresses such as Marilyn Monroe, Margot Robbie, Pamela Anderson, and Cindy Crawford,[57] along with musicians including Enya, Adele, Stephen Tyler, Slash, Taylor Swift, and many more.[58] There is a historical dimension as well. Nearly every, if not all, American president and First Lady is alleged to have been trans by some proponents of the theory.[59] These supposed truths are protected by a conspiracy of silence and misdirection—although the motives are not always clear, Bible quotes, references to demons, suspicion of biomedicine, and allegations of general celebrity depravity are often present.[60] The theory is sometimes called "Elite Gender Inversion" (EGI) and individual trans people are named with the slur "invert."[61] The origin of this term is unclear—"sexual inversion" was a nineteenth-century concept encompassing a variety of gender behaviors marked as deviant,[62] but "inversion" has also long been used to mark Satan-worshippers' supposed reversal of the order of creation given by God, including gender roles.[63]

At the time of writing, transvestigators form a relatively niche community even among other conspiracy theorists. They fit only on the margins of much broader anti-trans hatred that has become mainstream in the English-speaking world. However, it would be a mistake to dismiss transvestigation as an irrelevant fringe group. Despite limited uptake at present, a sincere, devoted community of transvestigators still exists. QAnon did not receive the attention it warranted early on either, and the larger ecosystem of anti-trans reactionary sentiments and conspiracy theories has created a potentially kairotic moment for this particular community. As Jules Gill-Peterson writes, anti-trans movements "demonstrate that conspiracy and disinformation are not outside of, but rather are central to, liberal political institutions. Indeed, anti-trans speech is increasingly the very means by which to launder extremism and conspiracy theory into democratic institutions, with disastrous results." While allusions to the "trans agenda" allow conspiracy theories to infiltrate other discourses, they in turn help to consolidate anti-trans opinions with more mainstream respectability, "the new anchor of anti-trans politics on the extremist right."[64] Examining such an unrefined part of anti-trans ideology before it has fully consolidated may give us insight into the larger economy of desire that underpins it.

That said, Transvestigation is not entirely reducible to right-wing hatred of trans people or QAnon worship of Donald Trump, although intersection with QAnon and amplification by Alex Jones created something qualitatively new. From a repeated narrative, transvestigators became an actual community, coming together across multiple Internet and social media platforms through a variety of media. Much of this activity is found on Facebook, where several public groups exist, the largest currently sporting around 26,000 members as of June 2024, with several more above 10,000 or in the four-digit range. Transvestigation accounts also exist on Twitter[65] and TikTok,[66] where the content is easily discoverable through tags. These are not huge numbers and the proportion of true believers to trolls cannot be determined, but the community is active enough to be self-sustaining and seems to grow over time. The relevant social media groups are international and identities are hard to discern, although they seem to skew North American, Christian, and White. Membership is informal and fairly turbulent—perhaps inevitably, scandals have erupted in which prominent transvestigators are accused by others of being trans themselves. Inanna Snow,[67] a prominent member of the movement who sometimes wore revealing clothing in her videos, perhaps in an effort to head off or preempt these accusations,[68] is among the most notable figures targeted by her peers. Although the community clearly skews right, it is not beholden to Donald Trump to the degree that some other variants of QAnon are. Some transvestigators have accused Trump himself of being trans.[69] Even Eugenia Cooney, an influencer mentioned in chapter 4,[70] and J. K. Rowling, a prominent anti-trans social media figure, have been accused of being transgender.[71]

The methods of transvestigation are not particularly sophisticated and rely almost entirely on visual interpretation, although common conspiracy fare shows up, such as distrust of people with "three names" or "three first names" (an observation often made of serial killers—John Wayne Gacy, Henry Lee Lucas, David Parker Ray, etc.) or etymological theories about "hiding in plain sight" (e.g., "bey" means "gentleman" in Turkish, so Beyoncé is teasing her trans identity). These activities are almost entirely performed on social media or through video sharing sites such as YouTube and Rumble. On Facebook or Twitter, users typically post still images of celebrities, either overlayed with lines showing supposedly opposite-sex physical characteristics or simply with appeals like "obviously a man/woman." Engaged commenters almost always express agreement with the transvestigator, although trolls and dissenters do sometimes comment (Mike Tyson and Elvis Presley, for example, are less likely to be unanimously declared trans than, say, Taylor Swift or Paul McCartney). Videos tend to have less of a community feel to them. Some are primarily voiceovers of a series of still images with the commentator offscreen.[72] Others, such as Inanna Snow's early content, are more interpretive or moralizing and focus on the commentator.[73]

Science plays an important legitimizing role. Photographs of celebrity bodies and faces overlaid with lines showing supposedly sex-specific bone structures are common. One post marks Ryan Gosling and Farah Fawcett as trans, for example, based on the angle of their clavicles,[74] while others show Q-angles (an actual hip measurement, but note the letter) to show that The Rock is actually a woman.[75] Superimposed lines purporting to identify the underlying structure of accentuating hips, spines, and shoulders show up everywhere, as do craniofacial comparisons. Journalist Patrick Lenton observes that beyond the references to Satanism and QAnon concepts, "the bread and butter of every post is essentially digital phrenology."[76] A TikTok user called Queen Awake briefly came to prominence on the basis that she could "help critical thinkers read skeletal markers" to identify secretly trans people before turning her account private.[77] Transvestigation resonates with the anti-trans catchphrase "we can always tell" in that it insists there are objective, scientific markers of sex that trans people cannot escape yet frequently try to conceal, a claim that shows the intersection between this community and the conspiracism of broader "mainstream" anti-trans politics, as British trans rights activist Katy Montgomerie has observed.[78] Doubt is occasionally expressed, but mostly to be immediately dismissed: The constant refrains "just look" and "use your eyes" again mirror those of Sandy Hook denialists and Žižek's Groucho Marx.[79]

The mixture of Science as justification and spirituality as a broader context in transvestigation recalls QAnon and other reactionary movements. Like QAnon, transvestigation draws heavily from Christian symbolism and terminology even as it mixes in New Age and pagan elements. Baphomet, a demon figure interpreted by transvestigators to have both male and female traits, shows up frequently, with supposedly trans celebrities accused of being influenced by, worshipping, or simply resembling the demon.[80] Satanism and Science intersect for QAnon in claims that celebrities harvest a chemical called adrenochrome from the pituitary glands of frightened children, who they sacrifice to demons.[81] Anti-trans agendas have gradually seeped into QAnon and merged with the antisemitic blood libel: now it is the global (Jewish) biomedical health apparatus that seeks to profit by influencing children to have sex reassignment surgeries.[82] "Natural" health and anti-vaccine messaging is a consistent QAnon thread allowing it to access a larger public than it otherwise might and shows up in transvestigation as hostility to the medical establishment, including gender-affirming surgery, plastic surgery, and drugs.

The pan-conspiracy networking of QAnon and its New Age influences are also evident in transvestigation. For example, Inanna Snow combines anti-vaccine, natural health, free energy, and flat earth messages.[83] While some elements of transvestigation discourse might seem avowedly anti-scientific, no contradiction is evident for transvestigators because they see various concepts (adrenochrome harvesting, alternative medicine, confluence of biological sex and gender) as "true" science, allowing the signifier to work its authority-consolidating power without producing too much cognitive dissonance. Thus, QAnon-supporting, evangelical Christian, reactionary Congresswoman Marjorie Taylor Greene can hang a sign declaring that there are only two genders saying "Trust the Science"—quotation marks in original—with no compunctions,[84] because Science operates differently in the context of anti-trans hatred and cannot be meaningfully disproven for its adherents.[85]

Fools, Knaves, and Dolts

Science plays a similar role in the discourses of White supremacists, incels, and transvestigators. In each of these cases, it serves as a legitimizing resource, something to anchor worldviews and give skittish subjects a sense of deeper meaning and belonging. This is Science the signifier: a means of *cutting off* one's feeling of uncertainty, of foreclosing the yawning chasm of nothingness that opens when we are forced to confront the essentially arbitrary nature of our choices in a world that can be so alien and complex that we may feel threatened with dissolution in it. Science as a mode of inquiry might exacerbate this feeling by endless questioning and challenges to human belief—as Yuri Gagarin was supposed to have reported upon leaving Earth's atmosphere for the first time, the scientist may report "I see no God up here."[86] Science as a signifier, however, arrests this process—once we "trust the science" as Marjorie Taylor Greene does, no more questions need be asked, and in fact we can return it to the function that God has played in some traditions, a final authority above questioning. White supremacists can avoid the vertigo (or anxiety, or cognitive dissonance) of recognizing that nothing special grounds them, and if they are "superior" to others it is due to an unequal distribution of violence, amidst which they are as mediocre as anyone else. Incels do not have to acknowledge chance or choice in their personal dating prospects, the groundlessness of male superiority, nor give up on the fantasy that a perfect relationship is possible (just not for them)—they can instead reduce everything to the iron laws of ethology and genetics. Transvestigators do not need to admit that "male" and "female" are cultural conventions and that all gender identities—including their own—are performances of shared fantasies.[87] Science becomes a site where subjects can profess certainty even if they must proclaim an alternative interpretation of "science" to square it with their religious or intuitive worldviews. As Wendy Chun notes, drawing from Natalie Wynn in a discussion of incels, this is precisely the appeal of bone as a signifier: It is unchanging, permanent, and solid, the ultimate defense against ambiguity and uncertainty.[88]

In its capacity to serve as an anchor for certainty, Science permits a discourse of the knave. Lacan described right-wing intellectuals as "knaves" and left-wing ones as "fools" in his seminar on the ethics of psychoanalysis, using the English terms in reference to a dramatic tradition of archetypes that he associated with Chaucer.[89] He returned to these ideas twelve years later and added the "dolt," suggesting that they remained useful for him even in the more matheme-centered later period of his thought.[90] The fool speaks truth to power but in such a way that it does not disrupt the status quo. The knave, on the other hand, insists on "realism" and when required "admits" to being "a crook."[91] The knave is always ready to echo the question "why do things have to be so bad" with a shifted emphasis, accepting that the truth might be unpleasant, but that there is nothing we can do to change it so evil behavior is inevitable. This is the general line behind pessimistic views of politics based on human nature—sure, (capitalism, militarism, intolerance . . .) might be bad, but since (God, human nature, evolution . . .) make them inevitable, there's nothing we can do, so we might as well (make money, embrace the patriarchy, hoard resources . . .). What "makes the politics of right-wing ideology so depressing," writes Lacan, is that while an individual knave might be worth a joke, a "herd of crooks" invariably turns to a problematic "collective foolery,"[92] meaning that these knaves eventually belie their fatalism and believe that they really are speaking the truth against a power that oppresses them.

Racial realism, the black pill, and the supposed objectivity of sex all become legible as specific instances of knavery through the appeal to Science. In addition to providing a sense of certainty, this quality of these discourses allows subjects to deflect desire. For White supremacists, Science determines that Black people are violent and less intelligent so their inferior position in society need no further justification. Worse performance in schools, for example, is framed as a regrettable inevitability that no change in social policy could remedy, not a product of inequality. This is where racial realism tips from knavery to collective foolery. Gatherings of these racist knaves in forums like *Mankind Quarterly* let them act like fools, in both the Lacanian sense and the more general one, by giving them a place to claim that they are speaking an uncomfortable suppressed truth, even though it is one no doubt quietly believed by many supposedly mainstream conservatives. The transition from knavery as a prop and shield to the "foolishness" of a "herd" of knaves helps to describe what changes about how individual subjects might speak and orient themselves toward their desire when they form a community. The fact that social consensus has eroded around some of their issues does not stop them from imagining it as a still-hegemonic force trying to suppress them: These are knaves acting like fools.

Science is not only a passive resource, however, even when understood as a rhetorical "poultice" to blunt the anguish of desire and the trauma of uncertainty.[93] The signifier of Science alters the discourse around it, creating some possibilities for rhetorical deployments while cutting off others. Once a discourse becomes "scientific," it must be accommodated to this organizing signifier and the displacements that it causes. For White supremacists, for example, when genetic tests turn up more diverse ancestry than expected some rhetorical resources are already closed off due to a prior declaration of commitment to Science. Simply claiming that race is a social category is no longer an option, nor is a wholly anti-scientific worldview. The concrete instance of speech reporting the results of a genetic test has to be reconciled in some way that avoids a confrontation with what Science was supposed to hide (i.e., the groundlessness of race), and must do so without forsaking some understanding of Science, since attachments to this signifier play a central part in the entire ideology. For racial realists, incels, and transvestigators, pseudoscience becomes a necessary component of their communities as a means of reconciling their commitments to Science with the powerful evidence against their views marshaled by actual scientific inquiry. In this way, the deployment of Science amongst reactionary communities differs from its distortion by fossil fuel interests and other propagandists: the latter misuse science, while the former are misused by it.[94]

Structure and Agency

With one major caveat, there are advantages to studying speaking subjects as media. One is the problem of linking speech to belief. In our everyday lives, if not in academia, we are accustomed to saying "so-and-so believes that . . ." on the basis of what they have said, and rhetoricians have traditionally focused on a speaker and their rhetorical situation, presuming the former to be a fairly stable, legible subject. But human subjects are black boxes, and we can never be sure what they mean, think, know, or plan. Speaking subjects are, at a minimum, capable of lying, and in some cases have to do so when propriety demands it. We might have evidence pointing toward sincerity—serpent handlers and pro-ana figures both risk death for little tangible reward, and some Sandy Hook conspiracists face ostracism or other social costs—but we can never be entirely sure. Similarly, we can believe P. T. Barnum, Alex Jones, or Donald Trump to be probable liars, but we could never *prove* that they don't believe what they say, even if it seems very unlikely. Even when someone thinks they are speaking the truth, it is impossible to "say the whole truth," as Lacan was fond of noting, and we could never be sure that what they say and we hear represent the same concepts.[95] Messages might be ironic or sarcastic, or communicated by trolls. They may be what Harry Frankfurt calls "bullshit," or things said without regard for truth to convey a message about the speaker, who may not even know whether they believe what they espouse.[96] This uncertainty characterizes much of Internet culture, where anything might mean anything, and the line between parody and sincerity might not even be apparent to the parodist. This issue is compounded in research on broader discourses because it is often difficult to measure how much any individual or even text represents an entire community.

Signifiers, on the other hand, order space and create the conditions into which subjects speak along with the resources available for them to do so. Signifiers like "Men" and "Women" order space and are materialized by power, dictating where some subjects are allowed and others are barred, how basically identical spaces (e.g., bathrooms) are understood as different. Millions of speaking subjects deploy them in different circumstances every day, making it difficult to locate their origins or meaning in anything but highly situational ways. Taking the signifier as the unit of analysis shifts our questions somewhat, leading us to ask how signifiers manifest in concrete instances, treating variations as differences in media that don't necessitate a focus on unknowable interiority of particular subjects, and facilitating a reading of signifiers as they cross between restricted economies of discourse.

So if individual subjects are media and signifiers speak through them, are the knaves right? No. This approach does not absolve individual subjects of responsibility for their choices—we might be media, but we are self-reflective media, even if our powers of understanding are more limited than we pretend they are. Studying media is in part about identifying how the media form matters, and this perspective is no different. Your television cannot stop you from watching trash or decide to interrogate its ethical comportment toward the question of difference, but whether you serve as a conduit for what you see is something over which you can exercise discipline. The unconscious as it exists from each individual's perspective is not fixed but partly a reflection of attention and effort such that more ethical choices are always possible. One of the affordances of speaking-subject media is a modicum of influence over how form and content mutually interact and spread to others. Nor does this approach necessarily eschew close reading—the material manifestations of our signifiers (Lacan's "letter") are how we see them act in particular places and times, and ultimately what we know about how about the unconscious constructions of symbolic networks relies on our interpretations of many such instances. Knavery is a parody of structuralism that should reveal the limits of its explanatory power and remind us why rhetoric insists on contingency and psychoanalysis insists on the subject.

This is the logical extension of the argument, made in the Introduction to this book, that there is a Faustian bargain innate to language. If we are interested in the discourse of a community, individual members and their choices do matter even if psychoanalysis might instill caution about where we locate the agency for those choices. But speakers are heavily constrained by the symbolic networks in which they participate. They must demonstrate fealty to certain beliefs to be considered members of a community at all and must have some mastery of its lexicon to ground their speech in legible ways. What is sayable, and even thinkable, is determined to some measure in advance by the well of signification from which they can draw. Attending to the concrete expressions of individuals might help us make inferences about what they personally believe, but if our interest is in the community itself, we must analyze its discourse as a shared entity that exceeds any single speaker. This is not to say that there is no point in comparing the ways that, say, James Fetzer and Alex Jones talk about Sandy Hook, just that such a comparison tells us more about individuals than a community, even if it facilitates some inferences about the larger milieu in which they speak. Some groups, such as the pro-ana community, are more horizontally structured, without a few defining leaders, and others, such as that of Holiness serpent handlers, demonstrate strong continuity over time despite having entirely different membership at different points. In other cases, such as the three treated in this chapter, the same signifier plays a nearly identical role in different communities. Examining its agency—or examining it as if it had agency, if one prefers—is therefore warranted, but doing so describes the terrain in which choice operates. It does not obviate it.

The agential balance between subject and signifiers demonstrates the potential of Lacan's dolt—someone who speaks the truth without knowing that they do so, sometimes surprising themselves in what they reveal.[97] The dolt may reveal the "obscene supplement," which is Žižek's name for the truth of a system, known to everyone, which it is forbidden to acknowledge, as in the story of the Emperor's new clothes. The dolt is a goldmine for psychoanalytic study because they accidentally announce the unconscious, acting as a conduit without the same obfuscating effects of desire in their speech.[98] The same subjects might cycle between knave, fool, and dolt, revealing a composite of how a discourse is organized unconsciously and consciously. Donald Trump is one example. Early in his political career, Trump seemed to relish the notion that his "Muslim ban" would violate the standards of political correctness, an example of playing the fool.[99] Trump's knavery was on display when asked during the 2020 pandemic about the death rate from Covid, to which he responded, "it is what it is," suggesting that the situation could not be controlled any more effectively than it had been.[100] Trump's announcement that "I will always tell you the truth" is,[101] in a certain way, true, as even mendacious enunciations reveal something about the order that the speaker channels, even if it is only their felt need to conceal it. In regards to race, Trump then plays the dolt. In a call to the widow of slain U.S. soldier La David Johnson, Trump stated that Johnson "knew what he was signing up for" and could not remember the young man's name.[102] This statement reveals a truth that one is not supposed to speak: Signing up for military service, perhaps especially as a young Black man, means accepting death for no discernable strategic purpose, a sacrifice that might not even be remembered by those who send you into harm's way.

The fool, knave, and dolt each describe how messages are shaped by the medium they pass through—their desires, capacities, and symbolic resources. In focusing on how the signifier Science operates in three distinct (but sometimes overlapping) communities, I aimed to show both how these communities are structurally similar in their refusal of threatening ambiguity and to suggest that signifiers might be an appropriate unit of analysis for some kinds of inquiry into how discourses form. My relatively quick sketches of these postsymbolic-demise communities nonetheless demonstrate that they bear striking resemblances not just to each other, but to the serpent handlers, pro-anorexic Internet figures, and conspiracists examined earlier in this book. I would like to consider what these parallels might mean for the theories applied here in media studies, rhetoric, cultural studies, and psychoanalysis; the possibility of using them in studies of other discourses; and their implications for how we might think about rhetoric as a comportment toward the world beyond its status as an academic discipline. That is the project of the conclusion.

Conclusion

The Ends of Rhetoric

It is November 2024. Donald J. Trump has recently won reelection as president of the United States on a platform openly embracing American division. In Pittsburgh, Pennsylvania, where I live, traffic has been catastrophic for months as one candidate or the other sends their avatars or manifests in the flesh. I have been exposed to millions of dollars' worth of political advertising and, out of a misguided sense of professional obligation, I watch, read, and listen to all of it. Perhaps the most impactful of these ads relied principally on transphobia to make its point about the so-called extremism of Kamala Harris, Trump's politically moderate Democratic opponent. "Kamala Harris is for they/them," it declared, "and Donald Trump is for us."[1] Conspiracy theorists, fundamentalists, anti-vaccine campaigners, xenophobes, and racists are set to populate the new administration. The importance of understanding how these discourses coalesce, survive, spread, and position their subjects should be clearer than it ever has been, not because of a single election but because of the underlying conditions of cultural turmoil of which it is only a symptom.

Donald Trump is a key figure in this age of anti-rhetoric.[2] He himself is capable of using rhetorical devices, of course, but much of his audience reads his discourse anti-rhetorically, insisting that they "just know" what he means, that they can "believe their eyes" and ignore claims to authority by establishment figures like doctors, generals, more moderate Republicans, and, of course, college professors. We have come full circle from Kellyanne Conway saying that "everyone knew" what she meant by "alternative facts," essentially an appeal to ignore evidence in front of one's eyes in favor of the administration's authority. That is no longer necessary, if it even was then. It makes almost no difference what Trump talks about—Hannibal Lecter, Arnold Palmer's genitals, electrocuted sharks, Black immigrants eating house pets—or whether he says nothing at all and just sways to music in front of an audience for forty minutes. True believers know that there is a hidden truth, even if they can't say exactly what it is, because to them Trump conveys meaningfulness and significance, so he doesn't always have to signify. Trump doesn't have to say that Kamala Harris is inferior because she is Black, a woman, or more dishonored than the sum of its parts, a Black woman. He doesn't have to say that the segment of his supporters who hate her for her identity should trust their eyes, literally look at her to discredit her, because the decline of symbolic efficiency has voided the signifiers of her ethos. Her degree, record as a prosecutor, legislative and executive experience—these things cannot be seen, but her bodily experience can be. Trump doesn't have to say that "they/them" can never be part of "us," either. For some of his supporters, that's plain to see.

Millions of Trump supporters no doubt cast their ballots for reasons other than anti-rhetorical readings of race, gender, and sexuality, but then again, millions of others did. There are also White supremacists, QAnon conspiracy descendants, and Internet-radicalized Christians. A great deal of media coverage treats the discourses of Trump and his followers rhetorically. Some outlets have identified Trump's comments about Haitian immigrants as racist enthymemes (without using the word), or fact-checked his statements, relying on the ethos of their sources to be persuasive. Academics will no doubt attend to his rhetoric. This is important work—rhetoric is certainly a prevalent way to read these discourses, and its disciplined study will produce important and interesting findings. However, to stop at rhetoric would miss much of the structure of desire that underpins modern politics and miss much of what Trump does for his followers psychically, what wound he covers or what lack he fills for those who read anti-rhetorically, which describes many of the erstwhile subcultures that have come increasingly into the light as older senses of propriety fail to constrain them. To understand conspiracy theorists, identitarian supremacists, and fundamentalist literalists requires that we realize that they themselves do not think of what they are doing as rhetorical, but revelatory.

Trump supporters are not the only anti-rhetorical readers, of course. In the days after Trump's second election, Reddit was full of self-identified liberals and Democrats mirroring Republican claims of 2020 that the election was rigged (although no one tried to storm the U.S. Capitol). Stories abounded during the COVID-19 pandemic of patients who swore at or spat on doctors because they believed the virus didn't exist. Others refused to vaccinate themselves or their children for reasons that required expertise they didn't see in Anthony Fauci, Bill Gates, or the CDC. QAnon has metastasized into innumerable conspiracy communities, many of which are indistinguishable from mainstream causes like children's welfare and natural wellness. There are still moon landing deniers, flat earthers, New Age apocalyptic movements, Groypers, Trad Caths, Gaylors, Orthobros, crystal healers, self-castrators, otherkin, David-Icke lizard alien enjoyers, and cults beyond measure. Some of these communities are self-reflexive and tongue in cheek. Most are not directly harmful and may even support individual autonomy and a sense of community. Some are open to productively rhetorical readings. Many, however, take themselves very seriously, believe they have access to privileged truth, and are willing to employ violence against those who threaten them. They are structured along the lines of anti-rhetorical reading, and because our world of declining symbolic efficiency is populated by ever more of them, understanding the commonalities of their structure is important for anyone who must navigate the symbolic landscape of the twenty-first century.

The communities analyzed in this book bear witness to commonalities in structure that may shed some light on these other groups, although none of the concepts developed here are meant to be definitive and there is no substitute for actually engaging with the details of each new discourse. Three of the parallels identified in the Introduction closely resemble the mechanism of psychosis: Foreclosure, novelty (or delusion), and certainty are all structural isomorphisms that were apparent early on. In the course of researching these communities, other parallels emerged, including the importance of death to subjectivity, the effect of different media forms, and the place of agency in anti-rhetorical discourses. In the section that follows, I will summarize these parallels before returning to the notion of propriety to suggest two functions for rhetoric amidst the decline of symbolic efficiency. I have chosen my title for this conclusion because I aim to think through the end of rhetoric in three senses: its boundary, its demise in anti-rhetorical interpretation, and its purpose as an attitude.

Foreclosure. Foreclosure is the refusal to "know anything about" some important signifier that provides structure and meaning to a discourse. In the pathology of patriarchy, that is the "Name of the Father," but any protocol for structuring meaning could be foreclosed. While the specific content of each discourse varies, the groups in this study all demonstrate a common refusal of ambiguity and complexity. Sandy Hook conspiracy theorists cannot tolerate the idea that the world is chaotic and that the death of children is possible at any time for no reason—or that their fetishized defense, guns, could be part of the problem. Serpent handlers, too, recoil in the face of directionless life. Everything happens for a reason, including sickness and death in the name of the Lord, but God's will remains inscrutable. The Holy Spirit is a part of daily life, and the possibility of a godless universe simply cannot be countenanced. The common denominator in pro-ana circles is control. Bodies are porous, depending on a constant influx of food from outside that contaminates us with otherness. Desire for any-thing inevitably falls short and forces us to depend on others, risking that contamination and loss of boundary. Biological racists cannot bear the notion that race, the foundation of their exceptionalism, is a social category and therefore arbitrary, a realization that would force them to confront the fact that they are simply like everyone else, and if their life outcomes are better that is a result of societal prejudice, not individual excellence. Incels similarly cannot confront the socially constructed nature of patriarchy nor acknowledge that they can be unsuccessful romantically for many reasons, including simple chance. Transvestigators exist in a society where people can look like one thing and be another, where the rigidity of sex and gender have given way to fluidity and multiplicity, where things are always in flux.

In all of these examples, subjects are exposed to a groundless, inhuman world where strict categories turn out to be arbitrary, indistinct, and subject to change. While Lacan thought that psychosis begins with a subject foreclosing an authoritative signifier (the Name of the Father), in the case of the groups examined here key signifiers had already eroded. They are then left to face the rudderless ambiguity that comes from being foreclosed on when symbolic efficiency begins to fade. As a result, uncertainty cannot be tolerated. It is not so much that a particular signifier is foreclosed as a strategy of reading that relies on some distance and possibility becomes unbearable. The sense of propriety shatters: One does not know how to read the signs anymore, so new, less ambiguous protocols emerge to prevent the subject from being lost among the noise.

Novelty. Every community in this book compensates for the vertigo of foreclosure by inventing a novel system of meaningful signifiers, either creating them from whole cloth or repurposing ones that already exist. Although psychoanalysis has tended to focus on words, the communities in this book often incorporate signifiers in other media as well. In many of these systems, a small number of these signifiers take prominence as central terms. For incels, biological White supremacists, and transvestigators, Science is one of those key signifiers, serving as a source of authority through subsidiary fixations like bones. Bone plays a role in pro-ana communities as well, along with Anorexia itself and words like "thin," "control," and "food." Sandy Hook denialists, who read photographs and videos of victims, officials, and the perpetrator as evidence, also attach to written signifiers, especially official documents. Serpent handlers valorize straightforward textual signifiers such as "serpent," "Satan," and "signs," but "God" (or maybe "Holy Ghost") are central terms, and they also adopt practices like "fleecing" and speaking in tongues. Each community develops its own complete argot but, importantly, tends to do so only in relation to the areas where they are most invested. Overall, they are capable of participating in other discourses in terms widely shared outside of their own, which supports the notion that subjects may read anti-rhetorically in one discourse and not another. Identifying which signifiers are almost never read rhetorically in their own discourses will help to distinguish "quilting points" from other ones that are less significant (in the psychoanalytic sense of that word).

Certainty. What turns novel symbols into anti-rhetorical devices is the absolute conviction that they are inherently signifying rather than arbitrary. It is a confusion of label and referent, even when the "true meaning" of the signifier is obscure to the subject of its discourse. Evidence for univocal reading practices comes from the discourses themselves. It is often announced that a signifier can "only mean one thing," or that polyvalent interpretations are necessarily wrong, as in the case of Sandy Hook identifications of the children. White supremacists are sometimes so sure that race is a biological reality—and that they belong to the best one—that they dismiss contrary genetic evidence as part of a Jewish plot. Serpent handlers have explicit protocols about how to read the Bible, citing passages within it to reveal the means of understanding text. Of course, sincerity is always a difficult issue—how can we be absolutely sure that someone really believes what they say they do? Perhaps we can't, but the communities in this book provide some compelling evidence. Sandy Hook theorists have ruined their personal lives, reputations, and finances in their commitment to their theories, which would be hard to imagine if they were just doing a bit. Incels and White supremacists have killed people. Serpent handlers suffer ostracism and knowingly risk their lives for no material gain, and most witness deaths by snakebite, sometimes of close family. Anorexics can live in constant physical distress and sometimes die. At the very least, these groups do not metaphorize their identities: Anorexics don't say that starvation is really just a metaphor for discipline, serpent handlers don't say that Mark 16:17–18 is allegorical, and Sandy Hook theorists don't say that the collusion of elites only resembles a shadow government. Their worlds revolve around the notion that these things are exactly and only what they are revealed to be.

Agency. Two more similarities—agency and death—are not structural per se but demonstrate cross-cutting ways that anti-rhetorical readings influence subjectivity.[3] Most of these communities also displace agency in ways that cast them as merely channels for some compelling outside power. I argued in the last chapter that signifiers do indeed speak through their subjects, but in psychotic communication this stance is taken to its extreme and any role for particular subjects in choosing what discourses to channel fades away. Serpent handlers claim to be "moved on" during their services by the Holy Spirit, although like most Christians they do have a developed concept of free will. Pro-ana communities personify Anorexia and live by a set of rules said to issue from it. They often write of anorexia as an irresistible force making them restrict. Transvestigators, White supremacists, and incels personify science as if he (of course) is a person they know—"science says," "trust science," "according to science," and so on. Their disavowal of agency is discussed in the preceding chapter, but it is worth noting here that the notion of outside agency is particularly important to their belief structure as it prevents a reckoning with the social injustices to which they actively contribute. Sandy Hook denialists sometimes double this move by claiming that they serve "the truth" or something similar while others are helpless tools of the conspirators. Paranoid conspiracy theories in general must assert that someone is pulling the strings, leaving us sheeple with no real choices other than to follow scripts of which we are unaware.

Death. It is perhaps impossible to overstate the importance of death for human religion, philosophy, and lived experience. Some relation to death is discoverable in any community if one looks hard enough, even if it is just the promise of immortality that comes from being part of a community that will survive even after the worms claim their triumph. In the case of the communities studied here, attitudes toward death were defining in many places. Sandy Hook conspiracy theorists seem unable to accept it, refusing to believe that the children are dead but simultaneously fixating on the morbid symbols of their bodies when they demand exhumations. Serpent handlers view their practices as the means to victory over death and life everlasting in Heaven. The serpents are both symbols of death and its direct agent. Pro-ana communities are full of bones, contemplations about mortality, and fears of corruption and defilement. The perfection of anorexic desire is potentially one response—as outlined in chapter 3, Other jouissance is equated to death in its yearning to unmake the subject. Incels frequently describe themselves as "rotting," describing upsetting reminders of their inferiority as "suicide fuel" and sometimes figuring "the rope" as the only solution. Belonging to "race" or "nation" is one means of transcending individual mortality, but White supremacists fret that non-White peoples will replace them, undoing their defense against death. Anti-trans conspiracy theorists, too, seem to worry about biological reproduction and the promise of the future in a similar vein, believing that their cultures are turning away from traditional cisgender heterosexual family structures and reproductive futurism. Believing that trans people prey on children is a way to figure them as threats to reproductive futurism.

Media. Traditional psychoanalysis and rhetoric both center on speech. Psychoanalysis is the "talking cure," after all, the familiar image of rhetoric's Greek past centers on words said in the agora. Much Lacanian thought still privileges speech, or at least words as signifiers. Psychosis itself, however, has changed along with new media technologies.[4] Jeffrey Sconce has argued that old fantasies like the "influencing machine" and thought insertion have analogues in the Internet and remote communication technology.[5] The notion that psychosis is defined in part by severing the social link does not survive modern scrutiny.

What once were relatively private experiences can now be shared as the kernel of new communities due to new media technologies.[6] Sandy Hook denialism is enabled by mixed-media presentations, online video platforming, and image manipulation technologies. Pro-ana communities rely heavily on microblogging and image sharing sites. Reactionary science communities organize on social media, where they share images, texts, and conversations. Incels and transvestigators in particular rely on marked up images and the interconnected platforms allowing them to be shared. We can stretch the notion of a signifier to any media and adapt the tools of textual criticism, but we should also attend to the unique affordances offered by distinct media as we analyze the groups employing them. Psychosis as a collective phenomenon is impossible without media technology, and the shape of each community is dictated in part by these affordances. In a structural analysis, media should be included as a layer between subject and discourse that substantially influences both.

Equipment for Living

I want to return to the double notion of propriety mentioned in the Introduction to this book. Propriety can be thought of as a set of rules or norms on the one hand and the capacity of an individual to navigate those norms on the other. Propriety is arguably the most important concept in rhetoric, one that underlies nearly all the others because it determines what tropes and figures are deemed appropriate and what means of persuasion are available in a given instance.[7] The decline of symbolic authority can be thought of as a weakening of propriety in the first sense, while anti-rhetorical readings are strategies available for subjects to "read" the new rules that arise in emergent communities. In conclusion, I will outline two implications of the structural similarities of anti-rhetorical communities for those who do not just study rhetoric but adopt it as a worldview. The first is critical: returning from the fringes with the notion of anti-rhetorical discourse to find lines of thought in the putative mainstream that are organized along similar lines and recognizing in them the potential to ossify their subjects. The second task is more hopeful: to cultivate rhetoric as an attitude toward ambiguity and uncertainty, a means of living in the world that does not require oracular truth or univocality.

Propriety, Symbolic Efficiency, Psychosis

As I have taken pains to repeat, everyone has psychotic attachments to something, but we overlook ones that are authorized by the remainder of the mainstream. What marks a belief as "crazy," "fringe," or "extreme" is only how it can be positioned relative to a concept of "normal." I have chosen communities that somehow lie outside of this sanction to highlight their structural elements, but many more based on anti-rhetorical readings merely hide behind propriety to escape judgment. The demise of symbolic efficiency has been a protracted and labored thing: Figures of authority may have faded, but we haven't entirely burned down the house just yet. One example of anti-rhetorical discourse is the insistence that we return to some imagined unity, what the Introduction calls "restorative nostalgia" following Svetlana Boym. This is a particularly insidious move because it relies on the same structures of certainty and delusion that underpin emergent communities, but its reactionary impulse asserts a common propriety absent in many other discourses. It is a promise to rebuild the tower with the same stones without recognizing that the tower itself was never really complete.

There is a role for rhetorical critique in exposing the arbitrariness of the mainstream so that we might develop reflexive attitudes to unquestioned orthodoxies. Doing so is valuable to the extent that we acknowledge that anti-rhetorical readings may bleed the color, delight, and surprise from our lives, undermine our capacity to live in common difference, and even create the conditions for organized violence. It should also destigmatize "fringe" communities, which does not mean automatically declaring them to be ethical and good, only creating a basis to make these judgments on grounds other than their perceived marginality. Recognizing the (perhaps increasing) ubiquity of anti-rhetorical discourse might help us to decouple it from problematic notions like "extremism" or the "far right," both common labels that convey a sense that some discourses belong together without pinning down how, precisely. "Reactionary," the label I chose in chapter 4, comes closer in my view, but may not include some radical or revolutionary discourses that ought to belong. While all of these labels are appropriate to different areas of study, analyzing anti-rhetoric as a throughline should demonstrate resonances between groups that would be figured as mainstream, extreme, moderate, far right, or whatever. The fact that they demonstrate anti-rhetorical readings is in itself worthy of attention, something that the operations of propriety might conceal.

Common understandings of what is delusional and what is acceptable are shaped in part by the *DSM-5-TR*, the primary value of which is not helping patients but revealing which ones psychologists think are beyond the pale. The *DSM* defines delusions as "fixed beliefs that are not amenable to change in light of conflicting evidence." These beliefs count as "bizarre" when they are "clearly implausible and not understandable to same-culture peers," although labeling delusions in people from different cultural environments can be "difficult," the *DSM* acknowledges, since their "religious and supernatural beliefs" (among others) may differ.[8] As Sconce notes, "bizarre" is a landmine of a concept that ultimately relies on the clinician's sense of what is possible and therefore their own knowledge of and adjustment to social consensus. Therefore, it is possible for one to hold powerful beliefs with absolute certainty in defiance of all evidence that are still not judged as delusional because they largely accord with social norms at a particular place and time. If an average person reports that the CIA is monitoring them around the clock with state-of-the-art technologies, they may be labeled delusional, Sconce argues, even though this is at least technologically plausible, and yet "as a society, we continue to go to great lengths to accommodate as sane those individuals who appear to truly believe God observes everyone all the time, even if most would (at this point in history) consider surveillance by the CIA more plausible."[9]

The Catholic cult of the Sacred Heart is one example. The autobiography of the seventeenth-century nun Margaret Mary Alacoque's is a key text for these believers and is interpreted literally. "When He desired something from me," wrote Margaret Mary, "He urged me so strongly that it was impossible for me to resist." One day, preparing to clean up the vomit of a sick person in her care, Margaret Mary reported that "I was constrained to take it up with my tongue and to swallow it, saying: 'Had I a thousand bodies, O my God, a thousand loves and a thousand lives, I would immolate them all to Thy service!'" She "experienced such delight in this action that I would have wished to meet every day with similar occasions, that I might thus learn to conquer myself, having God alone as witness."[10] Exhibiting this behavior today would almost certainly qualify as "bizarre," but her many followers would disagree. NIHIL OBSTAT, declares my copy of the book.

My point is not to disparage this group of believers, but only to point out that our notions of propriety determine what is acceptable and what is not, even where there are obvious structural similarities between groups that are on the inside (e.g., followers of Margaret Mary) and on the outside (e.g., followers of George Went Hensley). In both cases, what is at issue is not just the behaviors but the mode of reading of signifiers that lead to them, such as the religious visions both had. Attention to propriety should help us to see "fringe" groups differently, but perhaps more importantly, it should help us to identify anti-rhetorical structures in groups that are considered mainstream. That anti-rhetorical readings begin with foreclosure but do not preclude a position in mainstream culture, however broad, should perhaps lead us to ask whether propriety is akin to the unconscious—something shared but simultaneously unique to every subject based on their perspective within it. It should be clear that the efficiency of every symbol does not decline in the same way at the same rate for every subject in a discourse. Studying how and why they do in distinct cases should add complexity and nuance to our understanding of how symbolic efficiency, propriety, and psychosis as strategies of reading relate to one another.

Embracing Ambiguity

Rhetoric is a contested concept, but at some level it must be a means to embrace or at least navigate ambiguity and multiplicity. Rhetoric is about contingency, mutability, and possibility, and persuasion and judgment under conditions of uncertainty. All of these things run counter to the structure of psychosis. Many of us have cheered the demise of symbolic efficiency, and for good reason. Cultural conformity can be oppressive, and the norms of American culture have generated heartbreaking violence, quotidian and spectacular, for hosts of people disqualified from full humanity on the basis of gender, sex, sexuality, race, ability, religion, language, culture, ethnicity, and ideology, alone and in intersection, yesterday and today. This is why we should not lament the passing of the "good old days" before fragmentation and polarization—these were not days before our differences divided us, they were days when it was taboo to *say* that differences divided us, or indeed, to be different.

The demise of a symbolic order does not mean unmitigated liberation, however. Each community in this book foreclosed some shared understanding or was abandoned by it, but in its place each one erected some new edifice of meaning under which to labor. As Wendy Chun has argued, the decline of "mainstream" culture has produced agitated microcultures that still cohere into angry, reactionary ideologies, strung together by the notion that they are persecuted in common, not common persecutors.[11] To repeat the Introduction's ersatz Internet law: For every subjugated group that finds space for self-expression online, another finds space to advocate the extermination of that group. In the place of fraying conformism, we have let a thousand little tyrannies bloom. The mechanisms by which they do so are described above, but I believe that certainty is the key—recoiling from meaninglessness, these communities latch on to new symbols with such force that ambiguity and polysemy become impossible.

Academics cannot reforge symbolic efficiency like Andúril from the shards, and frankly, that's probably good. Not only are shared norms double-edged, but our own thinking sometimes runs toward the dogmatic and obscure (I'm looking at you, comrade Lacanians). College administrators have lately become enamored with "discourse and dialogue," and while these are noble (if vague) goals and places where communication scholarship is absolutely vital, the last thing we need is to be crafting norms in the service of powers that may be more concerned with preserving the status quo than enabling human flourishing. We shouldn't give up on being Archie Debunkers just to become Emily Post-Truths dishing out rules for polite conduct in the face of global catastrophes. Any kind of productive encounter, including discourse, dialogue, and debate, requires stasis not only in terms of topic but also protocols for understanding what constitutes proof. But stasis requires at least a tacit admission that other perspectives are *possible*, even if we don't agree with them. That is precisely what is refused by anti-rhetorical readings, which is why engaging the affordances of modes of interpretation is an issue prior to any narrower discussion with communities like those analyzed in this book.

There is a place for scholarly intervention here. Kenneth Burke famously described literature as "equipment for living" in the sense that identifying "strategies" within it would help us understand and navigate the world.[12] What we can do in recognition of our anti-rhetorical age is to find new justification for teaching multiplicitous interpretation as an orientation toward the world. Not every community that forms around anti-rhetorical readings necessarily has to be challenged, but some of them certainly do, and that task is not easy. Rhetoric's contingency should teach us that we are never absolutely certain, but constantly called to make judgments about likelihood, prudence, and ethics. We may stick strongly to our principles: The key difference between rhetorical and anti-rhetorical readings is more about truth and desire than it is about normative values. Understanding the intersection of rhetoric and culture requires engaging with other fields, not least media studies, cultural studies, and scholarship on race, gender, and sexuality across the humanities. Studies of mediation demonstrate that messages are never transmitted untouched but are shaped by the circumstances of their communication. Social categories are not given, but are the products of constant contestation, and as such they are changeable. Rather than push a new consensus, we might help to popularize the flexibility, distance, and judgment that enable us to navigate even within discourses that are not our own and work hard to understand them from the perspectives of those who live inside them. This means reframing the case for rhetoric as an orientation toward the world in the sense of subjective propriety, or our capacity to exercise informed judgments about our symbolic modes of engagement with enough distance not to swallow them whole when we should be taking them with a grain of salt.

Above all, we must remember that anti-rhetorical readings, like all symptoms, are spontaneous attempts at a cure. Psychotic communities begin their formation by recoiling against uncertainty and ambiguity. Rigid discourses paper over the vertigo caused by looking too deeply into the void, and to some extent, that works, so deconstructing the discourse before attending to its cause can be counterproductive. Instead of simply criticizing those makeshift solutions, we should guide the way toward new ones, recognizing that the disorientation faced by anti-rhetorical communities is real. We should help to provide the tools and attitudes that make our students, families, and humans in general able to embrace ambiguity more comfortably and see the limits of our knowledge and control as opportunities for surprise, exhilaration, and joy. Certainty has a powerful appeal, but so do creativity and curiosity, two traits anathematized by anti-rhetorical thought. It is not just about regurgitating Aristotelian proofs or quizzing students on Burke's pentad. Rhetoric makes every language many languages. It resists closure and certainty because it is a framework of encounter, not just a technical skill. The humanities may be in endless crisis, but opportunities do exist to shape more thoughtful, reflective, and intrepid subjects. We don't need to rebuild the tower or raise a new one in its place. We need to look on its *spolia* and wonder at all the possibilities without declaring that every nation must be united.

Acknowledgments

No book is written alone. This one is the product of many conversations with friends, students, mentors, colleagues, and even an actual rock star.

I am fortunate to have had so much support from Rutgers University Press. Nicole Solano made this book happen, with remarkable patience, practical advice, and good humor throughout the entire process. At Westchester Publishing Services, Arielle Lewis edited this manuscript with precision and care—if it does not read like a day-late undergraduate paper, credit goes to her, not me.

I wrote this book during my time as department chair at the University of Pittsburgh. Were it not for our departmental staff, Lauri Freund, Julie Rosol, and Brooke Stearns, this undertaking would have been literally impossible for me. Were I to disappear in the woods tomorrow, little would change in our department besides the occupant of my chair. Were Lauri, Julie, and Brooke to have been gone for more than a day, the fourteenth floor of the Cathedral of Learning would have descended into chaos like *Lord of the Flies*. I hope they know how much I appreciate their work. I also hope that they can't hear me muttering about phrenology and snakes in my office.

I am grateful for my current and past graduate students at the University of Pittsburgh who have suffered through my enthusiasm for conspiracy theories, Jacques Lacan, Russian cults, and wee babies looking in the mirror. Many of my faculty colleagues have done the same, and I have benefited greatly from it. Annette Vee and the Mid-Career Writing Accountability Group kept me actually writing on a schedule. Many at the Pittsburgh Psychoanalytic Center have been generous with their time and wisdom, especially Mario Fischetti, Elleanor Irwin, Ron Jalbert, Tom Janoski, Melissa Jenereski, Sharon Leak, Jeff McCurry, Janet Mooney, Noah Rahm, and Josie van Londen. The Beatrice Institute gave me opportunities to share my work and talk to very thoughtful, very smart people about theology, chief among them James DeMasi and Ryan McDermott. This book was also supported by a fellowship at Pitt's Humanities Center, which included the opportunity to hear Todd Ochoa's invaluable feedback on an early draft of my work on serpent handling. A generous internal grant from the University of Pittsburgh Arts & Humanities Microgrant program permitted me to do archival work, where I earned new debts to the librarians at the West Virginia State Archives and the family of Nathan and Louise Gerrard.

I am fortunate to have many great academic friends and interlocutors at other institutions. Jarrod Atchison is loyal and supportive to a fault, not to mention generous, insightful, and humble. I know that, more than being a good professor, being a good person means being like Jarrod, even though I don't usually do it. I have never stopped learning from Eric King Watts, who first introduced me with patient eloquence to many of the ideas I have no doubt subsequently mangled. Thanks also to Johanna Hartelius, Robert McDonald, Casey Ryan Kelly, Justin Eckstein, Mike Lee, Jake Cowan, Sheldon George, Clint Burnham, Josh Gunn, and Derek Hook, all of whom have contributed meaningfully to my thinking and made conferences much more productive and engaging. Tim Barouch and several members of the Co-Conspirators network read drafts of this work—thank you especially to Atilla Hallsby, Jennie Keohane, Kellie Marin, and Reed Van Schenck. Tim has talked me out of my worst ideas, all of which I immediately text to him without remorse. This book would be a lot clumsier without him, but I have no idea what he gets out of it.

My family has continued to support me, largely a low-return investment. Thanks Mom, Chris, Scott, Calum, Calum, Tess, Charlotte, and all the others. I will miss the snoring of my twenty-pound mutt and research assistant Ogopogo, who knew how to secure a luxurious life despite never working a single day or quite learning his own name.

My wife insists that she contributed nothing to this project. On the contrary, she is the reason I do anything. She is kinder than she admits, more brilliant than she knows, and funnier than I can believe. Without her I would probably never have conversations with people who exist outside of Reddit conspiracy forums. I love you, NKO.

Notes

Introduction

1 J. A. Black et al., *The Electronic Text Corpus of Sumerian Literature*, Oxford 1998–2006, accessed March 13, 2024, https://etcsl.orinst.ox.ac.uk/cgi-bin/etcsl.cgi?text=t.1.8.2.3#.
2 Genesis 11:1–7, KJV.
3 Umberto Eco, *The Search for the Perfect Language*, trans. James Fentress (Blackwell, 1995), 1.
4 Unless otherwise specified, I mean "signifier" in the broadest sense, not just words. As Colette Soler defines them, a signifier could be a gesture, image, video, or even a physical sensation: "Any discrete elements, which can be isolated and combined with other discrete elements, which can also be isolated, and can take on meaning, can be called a signifier." Colette Soler, *What Lacan Said about Women: A Psychoanalytic Study*, trans. John Holland (Other Press, 2006), 50.
5 Slavoj Žižek, *The Ticklish Subject: The Absent Centre of Political Ontology* (Verso, 1999), 323.
6 Žižek, *The Ticklish Subject*, 323; Jodi Dean, *Publicity's Secret: How Technoculture Capitalizes on Democracy* (Cornell University Press, 2002), 131–133; Marc Andrejevic, *Infoglut: How Too Much Information Is Changing the Way We Think and Know* (Routledge, 2013).
7 Joy Williams, *Harrow: A Novel* (Alfred A. Knopf, 2021), 131.
8 Alenka Zupančič, *The Odd One In: On Comedy* (MIT Press, 2008), 9–30.
9 A play on his so-called Name of the Father (*nom du père*).
10 Stephen J. McKenna, *Adam Smith: The Rhetoric of Propriety* (SUNY Press, 2006), 28–29. I am not claiming that propriety and symbolic efficiency are synonymous, although they are related. I think of symbolic efficiency as the authority of some signifiers to determine what is proper (i.e., what connections in the Symbolic order are legitimate and what belongs with what).
11 Elliot Hunt, "Trump's Inauguration Crowd: Sean Spicer's Claims versus the Evidence," *The Guardian*, January 22, 2017, https://www.theguardian.com/us-news/2017/jan/22/trump-inauguration-crowd-sean-spicers-claims-versus-the-evidence.

12 Aaron Blake, "Kellyanne Conway's Legacy: The 'Alternative Facts'-ification of the GOP," *Washington Post*, August 24, 2020, https://www.washingtonpost.com/politics/2020/08/24/kellyanne-conways-legacy-alternative-facts-ification-gop/.
13 See, for example, Ralph Benko, "The Left, Not Kellyanne Conway, Invented 'Alternative Facts,'" *Forbes*, February 11, 2017, https://www.forbes.com/sites/ralphbenko/2017/02/11/the-left-not-kellyanne-conway-invented-alternative-facts/?sh=6c6dfa2d658c.
14 Dan Rather, Facebook status update, January 22, 2017, https://m.facebook.com/story.php?story_fbid=10158087282405716&id=240857807158&__tn__=*s.
15 Dylan Stableford, "Kellyanne Conway Explains What She Meant by 'Alternative Facts,'" *Yahoo! News*, July 23, 2017, https://news.yahoo.com/kellyanne-conway-explains-meant-alternative-facts-194946959.html.
16 Jacques Ellul, *Propaganda: The Formation of Men's Attitudes*, trans. Konrad Kellen and Jean Lerner (Vintage Books, 1965).
17 Michael J. Lee and R. Jarrod Atchison, *We Are Not One People: Secession and Separatism in American Politics Since 1776* (Oxford University Press, 2022), 30–31.
18 Lee and Atchison, *We Are Not One People*, 6, 33.
19 Svetlana Boym, *The Future of Nostalgia* (Basic Books, 2001).
20 Arthur Herman, *The Idea of Decline in Western History* (Free Press, 1997).
21 Stephanie Coontz, *The Way We Never Were: American Families and the Nostalgia Trap* (Basic Books, 1992).
22 The British Museum, "brick," accessed March 18, 2024, https://www.britishmuseum.org/collection/object/W_1825-0503-37.
23 Paul O'Kane, "*Spolia* as Speculation," *Journal of Visual Art Practice* 15, no. 2–3 (2016), 206. Italics in original.
24 On interpretive communities, see Stanley Fish, *Is There a Text in this Class? The Authority of Interpretive Communities* (Harvard University Press, 1980), especially Part II.
25 Ian Bogost, "The Ugly Honesty of Elon Musk's Twitter Rebrand," *The Atlantic*, July 31, 2023, https://www.theatlantic.com/technology/archive/2023/07/twitter-x-rebrand-juvenile-internet-style/674875/.
26 Patricia Gherovici, *Transgender Psychoanalysis: A Lacanian Perspective on Sexual Difference* (Routledge, 2017), 101.
27 Alenka Zupančič, *What Is Sex?* (MIT Press, 2017), 48. Zupančič is sophisticated and erudite, and this reference comes from the 1939 film *Ninotchka*, but truth be told, the first example that comes to my mind is the Ancient Mystic Society of No Homers, from "Homer the Great," an episode of *The Simpsons*. It's not just that there happen to be no Homers in the club (there is one—Homer Glumplich), but that the club is defined by the absence of Homers.
28 This symbolic order of human experience is often stylized simply as the Symbolic, especially by Lacanians.
29 Silvia Rosman, "Introduction: Translating *Jouissance*," in Néstor A. Braunstein, *Jouissance: A Lacanian Concept*, trans. Silvia Rosman (SUNY Press, 2020), p. 340, n. 6.
30 Calum Lister Matheson, "Instance of the Letter in the Unconscious, or Reason Since Freud," in *Reading Lacan's Écrits: From "The Freudian Thing" to "Remarks on Daniel Lagache,"* eds. Derek Hook and Calum Neill (Routledge, 2019), 131–162.
31 Néstor A. Braunstein, *Jouissance: A Lacanian Concept*, trans. Silvia Rosman (SUNY Press, 2020), 69.

32 This idea can certainly be taken too far, as chapter 4 demonstrates. The reason psychoanalysts cling so stubbornly to a notion of the subject is that there *is* always something that escapes mediation by any particular discourse. No one matches up perfectly with an external signifier or can be dissolved into their shared discourse with no remainder, which creates the conditions for contingency that psychoanalysis relies upon. Similarly, the exercise of rhetorical agency would be impossible without some subjective position from which interpretation may occur. Otherwise, discourses would vary only synchronically, which is clearly not the case.

33 Kenneth Burke, *Language as Symbolic Action* (University of California Press, 1966), 16.

34 Jacques Lacan, *The Seminar of Jacques Lacan, Book III: The Psychoses*, ed. Jacques-Alain Miller, trans. Russell Grigg (W. W. Norton, 1993), 242–243.

35 Carlo Michelstaedter, *Persuasion and Rhetoric*, trans. Wilhelm Snyman and Guiseppe Stellardi (University of KwaZulu-Natal Press, 2007), 67.

36 Zupančič, *What Is Sex?*, 66.

37 Zupančič, *What Is Sex?*, 66.

38 Dr. Ronald Jalbert of the Pittsburgh Psychoanalytic Center, one of my colleagues and former instructors and a native speaker of both French and English, translates this as "scribes to the insane," a perhaps even more evocative phrase.

39 Zupančič, *What Is Sex?*, 206.

40 For all of its many strengths, Christian Lundberg's *Lacan in Public* comes close to this in its discussion of the Mexico Solidarity Network's demand to be recognized as dangerous on a list made by the Mexican government. Lundberg argues that this demand represents a "call for sanction and love by the governing order" on the basis of just two documents. Both are clearly tongue in cheek, a possibility that Lundberg acknowledges but does not further discuss, and only one was authored by the group or its members (who are actually calling for *others* to demand recognition). The other source is an article in a Portland newspaper mocking the inclusion of various academics on the list. The notion that these texts communicate a desire for their own repression may be a bit of theoretical parapraxis. See Christian Lundberg, *Lacan in Public: Psychoanalysis and the Science of Rhetoric* (University of Alabama Press, 2012), 167–168.

41 Jonathan Culler, *Structuralist Poetics: Structuralism, Linguistics, and the Study of Literature* (Cornell University Press, 1975), 261.

42 Shoshana Felman, *Writing and Madness (Literature/Philosophy/Psychoanalysis)*, trans. Martha Noel Evans and Others (Stanford University Press, 2003).

43 In Jacques Lacan, *Écrits: The First Complete Edition in English*, trans. Bruce Fink (Norton, 2006).

44 On being an "oppositional lurker," see Jessie Daniels, *Cyber Racism: White Supremacy Online and the New Attack on Civil Rights* (Rowman & Littlefield, 2009). "Evenly suspended attention" is a concept in psychoanalysis consistent with Lacan's injunction to be "secretaries to the insane."

45 Stijn Vanheule, *The Subject of Psychosis: A Lacanian Perspective* (Palgrave Macmillan, 2011), 10.

46 Calum Lister Matheson, *Desiring the Bomb: Communication, Psychoanalysis, and the Atomic Age* (University of Alabama Press, 2019).

47 As quoted passages below will reveal, what I refer to as "novelty" is typically called "delusion" in both medicalized and psychoanalytic discourse. My word choice is meant to emphasize that fantasy beliefs are universal, and what renders them

vulnerable to pathologization is largely cultural propriety, an argument that I will develop throughout this book. This is not to romanticize them. Novel interpretations of the world may cause their believers to suffer. Instead, I want to emphasize that normative interpretations of the world *also* cause suffering, and what we determine to be "delusional" is largely culturally dependent.

48 Lacan, *Seminar of Jacques Lacan, Book III*, 13.

49 Annie Rogers, *Incandescent Alphabets: Psychosis and the Enigma of Language* (Karnac Books, 2016), 74.

50 Lacan, *Seminar of Jacques Lacan, Book III*, 85.

51 Rogers, *Incandescent Alphabets*, 75.

52 Lacan, *Seminar of Jacques Lacan, Book III*, 78. Bollas, although not a Lacanian, uses the same language. Christopher Bollas, *When the Sun Bursts: The Enigma of Schizophrenia* (Yale University Press, 2015), 108.

53 Lacan, *Seminar of Jacques Lacan, Book III*, 33.

54 Rogers, *Incandescent Alphabets*, 3.

55 See, for example, Wesley Willis, "Chronic Schizophrenia," track 13 on *Rush Hour*, Alternative Tentacles, 2000. Lyrics available at https://www.songlyrics.com/wesley-willis/chronic-schizophrenia-lyrics/.

56 David J. Buck, "Rock On Chicago," *Tedium*, November 16, 2017, https://tedium.co/2017/11/16/wesley-willis-remembrance-history/.

57 Rogers, *Incandescent Alphabets*, 82–83.

58 Sigmund Freud, *The Complete Letters of Sigmund Freud to Wilhem Fliess 1887–1904*, trans. and ed. by Jeffrey Moussaieff Masson (Harvard University Press, 1985), 111. Italics in original.

59 Lacan, *Seminar of Jacques Lacan, Book III*, 122.

60 Lacan, *Seminar of Jacques Lacan, Book III*, 123.

61 Lacan, *Seminar of Jacques Lacan, Book III*, 74.

62 Lacan, *Seminar of Jacques Lacan, Book III*, 75.

63 The Name of the Father is also an example of a structuring signifier: "I'm not saying that the Name of the Father is the only one," Lacan clarified. "We can uncover this element whenever we apprehend something that is of the symbolic order properly so-called." Lacan, *Seminar of Jacques Lacan, Book III*, 316.

64 Clinical evidence suggests that people experiencing psychosis use metaphor less in speech (see, for example, Nilufar Mossaheb et al., "Comprehension of Metaphors in Patients with Schizophrenia-Spectrum Disorders," *Comprehensive Psychiatry* 55, no. 4 [2014]: 928–937; Felicity Deamer et al., "Non-Literal Understanding and Psychosis: Metaphor Comprehension in Individuals with a Diagnosis of Schizophrenia," *Schizophrenia Research: Cognition* 18, article no. 100159 [2019], https://doi.org/10.1016/j.scog.2019.100159), but the structural understanding of psychosis explains why some tropes and figures, including metaphor, are still available to subjects experiencing it: Only the specific metaphor foreclosed becomes unspeakable, and only the delusional argot that replaces it must be understood hyperliterally.

65 Jacques Lacan, *The Seminar of Jacques Lacan, Book V: Formations of the Unconscious*, ed. Jacques-Alain Miller, trans. Russell Grigg (Polity, 2017), 31–33.

66 Joshua Gunn, *Political Perversion: Rhetorical Aberration in the Time of Trumpeteering* (University of Chicago Press, 2020), xi. Emphasis in original.

67 Jodi Dean, *Democracy and Other Neoliberal Fantasies: Communicative Capitalism & Left Politics* (Duke University Press, 2009).

68 Darian Leader, *What Is Madness?* (Penguin Books, 2011), 11.
69 This is also why subjects who have psychotic attachments to some signifiers are capable of rhetorical ones elsewhere—individual subjects may tolerate metaphors even when a discourse does not.
70 Francesco Casetti, *Screening Fears: On Protective Media* (Zone Books, 2023), 13.
71 Casetti, *Screening Fears*, 116.

Chapter 1 Sandy Hook

1 Elizabeth Williamson, *Sandy Hook: An American Tragedy and the Battle for Truth* (Dutton, 2022), 99.
2 For the sake of brevity, I will refer to the 2012 mass shooting as the "Sandy Hook massacre" or just "Sandy Hook," recognizing the potential that naming has to relegate or make exceptional acts of violence when they are better understood in the context of larger systemic violence, as I believe is the case here. See Bernd Hüppauf, "Introduction: Modernity and Violence: Observations Concerning a Contradictory Relationship," in *War, Violence, and the Modern Condition*, ed. Bernd Hüppauf (De Gruyter, 1997). Sandy Hook *conspiracism* refers to the broader community espousing a broad range of conspiracy beliefs concerned with this event, while Sandy Hook *denialism* refers more narrowly to the belief that the shooting never occurred.
3 Amanda Crawford, "Opinion: Sandy Hook Was the Start of Misinformation Running Amok," *CNN*, December 14, 2022, https://www.cnn.com/2022/12/14/opinions/sandy-hook-shooting-anniversary-disinformation-misinformation-crawford/index.html.
4 Williamson, *Sandy Hook*, 2.
5 David Bauder, "Is Alex Jones Verdict the Death of Disinformation? Unlikely," *ABC News*, October 17, 2022, https://abc7amarillo.com/news/local/is-alex-jones-verdict-the-death-of-disinformation-unlikely-sandy-hook-elementary-conspiracy-theories-rebecca-adelman-mark-fenster-nicole-hemmer-seth-rich-fox-news-tucker-carlson-john-jackson-dominion-voting-systems.
6 Cheryl Teh, "Alex Jones Bizarrely Declared 'Victory for Truth' After Being Ordered to Pay $4.1 Million in Damages to Sandy Hook Parents," *Business Insider*, August 5, 2022, https://www.insider.com/alex-jones-declares-victory-pay-damages-sandy-hook-2022-8.
7 See, for example, Dean, *Democracy and Other Neoliberal Fantasies*; Andrejevic, *Infoglut*.
8 Katharina Thalmann, *The Stigmatization of Conspiracy Theory Since the 1950s: "A Plot to Make Us Look Foolish"* (Routledge, 2019).
9 Stephen J. Sedensky III, *Report of the State's Attorney for the Judicial District of Danbury on the Shootings at Sandy Hook Elementary School and 36 Yogananda Street, Newtown, Connecticut, on December 14, 2012*, Office of the State's Attorney, Judicial District of Danbury, November 25, 2013, https://portal.ct.gov/-/media/DCJ/SandyHookFinalReportpdf.pdf, 1.
10 Sedensky, *Report of the State's Attorney*, 3.
11 Abby Rogers, "These Are the Worst Errors Reported After the Sandy Hook Massacre," *Business Insider*, December 18, 2012, https://www.businessinsider.com/sandy-hook-shooting-media-inaccuracies-2012-12; David Folkenflik, "Coverage Rapid, and Often Wrong, in Tragedy's Early Hours," *NPR*, December 18, 2012,

https://www.npr.org/2012/12/18/167466320/coverage-rapid-and-often-wrong-in-tragedys-early-hours.

12 Williamson, *Sandy Hook*, 84.

13 Rob Brotherton, *Suspicious Minds: Why We Believe Conspiracy Theories* (Bloomsbury Sigma, 2015), 73.

14 Google Hollie Greig (GGT), "The Sandy Hook Shooting—Fully Exposed," BitChute.com, September 28, 2022, https://www.bitchute.com/video/RUOax1J5Qwd4/. This documentary was originally posted on YouTube—my citation is for one of many copies elsewhere. For background, see Max Read, "Behind the 'Sandy Hook Truther' Conspiracy Video That Five Eight Million People Have Watched in One Week," *Gawker*, January 15, 2013, https://www.gawkerarchives.com/5976204/behind-the-sandy-hook-truther-conspiracy-video-that-five-million-people-have-watched-in-one-week.

15 See, for example, MrStosh314, "We Need to Talk About Sandy Hook," uploaded to Rumble by False Flags, October 7, 2022, https://rumble.com/v1mysno-we-need-to-talk-about-sandy-hook.html.

16 MrStosh314, "We Need to Talk About Sandy Hook." Widening the mental health net and influencing school curriculums are sometimes named as part of the plan.

17 Sofia Smallstorm, "Unravelling Sandy Hook in 2, 3, 4 and 5 Dimensions," uploaded to Rumble by JBR1959, July 29, 2022, https://rumble.com/v1e2emn-sandy-hook-in-five-dimensions-by-sophia-smallstorm.html.

18 MrStosh314, "We Need to Talk About Sandy Hook."

19 Jim Fetzer and Mike Palecek, eds., *Nobody Died at Sandy Hook: It Was a FEMA Drill to Promote Gun Control* (Moon Rock Books, 2015).

20 Amanda J. Crawford, "Professor of Denial," *The Chronicle of Higher Education*, February 5, 2020, https://www.chronicle.com/article/the-professor-of-denial/. Pozner, whose son Noah died in the 2012 massacre, has managed to have much conspiracy-related media pushed into the darker parts of the Internet.

21 Fetzer, "Thinking About Sandy Hook: Reality or Illusion?" in *Nobody Died at Sandy Hook*, eds. Fetzer and Palecek, 4.

22 Fetzer, "Thinking About Sandy Hook," 4. Emphasis mine.

23 *PBS NewsHour*, "Watch Conn. Gov. Malloy and Conn. State Police Address Newtown School Shooting," YouTube video, December 14, 2012, 10:55, https://www.youtube.com/watch?v=xGm9CzrZdX4.

24 Fetzer, "Thinking About Sandy Hook," 8. Emphasis in original.

25 James F. Tracy, "Medical Examiner: More Questions than Answers," in *Nobody Died at Sandy Hook*, eds. Fetzer and Palecek, 20.

26 Vivian Lee, "Top Ten Reasons: Sandy Hook Was an Elaborate Hoax," in *Nobody Died at Sandy Hook*, eds. Fetzer and Palecek, 71.

27 Lee, "Top Ten Reasons," 80.

28 Allan William Powell, "Setting the Stage: Refurbishing the School," in *Nobody Died at Sandy Hook*, eds. Fetzer and Palecek.

29 Ben Carver, "'Turning Points': Plots in Conspiracy and Literature," in *Plots: Literary Form and Conspiracy Culture*, eds. Ben Carver et al. (Routledge, 2022), 26.

30 Luc Boltanski, *Mysteries and Conspiracies* (Polity, 2014).

31 Lee, "Top Ten Reasons," 57.

32 Michael Calvin McGee, "Text, Context, and the Fragmentation of Contemporary Culture," *Western Journal of Communication* 54, no. 3 (Summer 1990), 273.

33 Carver, "'Turning Points,'" 21.

34 See, for example, Jim Fetzer, "David Zublick' Awake Nation: 'Have I Been Played on Sandy Hook?' (20 April 2023) with Brian Davidson," BitChute.com, April 24, 2023, https://www.bitchute.com/video/jpPsw2RRu3Ok/.

35 See, for example, Powell, "Setting the Stage."

36 Gi Linda, "Sandy Hook: Fleecing the Asleeple!" *Not the News*, uploaded to Scribd by Gordon Duff, accessed October 13, 2023, https://www.scribd.com/document/249692922/Sandy-Hook-Fleecing-the-Sheeple.

37 Jason Koebler, "Where the 'Crisis Actor' Conspiracy Theory Comes From," *VICE*, February 22, 2018, https://www.vice.com/en/article/pammy8/what-is-a-crisis-actor-conspiracy-theory-explanation-parkland-shooting-sandy-hook.

38 See, for example, David, "False Flag Crisis Actors," *The Truthful One*, archived March 30, 2016, at https://web.archive.org/web/20160330124820/http://thetruthfulone.com/false-flag-crisis-actors/.

39 G. Courbon and P. Fail, "Syndrome d'illusion de Frégoli et schizophrénie," trans. Hadyn D. Ellis et al., *History of Psychiatry*, 5, no. 17 (1994), 134.

40 Elizabeth Kim et al., "DMS: Delusional Misidentification Syndrome or Dead Moneyman and Sex Offender? A Case Report of Reverse Capgras Syndrome," *Case Reports in Psychiatry* 22, no. 3 (2022), 3, https://doi.org/10.1155/2022/9703482.

41 It should be noted, however, that even psychotic delusions identified in individuals are heavily dependent on culture and media for their content, which suggests that if we do take them seriously (and we should), psychiatry alone provides an incomplete perspective. See Joel Gold and Ian Gold, *Suspicious Minds: How Culture Shapes Madness* (Free Press, 2014); Jeffrey Sconce, *The Technical Delusion: Electronics, Power, Insanity* (Duke University Press, 2019); Victoria Shepherd, *A History of Delusions: The Glass King, a Substitute Husband and a Walking Corpse* (Oneworld Publications, 2022).

42 Barry Soetoro, "Sandy Hook—David Wheeler Exposed as Actor and Fake FBI Sniper," uploaded to BitChute.com by Yanghis Khan, July 6, 2019, https://www.bitchute.com/video/HKrGqfLOhoXx/. "Barry Soetoro" is presumably a pseudonym that is also alleged by conspiracy theorists to be an alias of former president of the United States Barack Obama.

43 Dr. Eowyn, "Remarkable Resemblance of Sandy Hook Victims and Professional Crisis Actors," *Fellowship of the Minds*, January 11, 2013, archived March 17, 2016, at https://web.archive.org/web/20160317110501/http://fellowshipoftheminds.com/2013/01/11/remarkable-resemblance-of-sandy-hook-victims-and-professional-crisis-actors/.

44 Ed Chiarnini, "A MUST READ . . . Did the CT School Shootings 'Really' Happen? . . . Murdered School Children—Rockefeller Grandchild . . . You Decide," *Know the Lies*, December 17, 2012, archived March 14, 2013, at https://web.archive.org/web/20130314053347/http://www.knowthelies.com/node/8486. Chiarnini's page at Wellaware.com contains many other examples of Fregoli/impostor claims.

45 Ed Chiarnini, "Peter Lanza Father of Adam Lanza Is a FICTION?" *Know the Lies*, December 17, 2013, archived January 22, 2013, at https://web.archive.org/web/20130122182157/http://www.knowthelies.com/node/8487.

46 See, for example, Nick Kollerstrom, "The 20 Children and Their Homes," in *Nobody Died at Sandy Hook*, eds. Fetzer and Palecek. This idea demonstrates

Brotherton's observation that conspiracy theorists cast their enemies as both incompetent and near omnipotent at the same time, capable of organizing an event like Sandy Hook but too lazy, cheap, or stupid not to reuse the same child actors every time (see *Suspicious Minds*, 2015).

47 "Dr. Eowyn" is alleged by Williamson (*Sandy Hook*, 106) to be Maria Hsia Chang. No evidence suggests that she is the same Éowyn who led the civilians of Rohan to safety in the White Mountains before the Battle of Hornburg, much less slayed the Witch-king of Angmar before the Grond-shattered gates of Minas Tirith at the Battle of the Pelennor Fields.

48 Dr. Eowyn, "Proof from the Social Security Death Index," in *Nobody Died at Sandy Hook*, eds Fetzer and Palecek. For discussions regarding how the absence of evidence becomes evidence in conspiracy theories, see Jenny Rice, *Awful Archives: Conspiracy Theory, Rhetoric, and Acts of Evidence* (Ohio State Press, 2020), 107; Anastasiya Astapova, "In Pursuit of Nationhood vis-à-vis Russia: The Search for Lost Manuscripts in Post-Soviet Countries," in *Plots*, eds. Carver et al.

49 Soetoro, "Sandy Hook."

50 Žižek, *The Ticklish Subject*, 325–326.

51 Daniel Paul Schreber, *Memoirs of My Nervous Illness*, trans. and ed. Ida Macalpine and Richard A. Hunter (New York Review Books, 1955), p. 17, n. 1.

52 Lee, "Top Ten Reasons," 91. Emphasis mine.

53 Lee's citation of Holocaust denier and antisemite Michael A. Hoffman suggests that the character of this Other for her is specifically Jewish, as is the case in a great number of conspiracy theories over the centuries. The Fregoli delusion has a parallel in the antisemitic anxiety about the possibility that Jews could "pass" as gentiles, meaning that nearly anyone could secretly be a Jewish person in disguise.

54 Melanie Klein, "Notes on Some Schizoid Mechanisms," *Journal of Psychotherapy Practice and Research* 5, no. 2 (1996), 169; also see Bollas, *When the Sun Bursts*, 81–83.

55 Williamson, *Sandy Hook*, 125.

56 Williamson, *Sandy Hook*, 398.

57 Williamson, *Sandy Hook*, 143–148.

58 Lundberg, *Lacan in Public*, 85.

59 Cormac McCarthy, *Suttree* (Vintage International, 1979), 284.

60 One could think of this in terms of Deleuze and Guattari's striated and smooth spaces, with rhetorical usage representing the latter in its capacity to invite multiple interpretations and associations and literalism representing the former, striating space within a narrow band of acceptable interpretations and anti-rhetorical devices seeking to ossify that band altogether in the service of a grid. I must admit, however, that after an early flurry of enthusiasm, in most things Deleuze I now side with the later preferences of Melville's scrivener. See Gilles Deleuze and Félix Guattari, *A Thousand Plateaus*, trans. Brian Massumi (University of Minnesota Press, 1987).

61 Lacan, *Écrits*, 413. Italics in original.

62 Flitting between word associations is distinguished by Lacan from the sense of deep cryptic ties between words and things as two modes of psychotic speech—mania and *acedia* or depression—in his seminar *Television*, although literary and clinical experience confirms that both can be present in the same subject. This distinction is a potentially fruitful and underexplored opportunity for encounter between psychoanalysis and rhetoric. See Jacques Lacan, *Television: A Challenge to*

the Psychoanalytic Establishment, trans. Denis Hollier et al. (W. W. Norton, 1990), 22; Calum Lister Matheson, "Psychotic Discourse: The Rhetoric of the Sovereign Citizen Movement," *Rhetoric Society Quarterly* 48, no. 2 (2018): 187–206.

63 Oxford English Dictionary, s.v. "for," accessed April 17, 2025, https://doi.org/10.1093/OED/1589022754.

64 For a discussion of psychosis and anxiety in relation to the abstract qualities of financial and rhetorical exchange, see Calum Lister Matheson, "Filthy Lucre: Gold, Language, and Exchange Anxiety," *Review of Communication* 18, no. 4 (2018): 249–264.

65 Sharon Leak, email to faculty of the Pittsburgh Psychoanalytic Center, October 23, 2023.

66 Hugh Bredin, "The Literal and the Figurative," *Philosophy* 67, no. 269 (1992), 72.

67 Bredin, "Literal and the Figurative," 77.

68 Bredin, "Literal and the Figurative," 79.

69 Willful misreading of figurative language further muddies this distinction, as in the case of Warren Demesme, an accused criminal who asked for "a lawyer, dawg" and was denied one because no dogs are also lawyers, something that is extremely unlikely to be an honest mistake by the interrogating officers.

70 I mean *atropic* both in the sense of "without trope" and as a reference to Atropos, one of the Moirai or Fates in Greek myth that is associated with death and the end of possibility, partly because of the prominence of death in the various anti-rhetorical discourses studied in this book.

71 George N. Christodoulou, ed., *The Delusional Misidentification Syndromes* (Karger, 1986).

72 It might have been interesting to analyze the sovereign citizen movement in these terms as a kind of mirrored-self misidentification had I thought of it prior to having written an article on the subject (Matheson, "Psychotic Discourse.")

73 Wilfred Bion, "Attacks on Linking," in *The Complete Works of W. R. Bion*, vol. 6, ed. Chris Mawson (Routledge, 2014), 152.

74 Fetzer, "Thinking About Sandy Hook," 8. "Fifty photos" deserves special note: Jenny Rice argues that many conspiracy theorists rely on *megethos*, a quantity of evidence that takes on a special, overwhelming quality. It brings to mind a quote misattributed to Stalin: "Quantity has a quality all of its own." See Rice, *Awful Archives*, 66–69.

75 See, for example, Renee Pittman Books, "Mind Control and Mass Shooters . . . Is There a Connection?" YouTube video, September 3, 2023, 24:51, https://www.youtube.com/watch?v=MZEZfkKHgSM. Thought insertion and thought deletion, fantasies tied up in this species of discourse, are classic symptoms of psychosis that could perhaps be understood as literal figures, just as I have argued regarding the Fregoli delusion.

76 See, for example, Michael Collins Piper, *False Flags: Template for Terror* (American Free Press, 2019).

77 Alex Seitz-Wald, "Sandy Hook Truther Won't Quit," *Salon*, January 18, 2013, https://www.salon.com/2013/01/18/james_tracy_wont_back_down/.

78 Lacan, *Écrits*, 415.

79 Richard Serrano, "Lacan's Oriental Language of the Unconscious," *SubStance #84*, 26.3 (1997), 96.

80 Marshal McLuhan, *Understanding Media: The Extensions of Man* (MIT Press, 1994), 8.

81 Kathleen Stewart, "Conspiracy Theory's Worlds," in *Paranoia Within Reason: A Casebook on Conspiracy as Explanation*, ed. George E. Marcus (University of Chicago Press, 1999), 18.

82 Sarah Sharma, "Many McLuhans or None at All," *Canadian Journal of Communication* 44, no. 4 (2019), para. 5, https://doi.org/10.22230/cjc.2019v44n4a3621.

83 I chose the word *host* deliberately. Desire is parasitic on media: It depends on media to separate a subject from its objects and also to bring them closer in the endless alternation that sustains it. Desire is an effect of media and could not exist without it.

84 See Williamson, *Sandy Hook*, 168, 244.

85 Jon Rappoport, "Astonishing Hunger Games 'Coincidence,' and Killer's Mother Now a Doomsday Prepper?" *Prison Planet*, December 17, 2012, archived August 19, 2018, at https://web.archive.org/web/20180819235941/https://www.prisonplanet.com/newtown-murders-astonishing-hunger-games-coincidence-and-killers-mother-now-a-doomsday-prepper.html.

86 See Brotherton, *Suspicious Minds*.

87 Lacan, *Seminar of Jacques Lacan, Book III*, 85. This "enormous meaning" is discussed in the Introduction of this volume.

88 Lucas Ballestín, "Resistance and Revelation: Lacan on Defense," *European Journal of Psychoanalysis* 2, no. 2 (2021), https://www.journal-psychoanalysis.eu/articles/resistance-and-revelation-lacan-on-defense/.

89 Lacan, *Seminar of Jacques Lacan, Book III*, 86. Emphasis in original. In Lacan's sometimes frustrating circumlocution, "it wouldn't be useless" is high praise indeed.

90 Rappoport, "Hunger Games 'Coincidence'"; Matt McCarson, "Newtown Connecticut Elementary Shooting Is a Staged False Flag Against Gun Owners and Preppers," InfoSalvo.com, December 14, 2012, http://www.infosalvo.com/us-news/newton-connecticut-elementary-shooting-is-a-staged-false-flag/.

91 Clyde Lewis, "Mental Hopscotch," *Ground Zero*, April 12, 2013, archived March 5, 2014, at https://web.archive.org/web/20140305235005/http://www.groundzeromedia.org/mental-hopscotch/.

92 Fetzer, "Thinking About Sandy Hook," 14–16.

93 See, for example, "Israeli Death Squads Involved in Sandy Hook Bloodbath: Intelligence Analyst," PressTV.com, December 18, 2012, archived May 20, 2015, at https://web.archive.org/web/20150520144015/http://www.presstv.com/detail/2012/12/18/278706/israeli-squads-tied-to-newtown-carnage.

94 Williamson, *Sandy Hook*, 129.

95 "A Startling Fact & Gigantic 'Coincidence' About Friday's Mass Shooting in Connecticut," SGTReport.com, December 15, 2012, archived February 24, 2013, at https://web.archive.org/web/20130224033919/http://sgtreport.com/2012/12/a-startling-fact-gigantic-coincidence-about-fridays-mass-shooting/. This article also discusses a comment linking *Hunger Games* author Suzanne Collins to the shooting because children die in her books and she allegedly lives near Sandy Hook. This is an unusually clear example of metonymic connection in delusions, in this case by geographical proximity.

96 Reggie Ugwu, "Gunplay Says Government Behind Sandy Hook Shooting," BET.com, December 21, 2012, https://www.bet.com/article/6m8s5l/gunplay-says-government-behind-sandy-hook-shooting.

97 Stephen Marche, "Guns Are Beautiful," *Esquire*, February 11, 2013, https://www.esquire.com/news-politics/a19335/guns-are-beautiful-0313/.

98 David Yamane, "Psycho-Sexual Analysis of Guns, Part 2," *Gun Culture 2.0* (blog), April 16, 2015, https://gunculture2pointo.wordpress.com/2015/04/13/psycho-sexual-analysis-of-guns-part-2/.

99 Matthew Gault, "Here's Why Men Are Pointing Loaded Guns at Their Dicks," *VICE*, May 27, 2020, https://www.vice.com/en/article/k7q83v/heres-why-men-are-pointing-loaded-guns-at-their-dicks; "The TAC-SAC: Picatinny Rail Accessory," Unicun.com, accessed October 17, 2023, https://unicun.com/product/the-tac-sac-picatinny-rail-accessory/; Warren Blumenfeld, "How the Gun Lobby Turned a Fake Quote from Sigmund Freud into a Rallying Cry," *LGBTQ Nation*, October 5, 2017, https://www.lgbtqnation.com/2017/10/gun-lobby-turned-fake-quote-sigmund-freud-rallying-cry/.

100 Carina Hsieh, "'Dicks Out for Harambe': How 2 Average Guys Started the Year's Most Controversial Meme," *Cosmopolitan*, December 6, 2016, https://www.cosmopolitan.com/politics/a8354653/dicks-out-for-harambe-internets-most-fascinating/.

101 E. P. Evans, *The Criminal Prosecution and Capital Punishment of Animals: The Lost History of Europe's Animal Trials* (Faber & Faber, 1906), 184.

102 U.S. Department of Defense, "The USS *New York*: A City on the Sea," accessed October 17, 2023, https://www.defense.gov/Multimedia/Experience/USS-New-York-A-City-on-the-Sea.

103 "'Holy Grail' of Guns Made: Company Sells $4.5M Pistols Made from 4.5-billion-year-old meteorite," *Fox News*, April 26, 2018, https://www.foxnews.com/tech/holy-grail-of-guns-made-company-sells-4-5m-pistols-made-from-4-5-billion-year-old-meteorite.

104 Jacques Derrida, *Deconstruction in a Nutshell: A Conversation with Jacques Derrida*, ed. John D. Caputo (Fordham University Press, 1997), 107–108.

105 Many other scholars have analyzed the rhetoric of guns in more detail than I have done here and affirmed that guns operate as signifying objects that root durable, persistent fantasies. Nathan Bedsole has described the "the Firearm" as a "master signifier" within the discourse so named by Lacan, a cultural logic with a powerful hold on American imaginaries. Joshua Gunn has analyzed American gun culture, and especially mass shootings, in terms of perversion, arguing that guns are not quite transitional objects due to their explicitly violent function and "not meant to be played with like toys." Richard Branscomb has provided a rhetorical history of gun culture and conspiracism, while Justin Eckstein has analyzed the mediation of gun violence by its victims. Eric King Watts has analyzed guns in the context of anti-Black racism and a turn away from rhetoric, which influences my concept of anti-rhetorical devices that threads through this book. See Joshua Gunn, *Political Perversion*; Nathan H. Bedsole, "X, Analyst," *Quarterly Journal of Speech* 110, no. 2 (2023): 245; Richard Branscomb, "Taking Aim: Rhetorical Conspiracism, Far-Right Extremism, and the Narrative Politics of Guns" (PhD diss., Carnegie Mellon University, 2023); Justin Eckstein, "Sensing School Shootings," *Critical Studies in Media Communication* 37, no. 2 (2020): 161–173; Eric King Watts, "'Zombies Are Real': Fantasies, Conspiracies, and the Post-truth Wars," *Philosophy and Rhetoric* 51, no. 4 (2018): 441–470.

106 McCarson, "Newtown Connecticut Elementary Shooting." Emphasis mine.

107 Roxanne Dunbar-Ortiz, *Loaded: A Disarming History of the Second Amendment* (City Lights Books, 2018).

108 Calum Lister Matheson, "'What Does Obama Want of Me?' Anxiety and Jade Helm 15,'" *Quarterly Journal of Speech* 102, no. 2 (2015): 133–149.
109 Caroline Light, *Stand Your Ground: A History of America's Love Affair with Lethal Self-Defense* (Beacon Press, 2017), 3–5.
110 Watts, "'Zombies Are Real,'" 2018.
111 See Casey Ryan Kelly, *Apocalypse Man: The Death Drive and White Masculine Victimhood* (The Ohio State University Press, 2020).
112 Gunn, *Political Perversion*, 126. Emphasis in original.
113 Simone Weil, *Gravity and Grace*, trans. Arthur Willis (University of Nebraska Press, 1952), 200.
114 Thalmann, *Stigmatization of Conspiracy Theory*, 9.
115 Tony Polito, "Tony Polito, PhD," archived December 8, 2023, at https://web.archive.org/web/20231208205038/http://www.tonypolito.com/.
116 Florida Atlantic University, "James Tracy," FAU Dorothy F. Schmidt College of Arts and Letters School of Communication and Multimedia Studies, archived September 11, 2015, at https://web.archive.org/web/20150911021341/http://www.fau.edu/scms/tracy.php.
117 Sarah Lederer, "James H. Fetzer," University of Minnesota Duluth, accessed October 20, 2023, https://www.d.umn.edu/~jfetzer/.
118 Did "Dr. Eowyn" even read *The Silmarillion*? I mean, sure, Éowyn was great, no denying it, and maybe Galadriel is too on the nose for a pseudonym, but you could have been proud Haleth, Chieftain of the Haladin, or if you're totally metal, Ungoliant, mistress of webs, darkness, and other conspiracy-adjacent themes. No? Then at least get the diacritics right.
119 Eve Kosofsky Sedgwick, *Touching Feeling: Affect, Pedagogy, Performativity* (Duke University Press, 2003).
120 Though, as Lacan reminds us through the tale of a man who was convinced without evidence that his wife was having affair and just happened to be correct, just because we're right doesn't mean we aren't paranoid.
121 Lee Edelman, *Bad Education: Why Queer Theory Teaches Us Nothing* (Duke University Press, 2022), 23.

Chapter 2 Serpent Handlers

1 The only other rhetorical study of serpent handling that I uncovered is a 1980 MA thesis, which is a notable exception in that it focuses on the rhetorical situation of serpent handling without explicitly condemning or identifying a root cause of the practice, despite its unfortunate use of the term "cult" in the title. See Kala Van Hoorebeke, "The Rhetorical Paradigm in the Service of the Snake Handling Cult" (master's thesis, Western Illinois University, 1980).
2 The excessive weight given to single passages of the Bible without context is sometimes called *prooftexting*, a charge frequently made against serpent handlers—see, for example, Robert C. Crosby, "The Other Side of 'Proof-Texting,'" *Patheos* (blog), January 11, 2014, https://www.patheos.com/blogs/robertcrosby/2014/01/the-other-side-of-proof-texting/.
3 Quoted in Ralph Hood Jr. and W. Paul Williamson, *Them That Believe: The Power and Meaning of the Christian Serpent-Handling Tradition* (University of California Press, 2008), 9.
4 Hood and Williamson, *Them That Believe*, 23.

5 Estrelda Y. Alexander, *Black Fire: One Hundred Years of African American Pentecostalism* (InterVarsity Press, 2011), 21–22.
6 Michael J. McVicar, "Take Away the Serpents from Us: The Sign of Serpent Handling and the Development of Southern Pentecostalism," *Journal of Southern Religion* 15 (2013), http://jsr.fsu.edu/issues/vol15/mcvicar.html.
7 Thomas Burton, *Serpent-Handling Believers* (University of Tennessee Press, 1993), 32.
8 Burton, *Serpent-Handling Believers*, 32. The role of Hensley's wife Amanda perhaps deserves more attention: According to Steven Kane, she found and read the biblical texts that inspired her husband, who was illiterate. Steven Michael Kane, "Snake Handlers of Southern Appalachia," (PhD diss., Princeton University, 1979), 32–33.
9 Hood and Williamson, *Them That Believe*, 38.
10 Jimmy Morrow (with Ralph W. Hood Jr.), *Handling Serpents: Pastor Jimmy Morrow's Narrative History of His Appalachian Jesus' Name Tradition* (Mercer University Press, 2005), 2–5. "Kleinieck" is also spelled "Klienieck" in Morrow's account.
11 See Paul R. L. Vance, "A History of Serpent Handlers in Georgia, North Alabama and Southeastern Tennessee" (master's thesis, Georgia State University, 1975), 32–37.
12 Hood and Williamson, *Them That Believe*, 237.
13 Fred Brown and Jeanne McDonald, *The Serpent Handlers: Three Families and Their Faith* (John F. Blair, 2000), xiv.
14 Hood and Williamson, *Them That Believe*, 82. Copperheads and rattlesnakes seem to be the most common.
15 Hood and Williamson, *Them That Believe*, 82; Karen W. Carden and Robert W. Pelton, *The Persecuted Prophets: The Story of the Frenzied Serpent Handlers* (A. S. Barnes and Company, 1976), 31–50.
16 Eliot Wigginton, "The People Who Take Up Serpents," in *Foxfire 7*, ed. Paul F. Gillespie (Anchor Books, 1980), 370.
17 See Hood and Williamson, *Them That Believe*, for a researched list through the mid-to-late 2000s.
18 Hood and Williamson, *Them That Believe*, 150.
19 David Kimbrough, *Taking Up Serpents: Snake Handlers of Eastern Kentucky* (Mercer University Press, 2002), 187.
20 J. Wayne Flynt, quoted in Kimbrough, *Taking Up Serpents*, 189.
21 Weston La Barre, *They Shall Take Up Serpents: Psychology of the Southern Snake-Handling Cult* (Waveland Press, 1992), 169–170. In their unpublished work, sociologists Nathan and Louise Gerrard disagreed somewhat, arguing that because many believers came from mining communities and stayed in their hollows there was less disruption than La Barre claimed. Still, the sense that the secular world abandoned serpent handlers is evident in their sermons, songs, and interviews. See Nathan L. Gerrard and Louise B. Gerrard, *Scrabble Creek Folk*, vol. I, unpublished 1966 manuscript at the Schoenbaum Library, University of Charleston, 70–71.
22 Keith G. Tidball and Christopher P. Toumey, "Signifying Serpents: Hermeneutic Change in Appalachian Pentecostal Serpent Handling," in *Signifying Serpents and Mardi Gras Runners: Representing Identity in Selected Souths*, eds. Celeste Ray and Luke Eric Lassiter (University of Georgia Press, 2003), 7–8. For a brief

response, see Melanie Rae Harsha, "These Signs Shall Follow: Endangered Pentecostal Practices in Appalachia" (master's thesis, Appalachian State University, 2015), 73–75.

23 Walter J. Hollenweger, *The Pentecostals: The Charismatic Movement in the Churches* (Augsburg Publishing House, 1972), 300.

24 La Barre, *They Shall Take Up Serpents*, vii.

25 La Barre, *They Shall Take Up Serpents*, vii–viii.

26 La Barre, *They Shall Take Up Serpents*, viii–ix.

27 Wayne Flynt, *Dixie's Forgotten People: The South's Poor Whites* (Indiana University Press, 2004), 156.

28 Exemptions for serpent-handlers in West Virginia's wildlife laws are an example of the persistence of tolerance there. See John McCoy, "Box Turtle, Rattlesnake Collection Would Be Outlawed Under WV's Proposed New Regulation," *WVNews*, March 21, 2020, https://www.wvnews.com/box-turtle-rattlesnake-collection-would-be-outlawed-under-wvs-proposed-new-regulation/article_dddb0e43-d480-5387-8f37-0b305574ae43.html.

29 Georgia General Assembly, "Acts and Resolutions of the General Assembly of the State of Georgia 1941 [volume 1]," Digital Library of Georgia, University of Georgia University Libraries, https://dlg.usg.edu/record/dlg_zlgl_179513495#text; Hood and Williamson, *Them That Believe*, 215.

30 See, for example, Danny Cevallos, "Snakes and Church vs. State," *CNN*, May 28, 2014, https://www.cnn.com/2014/02/26/opinion/cevallos-snake-handling-law; Robert W. Kerns Jr., "Article: Protecting the Faithful from Their Faith: A Proposal for Snake-Handling Law in West Virginia," *West Virginia Law Review* 116, no. 2 (2013), 561.

31 Tamara Tabo, "Snakes in a Church: Should the Law Protect the Religious Liberty of Serpent-Handlers?" *Above the Law*, November 14, 2013, https://abovethelaw.com/2013/11/snakes-in-a-church-should-the-law-protect-the-religious-liberty-of-serpent-handlers/. For a somewhat less snarky defense of serpent handler's religious freedom, see Matthew M. Ball, "Targeting Religion: Analyzing Appalachian Proscriptions on Religious Snake Handling," *Boston University Law Review* 95 (2015): 1425–1450.

32 As evidence of the persistence of this phrase or its close variants, see Carden and Pelton, *The Persecuted Prophets*, 72, and, thirty-six years later, "Andrew Hamblin, Young Snake Handler in Tennessee, Grasps the Power of Faith," *USA Today*, June 6, 2012, https://www.huffpost.com/entry/andrew-hamblin-snake-handler_n_1572528.

33 Here serpent handling may have an odd resonance with Orthodox Christianity, which, while radically different in many respects, emphasizes Christ's "trampling down death by death," or triumph over death itself, especially at Pascha (Easter). See Richard Beck, "The Snake Handling Churches of Appalachia: Conclusion, Snakebite, Death and Victory," *Experimental Theology* (blog), January 9, 2010, http://experimentaltheology.blogspot.com/2010/01/snake-handling-churches-of-appalachia_09.html.

34 Morrow, *Handling Serpents*, 150.

35 A close runner-up would be the mistaken notion that Holiness Pentecostals worship the snakes they handle.

36 Brown and McDonald, *The Serpent Handlers*, 68–69.

37 Quoted in Carden and Pelton, *The Persecuted Prophets*, 66.
38 Brown and McDonald, *The Serpent Handlers*, 60–61. A common criticism of serpent handling by other Christians in similar traditions invokes the biblical injunction against "testing" or "tempting" God, to which this passage in Judges is potentially a response.
39 Hood and Williamson, *Them That Believe*, 158.
40 For the music of serpent-handling churches, see Hood and Williamson, *Them That Believe*; Ferrill Gibbs and Abe Partridge, *Alabama Astronaut: The Podcast*, September 14, 2022, https://alabamaastronaut.com/.
41 Brown and McDonald, *The Serpent Handlers*, 37.
42 Lacan, *Seminar of Jacques Lacan, Book III*, 167. The other category Lacan discusses in this passage is the "trace," a sign that signifies the absence of a missing object, as a footprint does for a foot. The various symbols of serpent handling are "signs" rather than "traces" because, for the serpent-handlers, the things they represent (God, the Devil, etc.) are actually present.
43 Although now dated, Kenneth Paul Ambrose's survey-based research supports this position based on the percentage of serpent handlers declaring that every miracle in the Bible was true. Kenneth Paul Ambrose, "A Survey of the Snake-Handling Cult of West Virginia" (master's thesis, Marshall University, 1970), 77.
44 Hood and Williamson, *Them That Believe*, 2.
45 Another feasible textual response not discussed here comes from Fr. Lawrence Farley, who argues that the signs of Mark are a prophecy fulfilled by the Apostles, which is a position distinct from the insistence that miracles are no longer possible. See Fr. Lawrence Farley, "Snake Handling," *Orthodox Christianity*, July 14, 2020, https://orthochristian.com/132600.html.
46 Hood and Williamson, *Them That Believe*, 76.
47 Burton's term.
48 Morrow, *Handling Serpents*, 94. Serpent handler Elzie Preast also politely disagreed with La Barre's psychoanalytic sexual explanations for the faith. See Robert Kelvin Holliday, *Tests of Faith* (Fayette Tribune Inc., 1966), 66–67.
49 Morrow, *Handling Serpents*, 73.
50 Julia C. Duin, *In the House of the Serpent Handler: A Story of Faith and Fleeting Fame in the Age of Social Media* (University of Tennessee Press, 2017), 108.
51 Andrea Shan Johnson, review of *In the House of the Serpent Handler*, by Julia C. Duin, *Pneuma* 41, no. 1 (2019): 149–151.
52 Carden and Pelton, *The Persecuted Prophets*, 49.
53 Jim Birckhead, "Reading 'Snake Handling': Critical Reflections," in *Anthropology of Religion: A Handbook*, ed. Stephen D. Glazier (Praeger, 1997), 70.
54 Jim Birckhead, "'Bizarre Snake Handlers': Popular Media and a Southern Stereotype," in *Images of the South: Constructing a Regional Culture on Film and Video*, ed. Karl G. Heider (University of Georgia Press, 1993), 172. When I recently mentioned in passing that a research trip to Alabama was related to serpent handlers, an otherwise very thoughtful and humane undergraduate cheerfully declared that they were "stupid f-ckers."
55 *National Geographic*, "A Family Tradition | Snake Salvation," YouTube video, September 4, 2013, 2:01, https://www.youtube.com/watch?v=k1-BhaX5GSE.
56 William S. Tribell, "Last Film Footage of Pastor Jamie Coots," YouTube video, March 23, 2014, 9:16, https://www.youtube.com/watch?v=5f4NyYqHXa8.

57 Although I have not been able to locate the full episode, clips are available on YouTube. An example of her interaction with Chafin is available at https://www.youtube.com/watch?v=8wSLcFd_Z6c&t=7s.
58 The bit appears on multiple albums but is also available on YouTube: https://www.youtube.com/watch?v=6NUAo-TRvec. For evidence of Bagwell's sentiment, see Vance, *History of Serpent Handlers*, 9.
59 Anthony Davis, *Eat Around It*, directed by Sheryl Drozen (Uproar Entertainment, 2020). Transcription mine.
60 Although it should be noted that not every media story does so. The more recent the coverage and more mainstream the reporting entity, the more accurate serpent-handling coverage seems to be.
61 "'Snake Salvation' Church Killer Rattler Rises Again!'" *TMZ on TV*, February 24, 2014, https://www.tmz.com/2014/02/24/snake-salvation-church-cody-coots-rattlesnake-returns-video-tmz-tv/.
62 *The Young Turks*, "Dead Snake Handler's Son Does Exactly What You Shouldn't Do [VIDEO]," YouTube video, February 24, 2014, 4:41, https://www.youtube.com/watch?v=3UiPmmte2XE.
63 *The Young Turks*, "Son of Dead Snake-Bitten Preacher Gets—You Guessed It—Bitten by a Snake!" YouTube video, June 1, 2014, 2:05, https://www.youtube.com/watch?v=hF548tUhgaA.
64 Birckhead, "Reading 'Snake Handling,'" 21.
65 Vance, *History of Serpent Handlers*, 1.
66 Deborah Vansau McCauley, *Appalachian Mountain Religion: A History* (University of Illinois Press, 1995), 17–18.
67 Isabel Machado, "Revisiting *Deliverance*: The Sunbelt South, the 1970s Masculinity Crisis, and the Emergence of the Redneck Nightmare Genre," *Study the South*, June 19, 2017, https://southernstudies.olemiss.edu/study-the-south/revisiting-deliverance/. Jim Birkhead, quoted in Machado, specifically recounts an instance of *Deliverance* being conflated with serpent-handling Holiness worship. It should be noted, however, that the disparagement of "White trash" and its racial ambiguities does not dissolve the power of whiteness as a social signifier but potentially cements it through hypervisibility: See Eric King Watts, "Border Patrolling and 'Passing' in Eminem's *8 Mile*," *Critical Studies in Media Communication* 22 (2005): 187–206.
68 David M. Brown, "Film's Casting Call Wants That 'Inbred' Look," TribLive.com, February 26, 2008, https://archive.triblive.com/news/films-casting-call-wants-that-inbred-look/.
69 Wiley Cash, *A Land More Kind Than Home* (Harper Collins, 2013).
70 *Them That Follow*, directed by Britt Poulton and Dan Madison Savage (1091 Media, 2019).
71 *The Campaign*, directed by Jay Roach (Warner Brothers Pictures, 2012). The film includes a scene where Ferrell bursts through the window of a church after being bitten, which may be an intertextual reference to Wendy Bagwell's skit, which includes a bit about breaking out of a serpent-handling church.
72 Duin, *House of the Serpent Handler*.
73 *Holy Ghost People*, directed by Peter Adair (Thistle Films, 1967). For a recent critical analysis, see Kathryn Lofton, "Observational Secular: Religion and Documentary Film in the United States," *Journal of Cinema and Media Studies* 60, no. 5 (2021): 99–120.

74 *Holy Ghost People*, directed by Mitchell Altieri (XLrator Media, 2014).

75 John F. Day, *Bloody Ground* (University of Kentucky Press, 1981), 9.

76 William Sargant, *The Mind Possessed: A Physiology of Possession, Mysticism, and Faith Healing* (J. B. Lippincott Company, 1974), 187.

77 La Barre, *They Shall Take Up Serpents*, viii. Serpent-handling churches predate this window by at least a few decades.

78 La Barre, *They Shall Take Up Serpents*, 167.

79 La Barre, *They Shall Take Up Serpents*, 167–168. Also see La Barre, p. 17.

80 Matt Wray, *Not Quite White: White Trash and the Boundaries of Whiteness* (Duke University Press, 2006). Fitting with the stereotype of other rural Appalachian people, serpent handlers are sometimes assumed to be racist as well. Although a study of serpent handling and race would be fascinating, I am not aware of one. However, La Barre's observations of church services provide some evidence of explicit attempts at racial integration in serpent-handling churches at the height of segregation, including an anti-segregation sermon at a serpent-handling church in the early 1960s. Survey results published by Ambrose in 1970 indicated more favorable views of desegregation amongst serpent handlers than the general population of their area, an attitude that he notes was supported by deeds. Similar accounts of anti-segregation sermons and integrated worship are relayed by Archie Robertson as far back as the 1940s, and there is evidence for the historical existence of at least one Black serpent-handling congregation (in North Carolina) in contact with the larger community, plus threats by the Ku Klux Klan against White serpent handlers, reports (sometimes self-reports) of Indigenous and Hispanic ancestry or familial relations among serpent handlers over the past few decades, and visual evidence from videos of contemporary serpent-handling worship that appear to show several Black worshippers currently participating in church services and in some cases actually handling serpents. Perhaps most significantly, the first pastor selected in 1956 for the new church building at Jolo, West Virginia, which became one of the best-known serpent-handling churches, was a Black pastor named Winford Dickerson, who later went on to join the West Virginia Legislature. See La Barre, *They Shall Take Up Serpents*, 4–5, 163; Carden and Pelton, *The Persecuted Prophets*, 43; Brown and McDonald, *The Serpent Handlers*, 79; Hood and Williamson, *Them That Believe*, p. 264, n. 7; Ambrose, "Survey of the Snake-Handling Cult of West Virginia," 91, 94; Archie Robertson, *That Old-Time Religion* (Houghton Mifflin Co., 1950), 161, 177; Holliday, *Tests of Faith*, 48–49.

81 Michael Noel Reid, "Cobb Creek Church: Changing Perspectives in a Serpent-Handling Congregation in East Tennessee" (master's thesis, University of Tennessee, Knoxville, 2013), 77–78. Although my own psychoanalytic approach differs from La Barre's in many ways, I have still described serpent-handling literalism in the mold of Lacanian psychosis. The key distinction, however, is that I do so not to single out the group but to demonstrate that this strategy of reading cannot be normatively "pathological" because *all* communities have some element of psychotic reading as defined by essentially arbitrary standards of propriety, and what interests me is signification per se, not some hidden phallic meaning of the serpent, the quest for which is in itself psychotic.

82 Bart Ehrman, "Snake-Handling and the Gospel of Mark," *Bart Ehrman Blog: The History & Literature of Early Christianity*, February 20, 2014, https://ehrmanblog.org/snake-handling-gospel-mark/.

83 Brown and McDonald, *The Serpent Handlers*, 275.
84 Robertson, *That Old-Time Religion*, 172.
85 Morrow, *Handling Serpents*, 93.
86 Birckhead, "Reading 'Snake Handling,'" 63.
87 See Dana Cloud, "The Irony Bribe and Reality Television: Investment and Detachment in *The Bachelor*," *Critical Studies in Media Communication* 27, no. 5 (2010): 413–437.
88 Calum Lister Matheson, "Liberal Tears and the Rogue's Yarn of Sadistic Conservativism," *Rhetoric Society Quarterly* 52, no. 4 (2022): 341–355.
89 J. B. Collins, *The Tennessee Snake Handlers* (Chattanooga News-Free Press, 1947).
90 Matheson, "Liberal Tears," 352.
91 Georges Bataille, *Erotism: Death & Sensuality*, trans. Mary Dalwood (City Lights Books, 1986), 11–13. For a more thorough treatment of religious ritual and "intimacy," see Georges Bataille, *Theory of Religion*, trans. Robert Hurley (Zone Books, 1992).
92 Harry Crews, *A Feast of Snakes: A Novel* (Simon and Schuster, 1976).
93 Burton, *Serpent-Handling Believers*, 4–5.
94 For more on the desire for unmediated communication, see John Durham Peters, *Speaking into the Air: A History of the Idea of Communication* (University of Chicago Press, 1999).
95 Dennis Covington, *Salvation on Sand Mountain: Snake Handling and Redemption in Southern Appalachia* (Hachette Books, 1995), p. 168–170.
96 Kimbrough, *Taking Up Serpents*, 185.
97 Colleen Sexton, *Blind Faith: Serpent Handling in West Virginia: An Outsider's Look into an Inside World* (Page Publishing, 2015), p. 26.
98 Birckhead, "Reading 'Snake Handling,'" 35.
99 Duin, *House of the Serpent Handler*, 40, 53.
100 Heard and seen by the author during a performance at Partridge's art exhibit in Mobile, Alabama, January 21, 2023.
101 Birckhead, "Reading 'Snake Handling,'" 33.
102 Lacan, *Écrits*, 417.
103 The only defense I have discovered on the Internet plausibly written by an actual serpent handler is an already dated page entitled "Official Website of Holiness Serpent Handlers," archived March 11, 2023, at https://web.archive.org/web/20230311054148/https://holiness-snake-handlers.webs.com/.
104 Kimbrough, *Taking Up Serpents*, 190; Nathan L. Gerrard, "The Serpent-Handling Religions of West Virginia," in *Poor Americans: How the White Poor Live*, eds. Marc Pilisuk and Phyllis Pilisuk (Aldine Publishing Company, 1971).
105 Lacan, *The Seminar of Jacques Lacan, Book XX: Encore*, trans. by Bruce Fink, ed. Jacques-Allain Miller (W. W. Norton, 1998), 13. Italics in original.
106 See, for example, Duin, *House of the Serpent Handler*, 60.
107 Birckhead, "'Bizarre Snake Handlers,'" 165.
108 Tidball and Toumey, "Signifying Serpents," 2.
109 For example, Duin, *House of the Serpent Handler*; Lauren Pond, *Test of Faith: Signs, Serpents, Salvation* (Duke University Press, 2017).
110 Duin, *House of the Serpent Handler*, 117, 134–135. Being treated as outcasts may also create a self-fulfilling prophecy when it comes to serpent handlers refusing medical care for bites: I have heard anecdotally of medical personnel mocking

victims who are bitten by snakes in church to such an extent that they vow not to seek emergency help in future. Also see Brown and McDonald, *The Serpent Handlers*, 187.

111 See the interviews in *Alabama Astronaut*.

112 Birckhead, "Reading 'Snake Handling,'" 68.

Chapter 3 Pro-Ana

1 Nathan Stormer, "An Appetite for Rhetoric," *Philosophy & Rhetoric* 48, no. 1 (2015), 101–102.

2 Elaine Scarry, *The Body in Pain: The Making and Unmaking of the World* (Oxford University Press, 1985).

3 Katherine Dee, "Pro-Anorexia Is the Nexus of All Online Communities," *default.blog*, October 22, 2021, https://default.blog/p/is-anorexia-is-the-nexus-of-all-online/comments.

4 Emma Seaber, "Reading Disorders: Pro-Eating Disorder Rhetoric and Anorexia Life-Writing," *Literature and Medicine* 34, no. 2 (2016): 484–508. Abigail Bray previously criticized the notion of anorexia as a "reading disorder," describing the notion that women "contract psychiatric diseases from television" as "science fiction." Seaber's usage of the term "reading disorder," which I follow here, does not assume that anorexics are passive readers (or exclusively women). Like both Seaber and Bray, I seek not to pathologize these communities or even "explain" individual anorexia but rather to better understand the cultural contexts that shape and influence them. See Abigail Bray, "The Anorexic Body: Reading Disorders," *Cultural Studies* 10, no. 3 (1996): 413–429.

5 Maud Ellmann, *The Hunger Artists: Starving, Writing & Imprisonment* (Virago Press, 1993), 3. Again, although anorexia cannot be reduced to pure signification, the object of study here is the mediated discourse that forms pro-ana communities, which are distinct.

6 Emmanuelle Desbordes, "Anorexia, Anxiety, and the Object," *The Psychoanalytic Review* 101, no. 4 (2007), 572.

7 See, for example, Blazej Meczekalski et al., "Long-Term Consequences of Anorexia Nervosa," *Maturitas* 75, no. 3 (July 2013): 215–220.

8 Sharon K. Farber et al., "Death and Annihilation Anxieties in Anorexia Nervosa, Bulimia, and Self-Mutilation," *Psychoanalytic Psychology* 24, no. 2 (2007): 289–305.

9 Kelsey Osgood, *How to Disappear Completely: On Modern Anorexia* (Overlook Duckworth, 2013), 89.

10 Osgood, *How to Disappear Completely*, 29.

11 I have chosen not to cite individual accounts on social media in this section unless they are particularly influential (e.g., Eugenia Cooney). Doing so risks overemphasizing the importance of obscure posters and encourages cherry-picking. The experience of navigating pro-ana content cannot be conveyed in citation anyway: Part of the effect is the endless progression of scrolling, which users can simulate for themselves. My claims about the structure of feeling on Tumblr and other sites can be checked by searching for pro-ana tags, if necessary, such as *thinspo, ana, pro-mia, proana, meanspo, malespo*, etc., including many variants designed to avoid social media filters.

12 Seaber, "Reading Disorders," 501.

13 Emma Seaber, "Occult Anorexia: The Unseen Forces of Anorexia Life-Writing" (PhD diss., King's College London, 2021), https://kclpure.kcl.ac.uk/portal/en/studentTheses/occult-anorexia.

14 Laura Stampler, "Inside Pinterest's Frightening Pro-Anorexia 'Thinspo' Cult," *Business Insider*, March 22, 2012, https://www.businessinsider.com/inside-pinterests-frightening-pro-anorexia-thinspo-cult-2012-3. Images in this article are a good sample of early 2010s "thinspiration" (*thinspo*).

15 Suku Sukunesan et al., "Examining the Pro-Eating Disorders Community on Twitter via the Hashtag #proana: Statistical Modeling Approach," *JMIR Mental Health* 8, no. 7 (July 2021), article e24340, https://doi.org/10.2196/24340.

16 Debbie Ging and Sarah Garvey, "'Written in These Scars Are the Stories I Can't Explain': A Content Analysis of Pro-Ana and Thinspiration Image Sharing on Instagram," *New Media & Society* 20, no. 3 (March 2018): 1181–1200.

17 CT Jones, "Eating Disorders Are Getting Worse. Is It Social Media's Fault?" *Rolling Stone*, November 1, 2024, https://www.rollingstone.com/culture/culture-features/eating-disorder-social-media-liv-schmidt-1235150121/.

18 Center for Countering Digital Hate, "Deadly By Design," December 2022, https://counterhate.com/research/deadly-by-design/; Tawnell D. Hobbs et al., "'The Corpse Bride Diet': How TikTok Inundates Teens with Eating-Disorder Videos," *Wall Street Journal*, December 17, 2021, https://www.wsj.com/articles/how-tiktok-inundates-teens-with-eating-disorder-videos-11639754848?reflink=desktopwebshare_permalink; Decca Muldowney, "TikTok Slammed for 'Doing Nothing' over Pro-Anorexia Content," *The Daily Beast*, March 3, 2023, https://www.thedailybeast.com/tiktok-slammed-for-doing-nothing-over-pro-anorexia-content-by-center-for-countering-digital-hate.

19 Cooney briefly discussed having had inpatient rehabilitation for an eating disorder in a video made by Shane Dawson, although the degree to which she avoids the topic when it is raised by followers is conspicuous.

20 Describing her experience on these sites, Lena Ma writes that "hundreds of Pro-Ana forums have been taken down, but more only pop up in their place." Lena Ma, *Shamefully Vanished: A Memoir of a Girl Out of Control* (independently published, 2020), 45.

21 This remains true in modern memoirs. See, for example, Nicole Lynn's many seductive photos in her memoir *Pink Poison: A Memoir of Anorexia Nervosa* (independently published, 2019).

22 See Calum Lister Matheson, "A Child Is Being Trafficked: The Figuration of Child Abuse and Desire in Right-Wing Extremist Discourses," in *Pleasure and Pain in U.S. Public Culture*, eds. Christopher J. Gilbert and John Louis Lucaites (University of Alabama Press, 2025).

23 Texts and images are overlapping and mutually constituting categories in these discourses. On "imagetexts" in pro-ana communities, see Robin E. Jensen, "The Eating Disordered Lifestyle: Imagetexts and the Performance of Similitude," *Argumentation & Advocacy* 42, no. 1 (2005): 1–18.

24 Osgood, *How to Disappear Completely*, 212. For examples, see Marya Hornbacher, *Wasted: A Memoir of Anorexia and Bulimia* (Harper Perennial, 2014); Andrijka Keller, *Thin, and I: A Memoir* (CreateSpace Independent Publishing, 2018).

25 Seaber, "Reading Disorders," 485–486.

26 Seaber, "Reading Disorders," 488.

27 Seaber, "Reading Disorders," 490. This "disordered reading" is evident in discussions about literature in anorexia memoirs, which themselves are read along these same lines. This resembles the hermeneutics of serpent-handling churches, in which the protocols for reading the Bible are fully contained in the text itself.

28 Emily T. Troscianko, "Literary Reading and Eating Disorders: Survey Evidence of Therapeutic Help and Harm," *Journal of Eating Disorders* 6, no. 8 (2018), https://doi.org/10.1186/s40337-018-0191-5.

29 Emily T. Troscianko, "Fiction-Reading for Good or Ill: Eating Disorders, Interpretation and the Case for Creative Bibliotherapy Research," *Medical Humanities* 44, no. 3 (2018), 202.

30 For a discussion of the denial of rhetorical agency to anorexic subjects through the assertion of a deficit, see Stephanie R. Larson, "The Rhetoricity of Fat Stigma: Mental Disability, Pain, and Anorexia Nervosa," *Rhetoric Society Quarterly* 51, no. 5 (2021), 396. As explained in the Introduction, my approach here is that all subjects have psychotic attachments to some symbols, which are only presented as deficits when they violate a hegemonic sense of propriety. No one is normal, we are all pathological, and we are all deficient, but the classificatory aspects of power conceal the universality of our shared deficits for those it elevates.

31 Michele Mason, *Annihilating Anorexia: A Memoir* (The Paper House Publishing, 2023).

32 Jen Dixon, *Bones: Anorexia, OCD, and Me* (JD Associates, 2023), 331.

33 Keller, *Thin, and I*, 2.

34 Brittany Burgunder, *Safety in Numbers: From 56 to 221 Pounds, My Battle with Eating Disorders* (Wheatmark, 2016), 406.

35 Karyn Stapleton et al., "Ana as God: Religion, Interdiscursivity and Identity on Pro-Ana Websites," *Discourse and Communication* 13, no. 3 (2019): 320–341. Also see Nadja Breneisson, "I Spent a Week Undercover in a Pro-Anorexia WhatsApp Group," *VICE*, July 8, 2015, https://www.vice.com/en/article/vdx7ex/i-spent-a-week-in-a-pro-ana-whatsapp-group-talking-to-the-goddess-of-emaciation-876.

36 Seaber, "Reading Disorders," 501.

37 Melissa Espinoza, *My Life, as Told by Anorexia: Essays from the Deep* (Amazon Digital Services, 2023), 12.

38 Burgunder, *Safety in Numbers*, 8.

39 This reliance on stable terms to ward off dissolution responds to a surplus of meaning, an excess that can overwhelm the subject, as much as it stabilizes the sense of individual identity against an empty void. In this way, the language of anorexia only intensifies the more general function of language to limit out surplus meaning. We are all in a sense restrictors defending against too much meaning even as we seek our own gluttonous contact with the pure excess of the Real.

40 Center for Countering Digital Hate, "AI and Eating Disorders: How Generative AI Enables and Promotes Harmful Eating Disorder Content," August 7, 2023, https://counterhate.com/research/ai-tools-and-eating-disorders/.

41 Carlo Lai et al., "Why People Join Pro-Ana Online Communities? A Psychological Textual Analysis of Eating Disorder Blog Posts," *Computers in Human Behavior* 124 (2021), article no. 106922, https://doi.org/10.1016/j.chb.2021.106922.

42 Burgunder, *Safety in Numbers*, 259.

43 Kerry McGregor et al., "Disordered Eating and Considerations for the Transgender Community: A Review of the Literature and Clinical Guidance for

Assessment and Treatment," *Journal of Eating Disorders* 11, article no. 75 (2023), https://doi.org/10.1186/s40337-023-00793-0; Sofie M. Rasmussen et al., "Eating Disorder Symptomatology Among Transgender Individuals: A Systematic Review and Meta-Analysis," *Journal of Eating Disorders* 11, article no. 84 (2023), https://www.ncbi.nlm.nih.gov/pmc/articles/PMC10214585/.

44 "Thinspo and Gender Goals: Musing on Two Internet Subcultures," *Hormone Hangover* (SubStack), October 31, 2021, https://hormonehangover.substack.com/p/thinspo-and-gender-goals.

45 Kai Schweizer, "Eating Disorders as DIY Medical Transition: An Interview with Katherine Dee," *default.blog*, January 19, 2022, https://default.blog/p/diy-medical-transition-and-eating?utm_source=publication-search.

46 See Seaber's extended critique of this notion in "Occult Anorexia."

47 See Jensen, "The Eating Disordered Lifestyle."

48 ~Goddess Annea~, "Please Read Before Making a 'Guess My BMI' Post," *ED Support Forum*, August 30, 2022, https://www.edsupportforum.com/threads/please-read-before-making-a-guess-my-bmi-post.4433232/. There are many good reasons to limit access to photographs of users' bodies besides the fear of deplatforming, including the prevalence of grooming and unwanted sexual attention primarily by nonanorexic men. See Emma Simmons et al., "Pro-Anorexia Coaches Prey on Individuals with Eating Disorders," *International Journal of Eating Disorders* 57, no. 1 (2024): 124–131. This is another reason I have avoided linking even anonymous social media posts.

49 Carrie Arnold and Spectrum, "Is There a Link Between Autism and Anorexia?" *The Atlantic*, February 18, 2016, https://www.theatlantic.com/health/archive/2016/02/anorexia-and-autism/463233/.

50 This represents a shift in media capacities and habits coinciding with the rise of social media—celebrity thinspo certainly made up a greater proportion of pro-ana content before image sharing was as easy as it is today.

51 Burgunder, *Safety in Numbers*, 26.

52 Su Holmes, "(Un)twisted: Talking Back to Media Representations of Eating Disorders," *Journal of Gender Studies* 27, no. 2 (2018): 149–164. Holmes, following Bray, criticizes the notion of anorexia as a "reading disorder" as pathologizing but, as explained above, I read the theory thus critiqued as distinct from what Seaber describes as a "reading disorder."

53 Su Holmes, "Talking Back: Responding to Media Images of Eating Disorders," Department of Film, Television, and Media Studies at the University of East Anglia Blog, July 31, 2015, https://filmtelevisionmediauea.wordpress.com/2015/07/31/talking-back-responding-to-media-images-of-eating-disorders/.

54 Carrie Arnold, "Let Me Repeat Myself: The Media Doesn't Cause EDs," *ED Bites*, March 6, 2013, archived October 29, 2013, at https://web.archive.org/web/20131029024435/http://edbites.com/2013/03/let-me-repeat-myself-the-media-doesnt-cause-eds/.

55 Emily Troscianko, "Taking, Losing, and Letting Go of Control in Anorexia," *Psychology Today*, October 24, 2023, https://www.psychologytoday.com/us/blog/a-hunger-artist/201508/taking-losing-and-letting-go-of-control-in-anorexia.

56 Domenico Cosenza, *A Lacanian Reading of Anorexia*, trans. Jonathan West (Routledge, 2024), 27. It would have made more sense for the labels "anorexia" (*an-* "without," *orexis* "appetite") and "bulimia" (*bous* "ox," *limos* "hunger") to be switched, as anorexics have an insatiable appetite for nothing and bulimics expel what they desire rather than keeping it.

57 Cosenza, *Lacanian Reading of Anorexia*, 111.
58 In Lacanian theory this is true of any object since, whatever it is, it stands in for an ideal *objet petit a* that would fill the lack but does not exist—as a result, desire is always without end as long as a subject exists, but the unique character of anorexic attachments may still tell us something novel about desire, as the rest of this section will hopefully demonstrate.
59 Kate Taylor, "Introduction," in *Going Hungry: Writers on Desire, Self-Denial, and Overcoming Anorexia*, ed. Kate Taylor (Anchor Books, 2008), xiii. Emphasis in original.
60 Cosenza, *Lacanian Reading of Anorexia*, 31.
61 Body checking also brings to mind various symptoms of bodily disintegration experienced by some psychotic subjects, reinforcing the case (which Cosenza advances) that anorexia sometimes overlaps with psychosis.
62 Cosenza, *Lacanian Reading of Anorexia*, 95.
63 Osgood, *How to Disappear Completely*, 68; Cosenza, *Lacanian Reading of Anorexia*, 67.
64 Cosenza, *Lacanian Reading of Anorexia*, 26.
65 Anna Shechtman, "Escaping into the Crossword Puzzle," *The New Yorker*, December 20, 2021, https://www.newyorker.com/magazine/2021/12/27/escaping-into-the-crossword-puzzle.
66 Shechtman, "Escaping." Metonymy is Lacan's favored description for the connections that psychotic subjects make to the exclusion of metaphor, which makes this description consistent with that mode of attachment despite its rhetorical terminology (Shechtman mentions Lacan in passing, although not in this connection).
67 Desire, as discussed below, is what a subject wants surplus to need. Someone *needs* food to survive, but *desires* a full Scottish breakfast, for example. Attachment to this surplus is what distinguishes sexuality from reproduction, among other things.
68 Cosenza, *Lacanian Reading of Anorexia*, 99.
69 Cosenza, *Lacanian Reading of Anorexia*, 98.
70 On perversion, see Gunn, *Political Perversion*; Dany Nobus, *The Law of Desire: On Lacan's "Kant with Sade"* (Springer, 2017); Stephanie S. Swales, *Perversion: A Lacanian Psychoanalytic Approach to the Subject* (Routledge, 2012).
71 For the relationship between feminine beauty standards and anti-Black racism, see Sabrina Strings, *Fearing the Black Body: The Racial Origins of Fat Phobia* (NYU Press, 2019).
72 Burke, Language as Symbolic Action, 16.
73 Leslie Heywood, *Dedication to Hunger: The Anorexic Aesthetic in Modern Culture* (University of California Press, 1996), 144.
74 For an example of work that does move in this direction, see Gherovici's, *Transgender Psychoanalysis*. Matthew Lovett has recently explicated the critique of Lacanian transphobia, focusing on the work of Slavoj Žižek and Jacques Allain Miller, while indicating the potential for a mutually beneficial intersection of trans studies and psychoanalysis. See Matthew Lovett, "Lacanian Anxieties: Trans Surgeries, Countertransference, and the Fantasy of the Whole," *Transgender Studies Quarterly* 11, no. 3 (2024): 458–480.
75 As his followers would elaborate in more detail, "men" and "women" were not biological categories for Lacan, and "phallus" does not mean "penis."

76 This description of Lacan's theory of masculine and feminine desire condenses Lacan, *Seminar of Jacques Lacan, Book XX*. See also Colette Soler, *What Lacan Said About Women*; Zupančič, *What Is Sex?*

77 Soler, *What Lacan Said About Women*, 18.

78 See the discussion of Bataille's *Erotism* in chapter 2.

79 Osgood, *How to Disappear Completely*, 29.

80 Katie Engelhart, "Should Patients Be Allowed to Die from Anorexia?" *New York Times Magazine*, January 3, 2024, https://www.nytimes.com/2024/01/03/magazine/palliative-psychiatry.html.

81 Cosenza, *Lacanian Reading of Anorexia*, 69.

82 Incidentally, the fluidity of sexual and gender identities among pro-ana community members is evidence that "psychosis" is a protocol for reading applied to some signifiers and not all—ultimately rhetorical attitudes of ambiguity, fluidity, and uncertainty about gender and/or sex may coexist with rigid, oracular readings of food, hunger, and thinness that broadly coincide with the structural aspects of psychosis. There would be no need for this book or any of the intersecting fields from which it draws if people were not complex.

83 Paul B. Preciado, *Can the Monster Speak? Report to an Academy of Psychoanalysts*, trans. Frank Wynne (Semiotext(e), 2021), 93–94.

84 See Lovett's analysis of Žižek and Miller.

85 Preciado, *Can the Monster Speak?* 81.

86 Rogers, *Incandescent Alphabets*, 121.

87 Zupančič, *What Is Sex?* 57.

88 Alenka Zupančič, "Why Is Sexual Difference Relevant for Philosophy?" Lecture at Carnegie Lecture Hall, Carnegie Museums of Pittsburgh, November 11, 2017. The string *LGBTQIA* may conflate sex, gender, and sexuality, but I read Zupančič's claim to be that all of these categories can be understood as reflexive performance conditioned by our various discursive communities.

89 Zupančič, *What Is Sex?* 7. Emphasis in original.

90 The existence of asexual and aromantic subjects is an issue that post-Freudian psychoanalysis has yet to fully confront. See Kevin Murphy, *Asexuality and Freudian-Lacanian Psychoanalysis: Towards a Theory of an Enigma* (Routledge, 2023). Murphy's discussion of asexuality and the "eating of nothing" (159) intersects with Cosenza's understanding of anorexia.

91 Sigmund Freud, *The Psychology of Love*, trans. Shaun Whiteside (Penguin, 2007), 118.

92 Freud, *Psychology of Love*, 128. See Cosenza, cited above, on the "orgasm" of hunger in anorexia.

93 Freud, *Psychology of Love*, 127.

94 See Dominique Laporte, *History of Shit*, trans. Nadia Benabid and Rodolphe el-Khoury (MIT Press, 2000).

95 In choosing a Greek myth I do not mean to suggest the universal cultural relevance of this tradition as Freud seems to do, merely to choose an example that particularly resonates with me as an auto-diagnosis of the aspirationally global neoliberal culture that grows partly out of a classical European tradition. Kahn-Tineta Horn has reappropriated "Windigo psychosis," a colonialist "culture-bound syndrome" supposedly involving cannibalistic delusions, as a descriptor of settler greed and genocide. See kahntineta, "Boogie Men," *Mohawk*

Nation News, March 14, 2013, https://mohawknationnews.com/blog/2013/03/14/boogie-men/; James B. Waldram, *Revenge of the Windigo: The Construction of the Mind and Mental Health of North American Aboriginal Peoples* (University of Toronto Press, 2004).

96 I have synthesized this account from ancient sources, relying primarily on Ovid despite my use of the original Greek epithets.

97 This concept is discussed more fully in the next chapter.

98 Similarities and differences between "anorexia nervosa" and "anorexia mirabilis" have been widely noted elsewhere. See, for example, Walter Vandereycken and Ron van Deth, *From Fasting Saints to Anorexic Girls: The History of Self-Starvation* (The Athlone Press, 1994); Rudolph M. Bell, *Holy Anorexia* (University of Chicago Press, 1985).

99 Evagrios the Solitary, "Texts on Discrimination in Respect of Passions and Thoughts," in *The Philokalia: The Complete Text*, vol. 1, eds. G.E.H. Palmer et al. (Farrar, Straus and Giroux, 1979), 38.

100 St. John Cassian, "On the Eight Vices," in *The Philokalia*, vol. 1, eds. G.E.H. Palmer et al., 74.

Chapter 4 Reactionary Science

1 For a critique of "toxic fandom" as a metaphor, see Max Dosser, "I'm Gonna Wreck It, Again: The False Dichotomy of 'Healthy' and 'Toxic' Masculinity in *Ralph Breaks the Internet*," *Critical Studies in Media Communication* 39, no. 4 (2022): 333–346.

2 For a discussion of the rhetoric of *Rick and Morty*, see Joseph Packer and Ethan Stoneman, *A Feeling of Wrongness: Pessimistic Rhetoric on the Fringes of Popular Culture* (Pennsylvania State University Press, 2018).

3 Throughout this chapter I have capitalized Science when referring to the signifier rather than to "science" as a field of knowledge or collection of protocols for inquiry.

4 See, for example, works on disinformation citing Naomi Oreskes and Erik M. Conway, *Merchants of Doubt: How a Handful of Scientists Obscured the Truth on Issues from Tobacco Smoke to Global Warming* (Bloomsbury, 2010).

5 There is not, however, a single scientific method. See Naomi Oreskes, *Why Trust Science?* (Princeton University Press, 2019).

6 The capacity of unconscious occupations to warp scientific outcomes even when relatively good procedures are followed is particularly well documented in the case of race science, as discussed in a later section. See Stephen Jay Gould, *The Mismeasure of Man*, revised and expanded (W. W. Norton, 1996).

7 Lacan, *Écrits*, 742.

8 Lacan, *Seminar of Jacques Lacan, Book III*, 149. Emphasis in original.

9 Lacan, *Écrits*, 742.

10 See, for example, the r/IncelTear subreddit.

11 My thinking on this point is influenced by Karen E. Fields and Barbara J. Fields, *Racecraft: The Soul of Inequality in American Life* (Verso, 2012). The biological consensus that race is not a natural category is explained by Jonathan Marks, Stephen Jay Gould, and Angela Saini, cited below.

12 For a more complete discussion of race, identity, and desire, see Kaplana Seshadri-Crooks, *Desiring Whiteness: A Lacanian Analysis of Race* (Routledge, 2000);

Sheldon George, *Trauma and Race: A Lacanian Study of African American Racial Identity* (Baylor University Press, 2016).

13 I also tend to use the term *White supremacist* instead of *White nationalist*, as this more accurately captures the ideology of the discursive community I discuss here.

14 For a history and critique of the *DSM*, see Gary Greenberg, *The Book of Woe: The DSM and the Unmaking of Psychiatry* (Penguin Group, 2013).

15 Lacan, *Écrits*, 413. Italics in original.

16 For more on Lacan's treatment of the letter in this essay, see Matheson, "Instance of the Letter."

17 Lacan, *Écrits*, 21. Emphasis in original.

18 Lacan, *Écrits*, 413.

19 Matheson, "Psychotic Discourse," 194.

20 Lacan, *Écrits*, 430.

21 This can be seen in the I/me distinction in English: *I* want, *I* demand, *I* love; give it to *me*, listen to *me*, love *me*. "I" is the speaking subject, like Freud's *id*, and "me" is the self as it relates to others (what Freud called the "I" and is generally translated as *ego*).

22 Kenneth Burke, *The Philosophy of Literary Form* (University of California Press, 1973), 110–11.

23 Marilyn Colaninno, "Today's Hot Topic: The White Coat Rule," ReedSmith .com, May 2, 2013, https://www.reedsmith.com/en/perspectives/2013/05/todays -hot-topic--the-white-coat-rule.

24 Jim Taylor, "The Woman Who Founded the 'Incel' Movement," *BBC*, August 29, 2018, https://www.bbc.com/news/world-us-canada-45284455.

25 William Costello et al., "Levels of Well-Being Among Men Who Are Incel (Involuntarily Celibate)," *Evolutionary Psychological Science* 8 (2022): 375–390.

26 Incels.is appears to be the largest, longest running, and highest engagement incel forum still active, and it is therefore my primary resource for incel culture, although other platforms exist, including a number of subreddits.

27 Nearly all the terminology in this section can be found on the Incel Wiki at https://incel.wiki/w/Main_Page.

28 See "Blackpill," "Scientific Blackpill," and "Scientific Blackpill (Supplemental)" on incel.wiki; see also the subreddit "Black Pill Science," archived at https://old .reddit.com/r/BlackPillScience/.

29 There is sometimes a contradiction in this line of thought as women are portrayed as stone-cold rational actors on the one hand and overly emotional on the other.

30 For a comprehensive study of the black pill, misogyny, and fascism in incel ideology from a psychoanalytic-rhetorical perspective, see Kelly, *Apocalypse Man*.

31 "A Few Millimeters of Bone," Knowyourmeme.com, October 27, 2017, accessed June 1, 2024, https://knowyourmeme.com/memes/millimeters-of-bone.

32 [Lukas] Castle. *The Blackpill Theory: Why Incels Are Right & You Are Wrong* (independently published, 2019), 234.

33 Andrew S. Curran, *The Anatomy of Blackness: Science and Slavery in an Age of Enlightenment* (Johns Hopkins University Press, 2011).

34 Gould, *The Mismeasure of Man*, 82–101.

35 Jonathan Marks, *Is Science Racist?* (Polity, 2017).

36 Aaron Panofsky and Joan Donovan, "Genetic Ancestry Testing Among White Nationalists: From Identity Repair to Citizen Science," *Social Studies in Science* 49, no. 5 (2019): 653–681. The Daily Stormer is aimed at a younger, more

Internet-hip crowd but does not tend to provoke sustained discussion about race and science on its own site. As it is for nearly all contemporary reactionary content, 4chan is a major locus of racial realism. Other sites include White Aryan Resistance (WAR, at resist.com), American Renaissance (amren.com), and the Colchester Collection of White books (colchestercollection.com).

37 See, for example, humanbiologicaldiversity.com, which contains an immense (if dated) set of links to race science resources.

38 Angela Saini, *Superior: The Return of Race Science* (Beacon Press, 2019), 70.

39 Marks, *Is Science Racist?* 7.

40 Marks, *Is Science Racist?* 42.

41 See, for example, Society for Nordish Physical Anthropology, "The Society for Nordish Physical Anthropology (SNPA)," July 23, 2006, accessed June 5, 2024, https://www.theapricity.com/snpa/index2.htm.

42 "Anthropology Enthusiasts." Stormfront web community, accessed June 5, 2024, https://www.stormfront.org/forum/group.php?groupid=147.

43 See, for example, Richard D. Fuerle, Erectus *Walks Among Us* (Spooner Press, 2008).

44 Other physical characteristics also show up, notably Black penises, an enduring interest among White supremacists from Louis Agassiz to John Philippe Rushton.

45 Iselin Gambert and Tobias Linné, "How the Alt-Right Uses Milk to Promote White Supremacy," *The Conversation*, April 18, 2018, https://theconversation.com/how-the-alt-right-uses-milk-to-promote-white-supremacy-94854.

46 Andrea Freeman, "Milk, a Symbol of Neo-Nazi Hate," *The Conversation*, August 30, 2017, https://theconversation.com/milk-a-symbol-of-neo-nazi-hate-83292.

47 Alex Swerdloff, "Got Milk? Neo-Nazi Trolls Sure as Hell Do," *VICE*, February 21, 2017, https://www.vice.com/en/article/kbka39/got-milk-neo-nazi-trolls-sure-as-hell-do.

48 Gould distinguishes between racist skull measurements aimed at general intelligence and the more disparate attributes supposedly measured in phrenology, but because the latter is sometimes invoked, it is worthwhile to know that it has been recently subjected to modern scientific inquiry and found wanting in a study that also contains an interesting argument for the value of empirically testing even outmoded pseudoscience. See Oiwi Parker Jones et al., "An Empirical, 21st Century Evaluation of Phrenology," *Cortex* 106 (September 2018): 26–35.

49 The consensus on Stormfront seems to be that only people with entirely European, non-Jewish ancestry count as "White," so any admixture disqualifies one from the race. See John Law, "Who's White?" *White Hot Radio Podcast*, November 3, 2006, https://www.stormfront.org/forum/t579652/.

50 Perhaps what is foreclosed by these White supremacists is precisely the truth identified by Fields and Fields in *Racecraft*: There is no truth to race prior to racism. The consequence of there being a lack of objective foundation for race is therefore unbearable, not the consequences of racial difference, which presuppose that race is real. Confronting the hollowness of race would dissolve the foundations of Whiteness and its attendant supremacism, exposing the kind of aporetic violence Derrida identified in "Force of Law" as the only explanation for racial inequalities, which could no longer be the product of natural order. In other words, the absence of race makes the individual subjects of White supremacism exceptional in no way other than their cruelty. See Jacques Derrida, "Force of Law: The 'Mystical Foundation of Authority,'" in *Deconstruction and the Possibility of Justice*, ed. Drucilla Cornell, et al. (Routledge, 1992), 1–67.

51 In Lacanian terms anxiety is the affect produced when the *fort-da* mechanism of fantasy breaks down and its object looms too close. For more on anxiety and White nationalism, see E. Chebrolu, "The Racial Lens of Dylann Roof: Racial Anxiety and White Nationalist Rhetoric on New Media," *Review of Communication* 20, no. 1 (2020): 47–68. Ed: I mean "affect" as in force that is a precursor to emotion," not "effect."

52 See Panofsky and Donovan, "Genetic Ancestry Testing."

53 Izz Scott LaMagdeleine, "Michelle Obama Isn't a Trans Woman. Here's Why Some People Believe Otherwise," Snopes.com, October 17, 2023, https://www.snopes.com/news/2023/10/17/michelle-obama-is-trans/.

54 InfoWars, "'Is Michelle Obama a Man?'—The Alex Jones Channel—2014," uploaded to Rumble by Info Worm, July 10, 2014, https://rumble.com/v3mkhxa-is-michelle-obama-a-man-the-alex-jones-channel-2014.html. Jones has repeated this claim in detail over the years—see following note.

55 Michele Theil, "Conspiracy Theorist Claims Michelle Obama Is Transgender and We're so Very, Very Tired," *Pink News*, January 7, 2020, https://www.thepinknews.com/2020/01/07/michelle-obama-alex-jones-conspiracy-theory-infowars-debunked-first-lady/.

56 See, for example, Testimony of the Two Witnesses, "IRREFUTABLE PROOF that Serena Williams IS A MAN (mirrored)," YouTube video, 26:43, February 25, 2015, https://www.youtube.com/watch?v=WqVdGV-N9wo.

57 These examples are drawn from a series of posts in a public Facebook group called "Transvestigation Disclosure NOW—Candid!" https://www.facebook.com/groups/1233124250960776/?hoisted_section_header_type=recently_seen&multi_permalinks=1435885507351315. My general approach in this chapter has been to rely more on representative content as a guide to finding additional content, rather than an exhaustive citation of transvestigation creative material. The user experience of transvestigation relies partly on immersion in a stream of images and videos that are individually unmemorable but accumulate into a distinct ecology of paranoia, which makes citation of any particular post or image insufficient to uphold the overall experience. Where possible, I have cited journalistic sources that reproduce and aggregate this content effectively for anyone wanting to familiarize themselves with the community without full immersion. An added benefit to this approach is that media articles document ephemeral content that might otherwise disappear or be rendered inaccessible by changed account settings. Where I do cite transvestigation content directly, I have chosen only to cite publicly available content.

58 These examples are drawn from a series of posts on a public Facebook group called "Famous Transgender Disclosure Transvestigation Transhumanism Transformers," https://www.facebook.com/groups/894093204681787/. Taylor Swift is also alleged here to be a clone of Zeena Schreck, daughter of Church of Satan founder Anton LaVey, but that separate thread more closely resembles the Fregoli delusion, analyzed in chapter 1.

59 An example is Sandra Martha T, who posted a YouTube video that has been removed for violating YouTube's Terms of Service: "Michael May Not Be the First Tranny in W House Part 2," November 20, 2016.

60 Patrick Lenton, "A Wild Investigation of Transvestigators, the People Who Think Celebs Are All Trans," *VICE*, February 8, 2024, https://www.vice.com/en/article

/jg54kd/a-wild-investigation-of-transvestigators-the-people-who-think-celebs-are-all-trans.

61 Heyden Vernon, "The Conspiracy Theorists Who Think All Celebrities Are Secretly Trans," *VICE*, September 21, 2023, https://www.vice.com/en/article/3ak5wk/conspiracy-theorists-believe-all-celebrities-are-secretly-trans.

62 George Chauncey Jr., "From Sexual Inversion to Homosexuality: Medicine and the Changing Conceptualization of Female Deviance," *Salmagundi* no. 58/59 (Fall/Winter 1982/1983): 114–146.

63 Stuart Clarke, "Inversion, Misrule and the Meaning of Witchcraft," *Past and Present* no. 87 (May 1980): 98–127.

64 Jules Gill-Peterson, "From Gender Critical to QAnon: Anti-Trans Politics and the Laundering of Conspiracy," *The New Inquiry*, September 13, 2021, https://thenewinquiry.com/from-gender-critical-to-qanon-anti-trans-politics-and-the-laundering-of-conspiracy/.

65 For example, The Son of Man, https://twitter.com/TheSon071468392. This appears to be the same user who goes by "Poncho Pete" on other platforms.

66 For example, nexwex011, https://www.tiktok.com/@nexwex011, accessed April 21, 2025. Much of this content is backed up on YouTube at https://www.youtube.com/channel/UCLUFidvWlVtjhulAWwsM9Dg.

67 Miles Klee, "Unhinged 'Transvestigators' Think They're the Only Cis People Left," *Mel Magazine*, July 18, 2022, https://melmagazine.com/en-us/story/transvestigator-celebrity-conspiracy-theories.

68 See, for example, Banned.Videos, "TRANSVESTIGATION 101," Bitchute.com, January 23, 2023, https://www.bitchute.com/video/kv7ActvYQvyN/.

69 See, for example, Nex Wex backup, "Donald Trump Transvestigation," YouTube video, 2:18, May 13, 2022, https://www.youtube.com/watch?v=aUFXaPzG1xg.

70 Nex Wex backup, "Let's See if Popular Youtubers are 'In the Club': Eugenia Cooney T-Investigation," YouTube video, 4:53, April 7, 2023, https://www.youtube.com/watch?v=cNsZInsZzMU. This account includes many other transvestigation videos and is largely representative of the form.

71 Klee, "Unhinged 'Transvestigators.'"

72 For example, Sandra Martha T, "Michael May Not Be."

73 For example, Banned.Videos, "TRANSVESTIGATION 101."

74 Klee, "Unhinged 'Transvestigators.'"

75 Vernon, "Conspiracy Theorists."

76 Lenton, "A Wild Investigation." Not to split hairs, but physiognomy might be a closer parallel.

77 Nick DiRamio, "Is Your Favorite Celeb a Transgender Satanist?! One Skeleton-Obsessed Influencer Thinks So," YouTube video, 39:19, May 19, 2023, https://www.youtube.com/watch?v=y1Gy8jLYOhs.

78 Katy Montgomerie, "No, You Can't Always Tell," *Medium*, August 10, 2020, https://katymontgomerie.medium.com/no-you-cant-always-tell-a5967cc55761.

79 There is an obvious contradiction in this stance in that transvestigation would not be necessary if no one could ever "pass."

80 Emily Mikkelsen, "What Are 'Transvestigators'? Conspiracy Alleges Numerous Celebrities, Politicians Secretly Transgender," *FOX 8 News*, August 29, 2022, https://myfox8.com/news/what-are-transvestigators/

81 See Matheson, "A Child Is Being Trafficked."

82 Lee Leveille, "The Mechanisms of TAnon: What Is 'Tanon'?" *Health Liberation Now!* April 12, 2021, https://healthliberationnow.com/2021/04/12/the-mechanisms-of-tanon-what-is-tanon/.
83 Inanna Snow, "Active vs Passive #Flatearth Free Energy, Lilith Attacking, & January 12 Warning," Bitchute.com, February 13, 2020, https://www.bitchute.com/video/p494xDk7dfGl/.
84 Chandelis Duster, "Marjorie Taylor Greene Posts Anti-Transgender Sign Across Hall from Lawmaker with Transgender Child," *CNN*, February 25, 2021, https://www.cnn.com/2021/02/25/politics/marjorie-taylor-greene-anti-transgender-sign/index.html.
85 Riley Black, "Stop Trying to Out-Science Transphobes," *Slate*, March 3, 2021, https://slate.com/technology/2021/03/transphobes-science-trap-basic-human-rights.html.
86 Gagarin probably did not say this, as it does not appear in the official transcript of the flight, and he was reputedly an Orthodox Christian. Valentin Petrov, "I Am Proud to Be Accused of Having Introduced Yury Gagarin to Orthodoxy," interview on Interfax.com, April 12, 2006, archived August 9, 2007, at https://web.archive.org/web/20070809215050/http://www.interfax-religion.com/?act=interview&div=24.
87 Transvestigation, to the extent that it is a reaction to anxiety caused by the uncertainty and formlessness of sexual identity, is truly *trans-phobic*: It fears trans-ness, not just in sexuality, but in general as a quality that escapes categorization and therefore symbolic control.
88 Wendy Hui Kyong Chun, *Discriminating Data: Correlation, Neighborhoods, and the New Politics of Recognition* (MIT Press, 2021), 221.
89 Jacques Lacan, *The Seminar of Jacques Lacan, Book VII: The Ethics of Psychoanalysis 1959–1960*, ed. Jacques-Alain Miller, trans. Dennis Porter (W. W. Norton, 1992), 182–184.
90 Jacques Lacan, *The Seminar of Jacques Lacan, Book XIX: . . . or Worse*, ed. Jacques-Alain Miller, trans. A. R. Price (Polity, 2018), 174–175.
91 Lacan, *Seminar of Jacques Lacan, Book VII*, 183.
92 Lacan, *Seminar of Jacques Lacan, Book VII*, 183.
93 Michelstaedter, *Persuasion and Rhetoric*, 67.
94 Oreskes and Conway, *Merchants of Doubt*.
95 As John Durham Peters puts it, "My nerve endings terminate in my own brain, not yours." Peters, *Speaking into the Air*, 6.
96 Harry G. Frankfurt, *On Bullshit* (Princeton University Press, 2005).
97 In Lacan's explanation, "like the conjurer who thinks he has put a rabbit in the top hat to emerge from it later, and out pops a rhinoceros instead." Lacan, *Seminar of Jacques Lacan, Book XIX*, 20.
98 Which is not to say that desire is absent, only that it does not effectively occlude the unconscious.
99 See Kat Chow, "'Politically Correct': The Phrase Has Gone from Wisdom to Weapon," *NPR*, December 14, 2016, https://www.npr.org/sections/codeswitch/2016/12/14/505324427/politically-correct-the-phrase-has-gone-from-wisdom-to-weapon. This form of organized right-wing knavery becoming foolishness intersects with the conservative imaginary of persecution, victimage, and defiance, exemplified by exaggerated seasonal displays responding to the "war against Christmas," deliberate misgendering of trans and nonbinary people, or

performative defiance of "wokeness." The point is not that the structures the fool defies are actually hegemonic, but that the fool's speech characterizes them as such, revealing something about their role within a discourse.

100 Devan Cole and Tara Subramaniam, "Trump on Covid Death Toll: 'It Is What It Is,'" *CNN*, September 3, 2020, https://www.cnn.com/2020/08/04/politics/trump-covid-death-toll-is-what-it-is/index.html.

101 Jeremy Diamond and David Mark, "Campaign Reboot: Trump Expresses Regret for Saying 'the Wrong Thing,' Doesn't Specify," *CNN*, August 19, 2016, https://www.cnn.com/2016/08/18/politics/trump-i-regret-sometimes-saying-wrong-thing/index.html.

102 "'I Was Very Angry' at Trump, says Myeshia Johnson, Widow of Fallen Soldier," *ABC News*, October 23, 2017, https://abcnews.go.com/US/fallen-soldiers-widow-angry-trumps-call-couldnt-remember/story?id=50655063.

Conclusion

1 Sarah Fortinsky, "Chris Christie: Most Effective Trump Ad Was 'Kamala Harris Is for They/Them,'" *The Hill*, November 11, 2024, https://thehill.com/homenews/campaign/4983706-chris-christie-donald-trump-win/.

2 Joshua Gunn (*Political Perversion*) has persuasively described the age of Trump as one of perversion. To privilege psychosis over perversion as I have is not to say that both are not important, because these structures are modes of attachment that can coexist in subjects and society at the same time. We're talking heuristics, not Truth.

3 The notion that one is compelled to act rather than making choices is common in people who experience psychosis, however. There are clear parallels between possession and the notion that one's acts are determined by outside forces in the Symbolic, for example. Death is common content in psychotic delusional systems—Schreber's, for example. See Schreber, *Memoirs of My Nervous Illness*.

4 Victoria Shepherd, *A History of Delusions: The Glass King, a Substitute Husband and a Walking Corpse* (Oneworld Publications, 2022).

5 Jeffrey Sconce, *The Technical Delusion: Electronics, Power, Insanity* (Duke University Press, 2019).

6 Daniel Frederick Beresheim, "Circulate Yourself: Targeted Individuals, the Yieldable Object & Self-Publication on Digital Platforms," *Critical Studies in Media Communication* 37, no. 5 (2020): 395–408.

7 I have made a more extensive theoretical case for propriety as central to rhetoric and psychoanalysis elsewhere. See Calum Lister Matheson, "How the Letter Works: Lacan and Contemporary Rhetorical Theory," *Psychoanalytische Perspectieven* 40, no. 4 (2022); Calum Lister Matheson, *Propriety, Metaphor, and Metonymy: Potential Contributions of Rhetorical Theory to Psychoanalysis* (graduation essay, Pittsburgh Psychoanalytic Center, 2022), http:/d-scholarship.pitt.edu/44829/3/PPC%20Graduation%20Paper--Matheson%20(2).pdf.

8 American Psychiatric Association, "Schizophrenia Spectrum and Other Psychotic Disorders," in *Diagnostic and Statistical Manual of Mental Disorders, Fifth Edition, Text Revision* (American Psychiatric Association Publishing, 2022), https://doi.org/10.1176/appi.books.9780890425787.x02_Schizophrenia_Spectrum. See section on "Delusion." For a history and critique of the *DSM*, see Greenberg, *The Book of Woe*.

9 Sconce, *The Technical Delusion*, 94.

10 Margaret Mary Alacoque, *The Autobiography of St. Margaret Mary Alacoque*, trans. Sisters of the Visitation (TAN Books, 2012), 68–69. A self-reported incident of coprophagia was omitted from the English edition. Either be thankful for my restraint, or see David Morgan, "Rhetoric of the Heart: Figuring the Body in Devotion to the Sacred Heart of Jesus," in *Things: Religion and the Question of Materiality*, eds. Dick Houtman and Birgit Meyer (Fordham University Press, 2012), 92.

11 Chun, *Discriminating Data*, 34.

12 Burke, *Philosophy of Literary Form*, 293.

Bibliography

ABC News. "'I Was Very Angry' at Trump, Says Myeshia Johnson, Widow of Fallen Soldier." October 23, 2017. https://abcnews.go.com/US/fallen-soldiers-widow-angry-trumps-call-couldnt-remember/story?id=50655063.

Adair, Peter, dir. *Holy Ghost People*. Thistle Films, 1967.

Alacoque, Margaret Mary. *The Autobiography of St. Margaret Mary Alacoque*. Translated by Sisters of the Visitation. TAN Books, 2012.

Alexander, Estrelda Y. *Black Fire: One Hundred Years of African American Pentecostalism*. InterVarsity Press, 2011.

Altieri, Mitchell, dir. *Holy Ghost People*. XLrator Media, 2014.

Ambrose, Kenneth Paul. "A Survey of the Snake-Handling Cult of West Virginia." Master's thesis, Marshall University, 1970.

American Psychiatric Association. "Schizophrenia Spectrum and Other Psychotic Disorders." In *Diagnostic and Statistical Manual of Mental Disorders, Fifth Edition, Text Revision*. American Psychiatric Association Publishing, 2022. https://doi.org/10.1176/appi.books.9780890425787.x02_Schizophrenia_Spectrum.

Andrejevic, Marc. *Infoglut: How Too Much Information Is Changing the Way We Think and Know*. Routledge, 2013.

"Anthropology Enthusiasts." Stormfront web community. Accessed June 5, 2024. https://www.stormfront.org/forum/group.php?groupid=147.

Arnold, Carrie. "Let Me Repeat Myself: The Media Doesn't Cause Eds." *ED Bites*, March 6, 2013. Archived October 29, 2013. https://web.archive.org/web/20131029024435/http://edbites.com/2013/03/let-me-repeat-myself-the-media-doesnt-cause-eds/.

Arnold, Carrie, and Spectrum. "Is There a Link Between Autism and Anorexia?" *The Atlantic*, February 18, 2016. https://www.theatlantic.com/health/archive/2016/02/anorexia-and-autism/463233/.

Astapova, Anastasiya. "In Pursuit of Nationhood vis-à-vis Russia: The Search for Lost Manuscripts in Post-Soviet Countries." In *Plots: Literary Form and Conspiracy Culture*, edited by Ben Carver, Dana Craciun, and Todor Hristov. Routledge, 2022.

Ball, Matthew M. "Targeting Religion: Analyzing Appalachian Proscriptions on Religious Snake Handling." *Boston University Law Review* 95 (2015): 1425–1450.

Ballestín, Lucas. "Resistance and Revelation: Lacan on Defense." *European Journal of Psychoanalysis* 2, no. 2 (2021). https://www.journal-psychoanalysis.eu/articles/resistance-and-revelation-lacan-on-defense/.

Banned.Videos. "TRANSVESTIGATION 101." Bitchute.com, January 23, 2023, https://www.bitchute.com/video/kv7ActvYQvyN/.

Bataille, Georges. *Erotism: Death & Sensuality*. Translated by Mary Dalwood. City Lights Books, 1986.

———. *Theory of Religion*. Translated by Robert Hurley. Zone Books, 1992.

Bauder, David. "Is Alex Jones Verdict the Death of Disinformation? Unlikely." *ABC News*, October 17, 2022. https://abcnews.go.com/Entertainment/wireStory/alex-jones-verdict-death-disinformation-91632771.

Beck, Richard. "The Snake Handling Churches of Appalachia: Conclusion, Snakebite, Death and Victory." *Experimental Theology* (blog), January 9, 2010. http://experimentaltheology.blogspot.com/2010/01/snake-handling-churches-of-appalachia_09.html.

Bedsole, Nathan H. "X, Analyst." *Quarterly Journal of Speech* 110, no. 2 (2023): 244–262.

Bell, Rudolph M. *Holy Anorexia*. University of Chicago Press, 1985.

Benko, Ralph. "The Left, Not Kellyanne Conway, Invented 'Alternative Facts.'" *Forbes*, February 11, 2017. https://www.forbes.com/sites/ralphbenko/2017/02/11/the-left-not-kellyanne-conway-invented-alternative-facts/?sh=6c6dfa2d658c.

Beresheim, Daniel Frederick. "Circulate Yourself: Targeted Individuals, the Yieldable Object & Self-Publication on Digital Platforms." *Critical Studies in Media Communication* 37, no. 5 (2020): 395–408.

Bion, Wilfred. "Attacks on Linking." In *The Complete Works of W. R. Bion*, vol. 6, edited by Chris Mawson. Routledge, 2014.

Birckhead, Jim. "'Bizarre Snake Handlers': Popular Media and a Southern Stereotype." In *Images of the South: Constructing a Regional Culture on Film and Video*, edited by Karl G. Heider. University of Georgia Press, 1993.

———. "Reading 'Snake Handling': Critical Reflections." In *Anthropology of Religion: A Handbook*, edited by Stephen D. Glazier. Praeger, 1997.

Black, J. A., G. Cunningham, J. Ebeling, et al. *The Electronic Text Corpus of Sumerian Literature*, Oxford 1998–2006. Accessed March 13, 2024. https://etcsl.orinst.ox.ac.uk/cgi-bin/etcsl.cgi?text=t.1.8.2.3#.

Black, Riley. "Stop Trying to Out-Science Transphobes." *Slate*, March 3, 2021. https://slate.com/technology/2021/03/transphobes-science-trap-basic-human-rights.html.

Blake, Aaron. "Kellyanne Conway's Legacy: The 'Alternative Facts'-ification of the GOP." *Washington Post*, August 24, 2020. https://www.washingtonpost.com/politics/2020/08/24/kellyanne-conways-legacy-alternative-facts-ification-gop/.

Blumenfeld, Warren. "How the Gun Lobby Turned a Fake Quote from Sigmund Freud into a Rallying Cry." *LGBTQ Nation*, October 5, 2017. https://www.lgbtqnation.com/2017/10/gun-lobby-turned-fake-quote-sigmund-freud-rallying-cry/

Bogost, Ian. "The Ugly Honesty of Elon Musk's Twitter Rebrand." *The Atlantic*, July 31, 2023. https://www.theatlantic.com/technology/archive/2023/07/twitter-x-rebrand-juvenile-internet-style/674875/.

Bollas, Christopher. *When the Sun Bursts: The Enigma of Schizophrenia*. Yale University Press, 2015.

Boltanski, Luc. *Mysteries and Conspiracies*. Polity, 2014.

Boym, Svetlana. *The Future of Nostalgia*. Basic Books, 2001.

Branscomb, Richard. "Taking Aim: Rhetorical Conspiracism, Far-Right Extremism, and the Narrative Politics of Guns." PhD diss., Carnegie Mellon University, 2023.

Braunstein, Néstor A. *Jouissance: A Lacanian Concept*. Translated by Silvia Rosman. SUNY Press, 2020.

Bray, Abigail. "The Anorexic Body: Reading Disorders." *Cultural Studies* 10, no. 3 (1996): 413–429.

Bredin, Hugh. "The Literal and the Figurative." *Philosophy* 67, no. 269 (1992): 69–80.

Breneisson, Nadja. "I Spent a Week Undercover in a Pro-Anorexia WhatsApp Group." *VICE*, July 8, 2015. https://www.vice.com/en/article/vdx7ex/i-spent-a-week-in-a-pro-ana-whatsapp-group-talking-to-the-goddess-of-emaciation-876.

British Museum, The. "brick." Accessed March 18, 2024. https://www.britishmuseum.org/collection/object/W_1825-0503-37.

Brotherton, Rob. *Suspicious Minds: Why We Believe Conspiracy Theories*. Bloomsbury Sigma, 2015.

Brown, David M. "Film's Casting Call Wants that 'Inbred' Look." TribLive.com, February 26, 2008. https://archive.triblive.com/news/films-casting-call-wants-that-inbred-look/.

Brown, Fred, and Jeanne McDonald. *The Serpent Handlers: Three Families and Their Faith*. John F. Blair, 2000.

Buck, David J. "Rock On Chicago." *Tedium*, November 16, 2017. https://tedium.co/2017/11/16/wesley-willis-remembrance-history/.

Burgunder, Brittany. *Safety in Numbers: From 56 to 221 Pounds, My Battle with Eating Disorders*. Wheatmark, 2016.

Burke, Kenneth. *Language as Symbolic Action*. University of California Press, 1966.

———. *The Philosophy of Literary Form*. University of California Press, 1973.

Burton, Thomas. *Serpent-Handling Believers*. University of Tennessee Press, 1993.

Carden, Karen W., and Robert W. Pelton. *The Persecuted Prophets: The Story of the Frenzied Serpent Handlers*. A. S. Barnes and Company, 1976.

Carver, Ben. "'Turning Points': Plots in Conspiracy and Literature." In *Plots: Literary Form and Conspiracy Culture*, edited by Ben Carver, Dana Craciun, and Todor Hristov. Routledge, 2022.

Casetti, Francesco. *Screening Fears: On Protective Media*. Zone Books, 2023.

Cash, Wiley. *A Land More Kind Than Home*. Harper Collins, 2013.

Cassian, St. John. "On the Eight Vices." In *The Philokalia: The Complete Text*, vol. 1, edited by G.E.H. Palmer, Philip Sherrard, and Kallistos Ware. Farrar, Straus and Giroux, 1979.

Castle, [Lukas]. *The Blackpill Theory: Why Incels Are Right & You Are Wrong*. Independently published, 2019.

Center for Countering Digital Hate. "AI and Eating Disorders: How Generative AI Enables and Promotes Harmful Eating Disorder Content." August 7, 2023. chrome- https://counterhate.com/research/ai-tools-and-eating-disorders/.

———. "Deadly by Design." December 2022. https://counterhate.com/research/deadly-by-design/.

Cevallos, Danny. "Snakes and Church vs. State." *CNN*, May 28, 2014. https://www.cnn.com/2014/02/26/opinion/cevallos-snake-handling-law.

Chauncey Jr., George. "From Sexual Inversion to Homosexuality: Medicine and the Changing Conceptualization of Female Deviance." *Salmagundi* no. 58/59 (Fall/Winter 1982/1983): 114–146.

Chebrolu, E. "The Racial Lens of Dylann Roof: Racial Anxiety and White Nationalist Rhetoric on New Media." *Review of Communication* 20, no. 1 (2020): 47–68.

Chiarnini, Ed. "A MUST READ . . . Did the CT School Shootings 'Really' Happen? . . . Murdered School Children—Rockefeller Grandchild . . . You Decide." *Know the Lies*, December 17, 2012. Archived March 14, 2013, https://web.archive.org/web/20130314053347/http://www.knowthelies.com/node/8486.

———. "Peter Lanza Father of Adam Lanza Is a FICTION?" *Know the Lies*, December 17, 2013. Archived January 22, 2013, https://web.archive.org/web/20130122182157/http://www.knowthelies.com/node/8487.

Chow, Kat. "'Politically Correct': The Phrase Has Gone from Wisdom to Weapon." *NPR*, December 14, 2016. https://www.npr.org/sections/codeswitch/2016/12/14/505324427/politically-correct-the-phrase-has-gone-from-wisdom-to-weapon.

Christodoulou, George N. (ed.). *The Delusional Misidentification Syndromes*. Karger, 1986.

Chun, Wendy Hui Kyong. *Discriminating Data: Correlation, Neighborhoods, and the New Politics of Recognition*. MIT Press, 2021.

Clarke, Stuart. "Inversion, Misrule and the Meaning of Witchcraft." *Past and Present* no. 87 (May 1980): 98–127.

Cloud, Dana. "The Irony Bribe and Reality Television: Investment and Detachment in *The Bachelor*." *Critical Studies in Media Communication* 27, no. 5 (2010): 413–437.

Colaninno, Marilyn. "Today's Hot Topic: The White Coat Rule." ReedSmith.com, May 2, 2013. https://www.reedsmith.com/en/perspectives/2013/05/todays-hot-topic--the-white-coat-rule.

Cole, Devan, and Tara Subramaniam, "Trump on Covid Death Toll: 'It Is What It Is.'" *CNN*, September 3, 2020. https://www.cnn.com/2020/08/04/politics/trump-covid-death-toll-is-what-it-is/index.html.

Collins, J. B. *The Tennessee Snake Handlers*. Chattanooga News-Free Press, 1947.

Coontz, Stephanie. *The Way We Never Were: American Families and the Nostalgia Trap*. Basic Books, 1992.

Cosenza, Domenico. *A Lacanian Reading of Anorexia*. Translated by Jonathan West. Routledge, 2024.

Costello, William, Vania Rolon, Andrew G. Thomas, David and Schmitt. "Levels of Well-Being Among Men Who Are Incel (Involuntarily Celibate)." *Evolutionary Psychological Science* 8 (2022): 375–390.

Courbon, G., and P. Fail. "Syndrome d'illusion de Frégoli et schizophrénie." Translated by Hadyn D. Ellis, Janet Whitley, and Jean-Pierre Luaute. *History of Psychiatry* 5, no. 17 (1994): 134–138.

Covington, Dennis. *Salvation on Sand Mountain: Snake Handling and Redemption in Southern Appalachia*. Hachette Books, 1995.

Crawford, Amanda J. "Opinion: Sandy Hook Was the Start of Misinformation Running Amok." *CNN*, December 14, 2022. https://www.cnn.com/2022/12/14/opinions/sandy-hook-shooting-anniversary-disinformation-misinformation-crawford/index.html.

———. "Professor of Denial." *The Chronicle of Higher Education*, February 5, 2020. https://www.chronicle.com/article/the-professor-of-denial/.

Crews, Harry. *A Feast of Snakes: A Novel*. Simon & Schuster, 1976.

Crosby, Robert C. "The Other Side of 'Proof-Texting.'" *Patheos*, January 11, 2014, https://www.patheos.com/blogs/robertcrosby/2014/01/the-other-side-of-proof-texting/.

Culler, Jonathan. *Structuralist Poetics: Structuralism, Linguistics, and the Study of Literature*. Cornell University Press, 1975.

Curran, Andrew S. *The Anatomy of Blackness: Science and Slavery in an Age of Enlightenment*. Johns Hopkins University Press, 2011.

Daniels, Jessie. *Cyber Racism: White Supremacy Online and the New Attack on Civil Rights*. Rowman & Littlefield, 2009.

David. "False Flag Crisis Actors." *The Truthful One*, archived March 30, 2016. https://web.archive.org/web/20160330124820/http://thetruthfulone.com/false-flag-crisis-actors/.

Davis, Anthony. *Eat Around It*. Sheryl Drozen, dir. Uproar Entertainment, 2020.

Day, John F. *Bloody Ground*. University of Kentucky Press, 1981.

Deamer, Felicity, Ellen Palmer, Quoc C. Vuong, et al. "Non-Literal Understanding and Psychosis: Metaphor Comprehension in Individuals with a Diagnosis of Schizophrenia." *Schizophrenia Research: Cognition* 18, article no. 100159 (2019). https://doi.org/10.1016/j.scog.2019.100159.

Dean, Jodi. *Democracy and Other Neoliberal Fantasies: Communicative Capitalism & Left Politics*. Duke University Press, 2009.

———. *Publicity's Secret: How Technoculture Capitalizes on Democracy*. Cornell University Press, 2002.

Dee, Katherine. "Pro-Anorexia Is the Nexus of All Online Communities." *default.blog*, October 22, 2021. https://default.blog/p/is-anorexia-is-the-nexus-of-all-online/comments.

Deleuze, Gilles, and Félix Guattari. *A Thousand Plateaus*, translated by Brian Massumi. University of Minnesota Press, 1987.

Derrida, Jacques. *Deconstruction in a Nutshell: A Conversation with Jacques Derrida*. Edited by John D. Caputo. Fordham University Press, 1997.

———"Force of Law: The 'Mystical Foundation of Authority.'" In *Deconstruction and the Possibility of Justice*, edited by Drucilla Cornell, Michel Rosenfeld, and David Gray Carlson. Routledge, 1992.

Desbordes, Emmanuelle. "Anorexia, Anxiety, and the Object." *The Psychoanalytic Review* 101, no. 4 (2007): 571–602.

Diamond, Jeremy, and David Mark. "Campaign Reboot: Trump Expresses Regret for Saying 'the Wrong Thing,' Doesn't Specify." *CNN*, August 19, 2016. https://www.cnn.com/2016/08/18/politics/trump-i-regret-sometimes-saying-wrong-thing/index.html.

DiRamio, Nick. "Is Your Favorite Celeb a Transgender Satanist?! One Skeleton-Obsessed Influencer Thinks So." YouTube video, May 19, 2023, 39:19. https://www.youtube.com/watch?v=y1Gy8jLYOhs.

Dixon, Jen. *Bones: Anorexia, OCD, and Me*. JD Associates, 2023.

Dosser, Max. "I'm Gonna Wreck It, Again: The False Dichotomy of 'Healthy' and 'Toxic' Masculinity in *Ralph Breaks the Internet*." *Critical Studies in Media Communication* 39, no. 4 (2022): 333–346.

Dr. Eowyn. "Proof from the Social Security Death Index." In *Nobody Died at Sandy Hook: It was a FEMA Drill to Promote Gun Control*, edited by Jim Fetzer and Mike Palecek. Moon Rock Books, 2015.

———. "Remarkable Resemblance of Sandy Hook Victims and Professional Crisis Actors." *Fellowship of the Minds*, January 11, 2013. Archived March 17, 2016, https://web.archive.org/web/20160317110501/http://fellowshipoftheminds.com/2013/01/11/remarkable-resemblance-of-sandy-hook-victims-and-professional-crisis-actors/.

Duin, Julia C. *In the House of the Serpent Handler: A Story of Faith and Fleeting Fame in the Age of Social Media*. University of Tennessee Press, 2017.

Dunbar-Ortiz, Roxanne. *Loaded: A Disarming History of the Second Amendment*. City Lights Books, 2018.

Duster, Chandelis. "Marjorie Taylor Greene Posts Anti-Transgender Sign Across Hall from Lawmaker with Transgender Child." *CNN*, February 25, 2021. https://www.cnn.com/2021/02/25/politics/marjorie-taylor-greene-anti-transgender-sign/index.html.

Eckstein, Justin. "Sensing School Shootings." *Critical Studies in Media Communication* 37, no. 2 (2020): 161–173.

Eco, Umberto. *The Search for the Perfect Language*. Translated by James Fentress. Blackwell, 1995.

Edelman, Lee. *Bad Education: Why Queer Theory Teaches Us Nothing*. Duke University Press, 2022.

Ehrman, Bart. "Snake-Handling and the Gospel of Mark." *Bart Ehrman Blog: The History & Literature of Early Christianity*, February 20, 2014. https:/ehrmanblog.org/snake-handling-gospel-mark/.

Ellmann, Maud. *The Hunger Artists: Starving, Writing & Imprisonment*. Virago Press, 1993.

Ellul, Jacques. *Propaganda: The Formation of Men's Attitudes*. Translated by Konrad Kellen and Jean Lerner. Vintage Books, 1965.

Engelhart, Katie. "Should Patients Be Allowed to Die from Anorexia?" *New York Times Magazine*, January 3, 2024. https://www.nytimes.com/2024/01/03/magazine/palliative-psychiatry.html.

Espinoza, Melissa. *My Life, as Told by Anorexia: Essays from the Deep*. Amazon Digital Services, 2023.

Evagrios the Solitary. "Texts on Discrimination in Respect of Passions and Thoughts." In *The Philokalia: The Complete Text*, vol. 1, edited by G.E.H. Palmer, Philip Sherrard, and Kallistos Ware. Farrar, Straus and Giroux, 1979.

Evans, E. P. *The Criminal Prosecution and Capital Punishment of Animals: The Lost History of Europe's Animal Trials*. Faber & Faber, 1906.

Farber, Sharon K., Craig C. Jackson, Johanna K. Tabin, & Eytan Bachar. "Death and Annihilation Anxieties in Anorexia Nervosa, Bulimia, and Self-Mutilation." *Psychoanalytic Psychology* 24, no. 2 (2007): 289–305.

Farley, Lawrence. "Snake Handling." *Orthodox Christianity*, July 14, 2020. https://orthochristian.com/132600.html.

Felman, Shoshana. *Writing and Madness (Literature/Philosophy/Psychoanalysis*. Translated by Martha Noel Evans and Others. Stanford University Press, 2003.

Fetzer, Jim. David Zublick' Awake Nation: 'Have I Been Played on Sandy Hook?' (20 April 2023) with Brian Davidson" BitChute.com, April 24, 2023. https://www.bitchute.com/video/jpPsw2RRu3Ok/.

———. "Thinking About Sandy Hook: Reality or Illusion?" In *Nobody Died at Sandy Hook: It Was a FEMA Drill to Promote Gun Control*, edited by Jim Fetzer and Mike Palecek. Moon Rock Books, 2015.

Fetzer, Jim, and Mike Palecek, eds. *Nobody Died at Sandy Hook: It Was a FEMA Drill to Promote Gun Control*. Moon Rock Books, 2015.

Fields, Karen E., and Barbara J. Fields. *Racecraft: The Soul of Inequality in American Life*. Verso, 2012.

Fish, Stanley. *Is There a Text in this Class? The Authority of Interpretive Communities*. Harvard University Press, 1980.

Florida Atlantic University. "James Tracy." FAU Dorothy F. Schmidt College of Arts and Letters School of Communication and Multimedia Studies, archived September 11, 2015. https://web.archive.org/web/20150911021341/http://www.fau.edu/scms/tracy.php.

Flynt, Wayne. *Dixie's Forgotten People: The South's Poor Whites*. Indiana University Press, 2004.

Folkenflik, David. "Coverage Rapid, and Often Wrong, in Tragedy's Early Hours." *NPR*, December 18, 2012. https://www.npr.org/2012/12/18/167466320/coverage-rapid-and-often-wrong-in-tragedys-early-hours.

Fortinsky, Sarah. "Chris Christie: Most Effective Trump Ad Was 'Kamala Harris Is for They/Them.'" *The Hill*, November 11, 2024. https://thehill.com/homenews/campaign/4983706-chris-christie-donald-trump-win/.

Fox News. "'Holy Grail' of Guns Made: Company Sells $4.5M Pistols Made from 4.5-Billion-Year-Old meteorite," April 26, 2018. https://www.foxnews.com/tech/holy-grail-of-guns-made-company-sells-4-5m-pistols-made-from-4-5-billion-year-old-meteorite.

Frankfurt, Harry G. *On Bullshit*. Princeton University Press, 2005.

Freeman, Andrea. "Milk, a Symbol of Neo-Nazi Hate." *The Conversation*, August 30, 2017. https://theconversation.com/milk-a-symbol-of-neo-nazi-hate-83292.

Freud, Sigmund. *The Complete Letters of Sigmund Freud to Wilhem Fliess 1887–1904*. Translated and edited by Jeffrey Moussaieff Masson. Harvard University Press, 1985.

———. *The Psychology of Love*. Translated by Shaun Whiteside. Penguin, 2007.

Fuerle, Richard D. Erectus *Walks Among Us*. Spooner Press, 2008.

Gambert, Iselin, and Tobias Linné. "How the Alt-Right Uses Milk to Promote White Supremacy." *The Conversation*, April 18, 2018. https://theconversation.com/how-the-alt-right-uses-milk-to-promote-white-supremacy-94854.

Gault, Matthew. "Here's Why Men Are Pointing Loaded Guns at Their Dicks." *VICE*, May 27, 2020. https://www.vice.com/en/article/k7q83v/heres-why-men-are-pointing-loaded-guns-at-their-dicks.

George, Sheldon. *Trauma and Race: A Lacanian Study of African American Racial Identity*. Baylor University Press, 2016.

Georgia General Assembly. "Acts and Resolutions of the General Assembly of the State of Georgia 1941 [volume 1]." Digital Library of Georgia, University of Georgia University Libraries. https://dlg.usg.edu/record/dlg_zlgl_179513495#text.

Gerrard, Nathan L. "The Serpent-Handling Religions of West Virginia." In *Poor Americans: How the White Poor Live*, edited by Marc Pilisuk and Phyllis Pilisuk. Aldine Publishing Company, 1971.

Gerrard, Nathan L., and Louise B. Gerrard. *Scrabble Creek Folk*, vol. I, unpublished 1966 manuscript. Schoenbaum Library, University of Charleston.

Gherovici, Patricia. *Transgender Psychoanalysis: A Lacanian Perspective on Sexual Difference*. Routledge, 2017.

Gibbs, Ferrill, and Abe Partridge. *Alabama Astronaut: The Podcast*. September 14, 2022. https://alabamaastronaut.com/.

Gill-Peterson, Jules. "From Gender Critical to QAnon: Anti-Trans Politics and the Laundering of Conspiracy." *The New Inquiry*, September 13, 2021.

https://thenewinquiry.com/from-gender-critical-to-qanon-anti-trans-politics-and-the-laundering-of-conspiracy/.

Ging, Debbie, and Sarah Garvey. "'Written in These Scars Are the Stories I Can't Explain': A Content Analysis of Pro-Ana and Thinspiration Image Sharing on Instagram." *New Media & Society* 20, no. 3 (March 2018): 1181–1200.

~Goddess Annea~. "Please Read Before Making a 'Guess My BMI' Post." *ED Support Forum*, August 30, 2022. https://www.edsupportforum.com/threads/please-read-before-making-a-guess-my-bmi-post.4433232/.

Gold, Joel, and Ian Gold. *Suspicious Minds: How Culture Shapes Madness*. Free Press, 2014.

Google Hollie Greig (GGT). "The Sandy Hook Shooting—Fully Exposed." BitChute.com, September 28, 2022. https://www.bitchute.com/video/RUOax1J5Qwd4/.

Gould, Stephen Jay. *The Mismeasure of Man*, revised and expanded. W. W. Norton, 1996.

Greenberg, Gary. *The Book of Woe: The* DSM *and the Unmaking of Psychiatry*. New York: Penguin Group, 2013.

Gunn, Joshua. *Political Perversion: Rhetorical Aberration in the Time of Trumpeteering*. University of Chicago Press, 2020).

Harsha, Melanie Rae. "These Signs Shall Follow: Endangered Pentecostal Practices in Appalachia." Master's thesis, Appalachian State University, 2015.

Herman, Arthur. *The Idea of Decline in Western History*. The Free Press, 1997.

Heywood, Leslie. *Dedication to Hunger: The Anorexic Aesthetic in Modern Culture*. University of California Press, 1996.

Hobbs, Tawnell D., Rob Barry, and Yoree Koh. "'The Corpse Bride Diet': How TikTok Inundates Teens with Eating-Disorder Videos." *Wall Street Journal*, December 17, 2021. https://www.wsj.com/articles/how-tiktok-inundates-teens-with-eating-disorder-videos-11639754848?reflink=desktopwebshare_permalink.

Hollenweger, Walter J. *The Pentecostals: The Charismatic Movement in the Churches*. Augsburg Publishing House, 1972.

Holliday, Robert Kelvin. *Tests of Faith*. Fayette Tribune Inc., 1966.

Holmes, Su. "Talking Back: Responding to Media Images of Eating Disorders." Department of Film, Television, and Media Studies at the University of East Anglia Blog, July 31, 2015. https://filmtelevisionmediauea.wordpress.com/2015/07/31/talking-back-responding-to-media-images-of-eating-disorders/.

———. "(Un)twisted: Talking Back to Media Representations of Eating Disorders." *Journal of Gender Studies* 27, no. 2 (2018): 149–164.

Hood, Ralph, and W. Paul Williamson. *Them That Believe: The Power and Meaning of the Christian Serpent-Handling Tradition*. University of California Press, 2008.

Hormone Hangover (SubStack). "Thinspo and Gender Goals: Musing on Two Internet Subcultures." October 31, 2021. https://hormonehangover.substack.com/p/thinspo-and-gender-goals.

Hornbacher, Marya. *Wasted: A Memoir of Anorexia and Bulimia*. Harper Perennial, 2014.

Hsieh, Carina. "'Dicks Out for Harambe': How 2 Average Guys Started the Year's Most Controversial Meme." *Cosmopolitan*, December 6, 2016. https://www.cosmopolitan.com/politics/a8354653/dicks-out-for-harambe-internets-most-fascinating/.

Hunt, Elliot. "Trump's Inauguration Crowd: Sean Spicer's Claims Versus the Evidence." *The Guardian*, January 22, 2017. https://www.theguardian.com/us-news/2017/jan/22/trump-inauguration-crowd-sean-spicers-claims-versus-the-evidence.

Hüppauf, Bernd. "Introduction: Modernity and Violence: Observations Concerning a Contradictory Relationship." In *War, Violence, and the Modern Condition*, edited by Bernd Hüppauf. De Gruyter, 1997.

InfoWars. "'Is Michelle Obama a Man?'—The Alex Jones Channel—2014." Uploaded to Rumble by Info Worm, July 10, 2014. https://rumble.com/v3mkhxa-is-michelle-obama-a-man-the-alex-jones-channel-2014.html.

Jensen, Robin E. "The Eating Disordered Lifestyle: Imagetexts and the Performance of Similitude." *Argumentation & Advocacy* 42 (2005): 1–18.

Johnson, Andrea Shan. Review of *In the House of the Serpent Handler: A Story of Fleeting Fame in the Age of Social Media*, by Julia C. Duin. *Pneuma* 41, no. 1 (2019): 149–151.

Jones, CT. "Eating Disorders Are Getting Worse. Is It Social Media's Fault?" *Rolling Stone*, November 1, 2024, https://www.rollingstone.com/culture/culture-features/eating-disorder-social-media-liv-schmidt-1235150121/.

Jones, Oiwi Parker, Fidel Alfaro-Almagro, and Saad Jbabdi. "An Empirical, 21st Century Evaluation of Phrenology." *Cortex* 106 (September 2018): 26–35.

Kahntineta. "Boogie Men." *Mohawk Nation News*, March 14, 2013. https://mohawknationnews.com/blog/2013/03/14/boogie-men/.

Kane, Steven Michael. "Snake Handlers of Southern Appalachia." PhD diss., Princeton University, 1979.

Keller, Andrijka. *Thin, and I: A Memoir*. CreateSpace Independent Publishing, 2018.

Kelly, Casey Ryan. *Apocalypse Man: The Death Drive and White Masculine Victimhood*. The Ohio State University Press, 2020.

Kerns Jr., Robert W. "Article: Protecting the Faithful from Their Faith: A Proposal for Snake-Handling Law in West Virginia." *West Virginia Law Review* 116, no. 2 (2013): 561–581.

Kim, Elizabeth, Rachel Murphy, and Maggie Driscoll. "DMS: Delusional Misidentification Syndrome or Dead Moneyman and Sex Offender? A Case Report of Reverse Capgras Syndrome." *Case Reports in Psychiatry* 22 (2022). https://doi.org/10.1155/2022/9703482.

Kimbrough, David. *Taking Up Serpents: Snake Handlers of Eastern Kentucky*. Mercer University Press, 2002.

Klee, Miles. "Unhinged 'Transvestigators' Think They're the Only Cis People Left." *Mel Magazine*, July 18, 2022. https://melmagazine.com/en-us/story/transvestigator-celebrity-conspiracy-theories.

Klein, Melanie. "Notes on Some Schizoid Mechanisms." *Journal of Psychotherapy Practice and Research* 5, no. 2 (1996): 160–179.

Knowyourmeme.com. "A Few Millimeters of Bone." October 27, 2017, accessed June 1, 2024. https://knowyourmeme.com/memes/millimeters-of-bone.

Koebler, Jason. "Where the 'Crisis Actor' Conspiracy Theory Comes From." *VICE*, February 22, 2018. https://www.vice.com/en/article/pammy8/what-is-a-crisis-actor-conspiracy-theory-explanation-parkland-shooting-sandy-hook.

Kollerstrom, Nick. "The 20 Children and Their Homes." in *Nobody Died at Sandy Hook: It Was a FEMA Drill to Promote Gun Control*, edited by Jim Fetzer and Mike Palecek. Moon Rock Books, 2015.

La Barre, Weston. *They Shall Take Up Serpents: Psychology of the Southern Snake-Handling Cult*. Waveland Press, 1992.

Lacan, Jacques. *Écrits: The First Complete Edition in English*. Translated by Bruce Fink. Norton, 2006.

———. *The Seminar of Jacques Lacan, Book III: The Psychoses*. Edited by Jacques-Alain Miller, translated by Russell Grigg. W. W. Norton, 1993.

———. *The Seminar of Jacques Lacan, Book V: Formations of the Unconscious*. Edited by Jacques-Alain Miller, translated by Russell Grigg. Polity, 2017.

———. *The Seminar of Jacques Lacan, Book VII: The Ethics of Psychoanalysis 1959–1960*. Edited by Jacques-Alain Miller, translated by Dennis Porter. W. W. Norton, 1992.

———. *The Seminar of Jacques Lacan, Book XIX: . . . or Worse*. Edited by Jacques-Alain Miller, translated by A. R. Price. Polity, 2018.

———. *The Seminar of Jacques Lacan, Book XX: Encore*. Edited by Jacques-Alain Miller, translated by Bruce Fink. W. W. Norton, 1998.

———. *Television: A Challenge to the Psychoanalytic Establishment*. Translated by Denis Hollier, Rosalind Krauss, and Annette Michelson. W.W. Norton, 1990.

Lai, Carlo, Romana Pellicano, Gaia Iuliano, et al. "Why People Join Pro-Ana Online Communities? A Psychological Textual Analysis of Eating Disorder Blog Posts." *Computers in Human Behavior* 124, article no. 106922 (2021). https://doi.org/10.1016/j.chb.2021.106922.

LaMagdeleine, Izz Scott. "Michelle Obama Isn't a Trans Woman. Here's Why Some People Believe Otherwise," Snopes.com, October 17, 2023. https://www.snopes.com/news/2023/10/17/michelle-obama-is-trans/.

Laporte, Dominique. *History of Shit*. Translated by Nadia Benabid and Rodolphe el-Khoury. MIT Press, 2000.

Larson, Stephanie R. "The Rhetoricity of Fat Stigma: Mental Disability, Pain, and Anorexia Nervosa." *Rhetoric Society Quarterly* 51, no. 5 (2021): 392–406.

Law, John. "Who's White?" *White Hot Radio Podcast*, November 3, 2006. https://www.stormfront.org/forum/t579652/.

Leader, Darian. *What Is Madness?* Penguin Books, 2011.

Leak, Sharon. Email to faculty of the Pittsburgh Psychoanalytic Center, October 23, 2023.

Lederer, Sarah. "James H. Fetzer." University of Minnesota Duluth, accessed October 20, 2023. https://www.d.umn.edu/~jfetzer/.

Lee, Michael J., and R. Jarrod Atchison. *We Are Not One People: Secession and Separatism in American Politics Since 1776*. Oxford University Press, 2022.

Lee, Vivian. "Top Ten Reasons: Sandy Hook Was an Elaborate Hoax." In *Nobody Died at Sandy Hook: It was a FEMA Drill to Promote Gun Control*, edited by Jim Fetzer and Mike Palecek. Moon Rock Books, 2015.

Lenton, Patrick. "A Wild Investigation of Transvestigators, the People Who Think Celebs Are All Trans." *VICE*, February 8, 2024. https://www.vice.com/en/article/jg54kd/a-wild-investigation-of-transvestigators-the-people-who-think-celebs-are-all-trans.

Leveille, Lee. "The Mechanisms of TAnon: What Is 'Tanon'?" *Health Liberation Now!* April 12, 2021. https://healthliberationnow.com/2021/04/12/the-mechanisms-of-tanon-what-is-tanon/.

Lewis, Clyde. "Mental Hopscotch." *Ground Zero*, April 12, 2013. Archived March 5, 2014. https://web.archive.org/web/20140305235005/http://www.groundzeromedia.org/mental-hopscotch/.

Light, Caroline. *Stand Your Ground: A History of America's Love Affair with Lethal Self-Defense*. Beacon Press, 2017.

Linda, Gi. "Sandy Hook: Fleecing the Asleeple!" *Not the News*. Uploaded to Scribd by Gordon Duff, accessed October 13, 2023. https://www.scribd.com/document/249692922/Sandy-Hook-Fleecing-the-Sheeple.

Lofton, Kathryn. "Observational Secular: Religion and Documentary Film in the United States." *Journal of Cinema and Media Studies* 60, no. 5 (2021): 99–120.

Lovett, Matthew. "Lacanian Anxieties: Trans Surgeries, Countertransference, and the Fantasy of the Whole," *Transgender Studies Quarterly* 11, no. 3 (2024): 458–480.

Lundberg, Christian O. *Lacan in Public: Psychoanalysis and the Science of Rhetoric.* University of Alabama Press, 2012.

Lynn, Nicole. *Pink Poison: A Memoir of Anorexia Nervosa.* Independently published, 2019.

Ma, Lena. *Shamefully Vanished: A Memoir of a Girl Out of Control.* Independently published, 2020).

Machado, Isabel. "Revisiting Deliverance: The Sunbelt South, the 1970s Masculinity Crisis, and the Emergence of the Redneck Nightmare Genre." *Study the South,* June 19, 2017. https://southernstudies.olemiss.edu/study-the-south/revisiting-deliverance/.

Marche, Stephen. "Guns Are Beautiful." *Esquire,* February 11, 2013. https://www.esquire.com/news-politics/a19335/guns-are-beautiful-0313/.

Marks, Jonathan. *Is Science Racist?* Polity, 2017.

Mason, Michele. *Annihilating Anorexia: A Memoir.* The Paper House Publishing, 2023.

Matheson, Calum Lister. "A Child Is Being Trafficked: The Figuration of Child Abuse and Desire in Right-Wing Extremist Discourses." In *Pleasure and Pain in U.S. Public Culture,* edited by Christopher Gilbert and John Lucaites. University of Alabama Press, 2025.

———. *Desiring the Bomb: Communication, Psychoanalysis, and the Atomic Age.* University of Alabama Press, 2019.

———. "Filthy Lucre: Gold, Language, and Exchange Anxiety." *Review of Communication* 18, no. 4 (2018): 249–264.

———. "How the Letter Works: Lacan and Contemporary Rhetorical Theory." *Psychoanalytische Perpectieven* 40, no. 4 (2022). www.psychoanalytischeperspectieven.be/vol-40-4-2022/how-the-letter-works-lacan-and-contemporary-rhetorical-theory.

———. "Instance of the Letter in the Unconscious, or Reason Since Freud." In *Reading Lacan's Écrits: From "The Freudian Thing" to "Remarks on Daniel Lagache,"* edited by Derek Hook and Calum Neill. Routledge, 2019.

———. "Liberal Tears and the Rogue's Yarn of Sadistic Conservativism." *Rhetoric Society Quarterly* 52, no. 4 (2022): 341–355.

———. *Propriety, Metaphor, and Metonymy: Potential Contributions of Rhetorical Theory to Psychoanalysis.* Graduation essay, Pittsburgh Psychoanalytic Center, 2022. http://d-scholarship.pitt.edu/44829/3/PPC%20Graduation%20Paper--Matheson%20(2).pdf.

———. "Psychotic Discourse: The Rhetoric of the Sovereign Citizen Movement." *Rhetoric Society Quarterly* 48, no. 2 (2018): 187–206.

———. "'What Does Obama Want of Me?' Anxiety and Jade Helm 15." *Quarterly Journal of Speech* 102, no. 2 (2015): 133–149.

McCarson, Matt. "Newtown Connecticut Elementary Shooting Is a Staged False Flag Against Gun Owners and Preppers." InfoSalvo.com, December 14, 2012. http://www.infosalvo.com/us-news/newton-connecticut-elementary-shooting-is-a-staged-false-flag/

McCarthy, Cormac. *Suttree.* Vintage International, 1979.

McCauley, Deborah Vansau. *Appalachian Mountain Religion: A History*. University of Illinois Press, 1995.

McCoy, John. "Box Turtle, Rattlesnake Collection Would Be Outlawed Under WV's Proposed New Regulation." *WVNews*, March 21, 2020. https://www.wvnews.com/box-turtle-rattlesnake-collection-would-be-outlawed-under-wvs-proposed-new-regulation/article_dddb0e43-d480-5387-8f37-0b305574ae43.html.

McGee, Michael Calvin. "Text, Context, and the Fragmentation of Contemporary Culture." *Western Journal of Communication* 54, no. 3 (Summer 1990): 274–289.

McGregor, Kerry, John L. McKenna, Ellis P. Barrera, Coleen R. Williams, Sydney M. Hartman-Munick, and Carly E. Guss. "Disordered Eating and Considerations for the Transgender Community: A Review of the Literature and Clinical Guidance for Assessment and Treatment." *Journal of Eating Disorders* 11, article no. 75 (2023). https://doi.org/10.1186/s40337-023-00793-0.

McKenna, Stephen J. *Adam Smith: The Rhetoric of Propriety*. SUNY Press, 2006.

McLuhan, Marshal. *Understanding Media: The Extensions of Man*. MIT Press, 1994.

McVicar, Michael J. "Take Away the Serpents from Us: The Sign of Serpent Handling and the Development of Southern Pentecostalism." *Journal of Southern Religion* 15 (2013). http://jsr.fsu.edu/issues/vol15/mcvicar.html.

Meczekalski, Blazej, Agnieszka Podfigurna-Stopa, and Krzysztof Katulski. "Long-Term Consequences of Anorexia Nervosa." *Maturitas* 75, no. 3 (July 2013): 215–220.

Michelstaedter, Carlo. *Persuasion and Rhetoric*. Translated by Wilhelm Snyman and Guiseppe Stellardi. University of KwaZulu-Natal Press, 2007.

Mikkelsen, Emily. "What Are 'Transvestigators'? Conspiracy Alleges Numerous Celebrities, Politicians Secretly Transgender." *FOX 8 News*, August 29, 2022. https://myfox8.com/news/what-are-transvestigators/.

Montgomerie, Katy. "No, You Can't Always Tell." *Medium*, August 10, 2020. https://katymontgomerie.medium.com/no-you-cant-always-tell-a5967cc55761.

Morgan, David. "Rhetoric of the Heart: Figuring the Body in Devotion to the Sacred Heart of Jesus." In *Things: Religion and the Question of Materiality*, edited by Dick Houtman and Birgit Meyer. Fordham University Press, 2012).

Morrow, Jimmy (with Ralph W. Hood Jr.). *Handling Serpents: Pastor Jimmy Morrow's Narrative History of His Appalachian Jesus' Name Tradition*. Mercer University Press, 2005.

Mossaheb, Nilufar, Harald N. Aschauer, Susanne Stoettner, et al. "Comprehension of Metaphors in Patients with Schizophrenia-Spectrum Disorders." *Comprehensive Psychiatry* 55 (2014): 928–937.

MrStosh314. "We Need to Talk About Sandy Hook." Uploaded to Rumble by False Flags, October 7, 2022. https://rumble.com/v1mysno-we-need-to-talk-about-sandy-hook.html.

Muldowney, Decca. "TikTok Slammed for 'Doing Nothing' over Pro-Anorexia Content." *The Daily Beast*, March 3, 2023. https://www.thedailybeast.com/tiktok-slammed-for-doing-nothing-over-pro-anorexia-content-by-center-for-countering-digital-hate.

Murphy, Kevin. *Asexuality and Freudian-Lacanian Psychoanalysis: Towards a Theory of an Enigma*. Routledge, 2023.

National Geographic. "A Family Tradition | Snake Salvation." YouTube video, September 4, 2013, 2:01. https://www.youtube.com/watch?v=k1-BhaX5GSE.

Nex Wex backup. "Donald Trump Transvestigation." YouTube video, May 13, 2022, 2:18. https://www.youtube.com/watch?v=aUFXaPzG1xg.

———. "Let's See if Popular Youtubers Are 'In the Club': Eugenia Cooney T-Investigation." YouTube video, April 7, 2023, 4:53. https://www.youtube.com/watch?v=cNsZInsZzMU.

Nobus, Dany. *The Law of Desire: On Lacan's "Kant with Sade."* Springer, 2017.

O'Kane, Paul. "*Spolia* as Speculation." *Journal of Visual Art Practice* 15, no. 2–3 (2016): 204–213.

Oreskes, Naomi. *Why Trust Science?* Princeton University Press, 2019.

Oreskes, Naomi, and Erik M. Conway. *Merchants of Doubt: How a Handful of Scientists Obscured the Truth on Issues from Tobacco Smoke to Global Warming.* Bloomsbury, 2010.

Osgood, Kelsey. *How to Disappear Completely: On Modern Anorexia.* Overlook Duckworth, 2013.

Oxford English Dictionary, s.v. "for." Accessed April 17, 2025. https://doi.org/10.1093/OED/1589022754.

Packer, Joseph, and Ethan Stoneman. *A Feeling of Wrongness: Pessimistic Rhetoric on the Fringes of Popular Culture.* Pennsylvania State University Press, 2018.

Panofsky, Aaron, and Joan Donovan. "Genetic Ancestry Testing Among White Nationalists: From Identity Repair to Citizen Science." *Social Studies in Science* 49, no. 5 (2019): 653–681.

PBS Newshour. "Watch Conn. Gov. Malloy and Conn. State Police Address Newtown School Shooting." YouTube video, December 14, 2012, 10:55. https://www.youtube.com/watch?v=xGm9CzrZdX4.

Peters, John Durham. *Speaking into the Air: A History of the Idea of Communication.* University of Chicago Press, 1999.

Petrov, Valentin. "I Am Proud to Be Accused of Having Introduced Yury Gagarin to Orthodoxy." Interview on Interfax.com, April 12, 2006. Archived August 9, 2007. https://web.archive.org/web/20070809215050/http://www.interfax-religion.com/?act=interview&div=24.

Piper, Michael Collins. *False Flags: Template for Terror.* American Free Press, 2019.

Polito, Tony. "Tony Polito, PhD." Archived December 8, 2023. https://web.archive.org/web/20231208205038/http://www.tonypolito.com/.

Pond, Lauren. *Test of Faith: Signs, Serpents, Salvation.* Duke University Press, 2017.

Poulton, Britt, and Dan Madison Savage, dirs. *Them That Follow.* 1091 Media, 2019.

Powell, Adam William. "Setting the Stage: Refurbishing the School." In *Nobody Died at Sandy Hook: It was a FEMA Drill to Promote Gun Control,* edited by Jim Fetzer and Mike Palecek. Moon Rock Books, 2015.

Preciado, Paul B. *Can the Monster Speak? Report to an Academy of Psychoanalysts.* Translated by Frank Wynne. Semiotext(e), 2021.

PressTV.com. "Israeli Death Squads Involved in Sandy Hook Bloodbath: Intelligence Analyst." December 18, 2012, archived May 20, 2015. https://web.archive.org/web/20150520144015/http://www.presstv.com/detail/2012/12/18/278706/israeli-squads-tied-to-newtown-carnage.

Rappoport, Jon. "Astonishing Hunger Games 'Coincidence,' and Killer's Mother Now a Doomsday Prepper?" *Prison Planet,* December 17, 2012. Archived August 19, 2018. https://web.archive.org/web/20180819235941/https://www.prisonplanet.com/newtown-murders-astonishing-hunger-games-coincidence-and-killers-mother-now-a-doomsday-prepper.html.

Rasmussen, Sofie M., Martin K. Dalgaard, Mia Roloff, et al. "Eating Disorder Symptomatology Among Transgender Individuals: A Systematic Review and

Meta-Analysis." *Journal of Eating Disorders* 11, article no. 84 (2023). https://www.ncbi.nlm.nih.gov/pmc/articles/PMC10214585/.

Rather, Dan. Facebook status update, January 22, 2017. https://m.facebook.com/story.php?story_fbid=10158087282405716&id=24085780715&__tn__=*s.

Read, Max. "Behind the 'Sandy Hook Truther' Conspiracy Video That Five Eight Million People Have Watched in One Week." *Gawker*, January 15, 2013. https://www.gawker.com/5976204/behind-the-sandy-hook-truther-conspiracy-video-that-five-million-people-have-watched-in-one-week.

Reid, Michael Noel. "Cobb Creek Church: Changing Perspectives in a Serpent-Handling Congregation in East Tennessee." Master's thesis, University of Tennessee, Knoxville, 2013.

Renee Pittman Books. "Mind Control and Mass Shooters . . . Is There a Connection?" YouTube video, September 3, 2023, 24:51. https://www.youtube.com/watch?v=MZEZfkKHgSM.

Rice, Jenny. *Awful Archives: Conspiracy Theory, Rhetoric, and Acts of Evidence*. Ohio State Press, 2020.

Roach, Jay, dir. *The Campaign*. Warner Brothers Pictures, 2012

Robertson, Archie. *That Old-Time Religion*. Houghton Mifflin Co., 1950.

Rogers, Abby. "These Are the Worst Errors Reported After the Sandy Hook Massacre." *Business Insider*, December 18, 2012. https://www.businessinsider.com/sandy-hook-shooting-media-inaccuracies-2012-12.

Rogers, Annie. *Incandescent Alphabets: Psychosis and the Enigma of Language*. Karnac Books, 2016.

Rosman, Silvia. "Introduction: Translating *Jouissance*." In Néstor A. Braunstein, *Jouissance: A Lacanian Concept*, translated by Silvia Rosman. SUNY Press, 2020.

Saini, Angela. *Superior: The Return of Race Science*. Beacon Press, 2019.

Sandra Martha T. "Michael May Not Be the First Tranny in W House Part 2." YouTube video, November 20, 2016. https://www.youtube.com/watch?v=-1j4ySRc7dI&t=8s.

Sargant, William. *The Mind Possessed: A Physiology of Possession, Mysticism, and Faith Healing*. J. B. Lippincott Company, 1974.

Scarry, Elaine. *The Body in Pain: The Making and Unmaking of the World*. Oxford University Press, 1985.

Schreber, Daniel Paul. *Memoirs of My Nervous Illness*. Translated and edited by Ida Macalpine and Richard A. Hunter. New York Review Books, 1955.

Schweizer, Kai. "Eating Disorders as DIY Medical Transition: An Interview with Katherine Dee." *default.blog*, January 19, 2022. https://default.blog/p/diy-medical-transition-and-eating?utm_source=publication-search.

Sconce, Jeffrey. *The Technical Delusion: Electronics, Power, Insanity*. Duke University Press, 2019.

Seaber, Emma. "Occult Anorexia: The Unseen Forces of Anorexia Life-Writing." PhD diss., King's College London, 2021. https://kclpure.kcl.ac.uk/portal/en/studentTheses/occult-anorexia.

———. "Reading Disorders: Pro-Eating Disorder Rhetoric and Anorexia Life-Writing." *Literature and Medicine* 34, no. 2 (2016): 484–508.

Sedensky III, Stephen J. *Report of the State's Attorney for the Judicial District of Danbury on the Shootings at Sandy Hook Elementary School and 36 Yogananda Street, Newtown, Connecticut, on December 14, 2012*. Office of the State's Attorney,

Judicial District of Danbury, November 25, 2013. https://portal.ct.gov/-/media/DCJ/SandyHookFinalReportpdf.pdf.

Sedgwick, Eve Kosofsky. *Touching Feeling: Affect, Pedagogy, Performativity*. Duke University Press, 2003.

Seitz-Wald, Alex. "Sandy Hook Truther Won't Quit." *Salon*, January 18, 2013. https://www.salon.com/2013/01/18/james_tracy_wont_back_down/.

Serrano, Richard. "Lacan's Oriental Language of the Unconscious." *SubStance #84*, 26.3, (1997): 90–106.

Seshadri-Crooks, Kaplana. *Desiring Whiteness: A Lacanian Analysis of Race*. Routledge, 2000.

Sexton, Colleen. *Blind Faith: Serpent Handling in West Virginia: An Outsider's Look into an Inside World*. Page Publishing, 2015.

SGTreport.com. "A Startling Fact & Gigantic 'Coincidence' About Friday's Mass Shooting in Connecticut." December 15, 2012. https://web.archive.org/web/20130224033919/http://sgtreport.com/2012/12/a-startling-fact-gigantic-coincidence-about-fridays-mass-shooting/.

Sharma, Sarah. "Many McLuhans or None at All." *Canadian Journal of Communication* 44, no. 4 (2019). https://doi.org/10.22230/cjc.2019v44n4a3621.

Shechtman, Anna. "Escaping into the Crossword Puzzle." *The New Yorker*, December 20, 2021. https://www.newyorker.com/magazine/2021/12/27/escaping-into-the-crossword-puzzle.

Shepherd, Victoria. *A History of Delusions: The Glass King, a Substitute Husband and a Walking Corpse*. Oneworld Publications, 2022.

Simmons, Emma, Frank Noteboom, and Eric F. van Furth. "Pro-Anorexia Coaches Prey on Individuals with Eating Disorders." *International Journal of Eating Disorders* 57, no. 1 (2024): 124–131.

Smallstorm, Sofia. "Unravelling Sandy Hook in 2, 3, 4 and 5 Dimensions." Uploaded to Rumble by JBR1959, July 29, 2022. https://rumble.com/v1e2emn-sandy-hook-in-five-dimensions-by-sophia-smallstorm.html.

Snow, Inanna. "Active vs Passive #Flatearth Free Energy, Lilith Attacking, & January 12 Warning." Bitchute.com, February 13, 2020. https://www.bitchute.com/video/p494xDk7dfGl/.

Society for Nordish Physical Anthropology. "The Society for Nordish Physical Anthropology (SNPA)." July 23, 2006, accessed June 5, 2024. https://www.theapricity.com/snpa/index2.htm.

Soetoro, Barry. "Sandy Hook—David Wheeler Exposed as Actor and Fake FBI Sniper." Uploaded to BitChute.com by Yanghis Khan, July 6, 2019. https://www.bitchute.com/video/HKrGqfLOhoXx/.

Soler, Colette. *What Lacan Said About Women: A Psychoanalytic Study*. Translated by John Holland. Other Press, 2006.

Stableford, Dylan. "Kellyanne Conway Explains What She Meant by 'Alternative Facts.'" *Yahoo! News*, July 23, 2017. https://news.yahoo.com/kellyanne-conway-explains-meant-alternative-facts-194946959.html.

Stampler, Laura. "Inside Pinterest's Frightening Pro-Anorexia 'Thinspo' Cult." *Business Insider*, March 22, 2012. https://www.businessinsider.com/inside-pinterests-frightening-pro-anorexia-thinspo-cult-2012-3.

Stapleton, Karyn, Sarah Evans, and Catrin Rhys. "Ana as God: Religion, Interdiscursivity and Identity on Pro-Ana Websites." *Discourse and Communication* 13, no. 3 (2019): 320–341

Stewart, Kathleen. "Conspiracy Theory's Worlds." In *Paranoia Within Reason: A Casebook on Conspiracy as Explanation*, edited by George E. Marcus. University of Chicago Press, 1999.

Stormer, Nathan. "An Appetite for Rhetoric." *Philosophy & Rhetoric* 48, no. 1 (2015): 99–106.

Strings, Sabrina. *Fearing the Black Body: The Racial Origins of Fat Phobia*. NYU Press, 2019.

Sukunesan, Suku, Minh Huynh, and Gemma Sharp. "Examining the Pro-Eating Disorders Community on Twitter via the Hashtag #proana: Statistical Modeling Approach." *JMIR Mental Health* 8, no. 7 (July 2021), article e24340. https://doi .org/10.2196/24340.

Swales, Stephanie S. *Perversion: A Lacanian Psychoanalytic Approach to the Subject*. Routledge, 2012.

Swerdloff, Alex. "Got Milk? Neo-Nazi Trolls Sure as Hell Do." *VICE*, February 21, 2017. https://www.vice.com/en/article/kbka39/got-milk-neo-nazi-trolls-sure-as -hell-do.

Tabo, Tamara. "Snakes in a Church: Should the Law Protect the Religious Liberty of Serpent-Handlers?" *Above the Law*, November 14, 2013. https://abovethelaw.com /2013/11/snakes-in-a-church-should-the-law-protect-the-religious-liberty-of-serpent -handlers/.

Taylor, Jim. "The Woman Who Founded the 'Incel' Movement." *BBC*, August 29, 2018. https://www.bbc.com/news/world-us-canada-45284455.

Taylor, Kate. "Introduction." In *Going Hungry: Writers on Desire, Self-Denial, and Overcoming Anorexia*, edited by Kate Taylor. Anchor Books, 2008.

Teh, Cheryl. "Alex Jones Bizarrely Declared 'Victory for Truth' After Being Ordered to Pay $4.1 Million in Damages to Sandy Hook Parents." *Business Insider*, August 5, 2022. https://www.insider.com/alex-jones-declares-victory-pay-damages -sandy-hook-2022-8.

Testimony of the Two Witnesses. "IRREFUTABLE PROOF That Serena Williams IS A MAN (mirrored)." YouTube video, February 25, 2015, 26:43. https://www .youtube.com/watch?v=WqVdGV-N9wo.

Thalmann, Katharina. *The Stigmatization of Conspiracy Theory Since the 1950's: "A Plot to Make Us Look Foolish."* Routledge, 2019.

Theil, Michele. "Conspiracy Theorist Claims Michelle Obama Is Transgender and We're so Very, Very Tired." *Pink News*, January 7, 2020. https://www.thepinknews .com/2020/01/07/michelle-obama-alex-jones-conspiracy-theory-infowars -debunked-first-lady/.

Tidball, Keith G., and Christopher P. Toumey. "Signifying Serpents: Hermeneutic Change in Appalachian Pentecostal Serpent Handling." In *Signifying Serpents and Mardi Gras Runners: Representing Identity in Selected Souths*, edited by Celeste Ray and Luke Eric Lassiter. University of Georgia Press, 2003.

TMZ on TV. "'Snake Salvation' Church Killer Rattler Rises Again!" February 24, 2014. https://www.tmz.com/2014/02/24/snake-salvation-church-cody-coots -rattlesnake-returns-video-tmz-tv/.

Tracy, James F. "Medical Examiner: More Questions Than Answers." In *Nobody Died at Sandy Hook: It was a FEMA Drill to Promote Gun Control*, edited by Jim Fetzer and Mike Palecek. Moon Rock Books, 2015.

Tribell, William S. "Last Film Footage of Pastor Jamie Coots." YouTube video, March 23, 2014, 9:16. https://www.youtube.com/watch?v=5f4NyYqHXa8.

Troscianko, Emily T. "Fiction-Reading for Good or Ill: Eating Disorders, Interpretation and the Case for Creative Bibliotherapy Research." *Medical Humanities* 44, no. 3 (2018): 201–211.

———. "Literary Reading and Eating Disorders: Survey Evidence of Therapeutic Help and Harm." *Journal of Eating Disorders* 6, no. 8 (2018). https://doi.org/10.1186/s40337-018-0191-5.

———. "Taking, Losing, and Letting Go of Control in Anorexia." *Psychology Today*, October 24, 2023. https://www.psychologytoday.com/us/blog/a-hunger-artist/201508/taking-losing-and-letting-go-of-control-in-anorexia.

Ugwu, Reggie. "Gunplay Says Government Behind Sandy Hook Shooting." BET.com, December 21, 2012. https://www.bet.com/article/6m8s5l/gunplay-says-government-behind-sandy-hook-shooting.

Unicun.com. "The TAC-SAC: Picatinny Rail Accessory." Accessed October 17, 2023. https://unicun.com/product/the-tac-sac-picatinny-rail-accessory/.

USA Today. "Andrew Hamblin, Young Snake Handler in Tennessee, Grasps the Power of Faith." June 6, 2012. https://www.huffpost.com/entry/andrew-hamblin-snake-handler_n_1572528.

U.S. Department of Defense. "The USS *New York*: A City on the Sea." Accessed October 17, 2023, https://www.defense.gov/Multimedia/Experience/USS-New-York-A-City-on-the-Sea/#:~:text=Never%20forget.%22,Big%20Apple%20wherever%20it%20travels.

Vance, Paul R. L. "A History of Serpent Handlers in Georgia, North Alabama and Southeastern Tennessee." Master's thesis, Georgia State University, 1975.

Vandereycken, Walter, and Ron van Deth. *From Fasting Saints to Anorexic Girls: The History of Self-Starvation*. The Athlone Press, 1994.

Vanheule, Stijn. *The Subject of Psychosis: A Lacanian Perspective*. Palgrave Macmillan, 2011.

Van Hoorebeke, Kala. "The Rhetorical Paradigm in the Service of the Snake Handling Cult." Master's thesis, Western Illinois University, 1980.

Vernon, Heyden. "The Conspiracy Theorists Who Think All Celebrities Are Secretly Trans." *VICE*, September 21, 2023. https://www.vice.com/en/article/3ak5wk/conspiracy-theorists-believe-all-celebrities-are-secretly-trans.

Waldram, James B. *Revenge of the Windigo: The Construction of the Mind and Mental Health of North American Aboriginal Peoples*. University of Toronto Press, 2004.

Watts, Eric King. "Border Patrolling and 'Passing' in Eminem's *8 Mile*." *Critical Studies in Media Communication* 22 (2005): 187–206.

———. "'Zombies Are Real': Fantasies, Conspiracies, and the Post-Truth Wars." *Philosophy and Rhetoric* 51, no. 4 (2018): 441–470.

Weil, Simone. *Gravity and Grace*. Translated by Arthur Willis. University of Nebraska Press, 1952.

Wigginton, Eliot. "The People Who Take Up Serpents." *Foxfire 7*, edited by Paul F. Gillespie. Anchor Books, 1980.

Williams, Joy. *Harrow: A Novel*. Alfred A. Knopf, 2021.

Williamson, Elizabeth. *Sandy Hook: An American Tragedy and the Battle for Truth*. Dutton, 2022.

Willis, Wesley. "Chronic Schizophrenia." *Rush Hour* (CD), Alternative Tentacles, 2000.

Wray, Matt. *Not Quite White: White Trash and the Boundaries of Whiteness*. Duke University Press, 2006.

Yamane, David. "Psycho-Sexual Analysis of Guns, Part 2." *Gun Culture 2.0* (blog), April 16, 2015. https://gunculture2point0.wordpress.com/2015/04/13/psycho-sexual-analysis-of-guns-part-2/.

Young Turks, The. "Dead Snake Handler's Son Does Exactly What You Shouldn't Do [VIDEO]." YouTube video, February 24, 2014, 4:41. https://www.youtube.com/watch?v=3UiPmmte2XE.

———. "Son of Dead Snake-Bitten Preacher Gets—You Guessed It—Bitten by a Snake!" YouTube video, June 1, 2014, 2:05. https://www.youtube.com/watch?v=hF548tUhgaA.

Žižek, Slavoj. *The Ticklish Subject: The Absent Centre of Political Ontology*. Verso, 1999.

Zupančič, Alenka. *The Odd One In: On Comedy*. MIT Press, 2008.

———. *What is Sex?* MIT Press, 2017.

———. "Why Is Sexual Difference Relevant for Philosophy?" Lecture at Carnegie Lecture Hall, Carnegie Museums of Pittsburgh, November 11, 2017.

Index

About the Author

CALUM LISTER MATHESON is associate professor and chair of the Department of Communication at the University of Pittsburgh. He is also a graduate and faculty member of the Pittsburgh Psychoanalytic Institute. Matheson works at the intersections of rhetoric, media studies, cultural studies, and psychoanalysis. He is author of *Desiring the Bomb: Psychoanalysis, Communication, and the Atomic Age*, an analysis of apocalyptic fantasies and the limits of communication. His more recent work on conspiracy theories, reactionary discourses, and Internet culture has appeared in journals such as *Rhetoric Society Quarterly*; *Review of Communication*; *Philosophy and Rhetoric*; and *Quarterly Journal of Speech*.